For those who served, known and unknown...
and who defended their countries...

THREE FINGERS OF DEATH
2K12 KUB (SA-6 GAINFUL)
MISSILE SYSTEM

Danko Borojević Mihajlo (Mike) Mihajlović Zoran Vukosavljević

THREE FINGERS OF DEATH
2K12 KUB (SA-6 GAINFUL)
MISSILE SYSTEM

The extraordinary story of one of the most successful air defense missile systems in history and eyewitness accounts from those who fought with and against this system.

Danko Borojević   Mihajlo (Mike) Mihajlović   Zoran Vukosavljević

MSM Publishing, Toronto, Canada 2022

Three Fingers of Death: 2K12 Kub (SA-6 Gainful) Missile System: Eyewitness accounts from those who fought with and against this system.
Copyright @ 2021 by MSM, All rights reserved. Printed in Canada and US.
No part of this book may be used or reproduced in any matter whatsoever without written permission except in the brief quotations embodied in critical articles and reviews.
For information address MSMpublishing.canada@gmail.com.

MSM book may be purchased for educational, business, or sales promotional use. For information please email MSM at:
MSMpublishing.canada@gmail.com.

The Authors hereby assert their moral right to be identified as the authors of the Work. "The right of DANKO BOROJEVIĆ, MIHAJLO (MIKE) S MIHAJLOVIĆ and ZORAN VUKOSAVLJEVIĆ to be identified as the authors of this Work has been asserted by them in accordance with the Copyright, Designs and Patents Act 1988"; to make a condition of contract with any licensee concerning any edition of the Work to be published throughout the world that a notice of assertion in the same terms, as above, shall be printed with due prominence in every edition published by or further licensed by such licensee.

FIRST CANADIAN EDITION

Designed by Mike Mihajlović

Library and Archives Canada

ISBN: 978-1-7753953-8-6 Printed edition

'The man who ventures to write a contemporary history must expect to be criticized both for everything he has said and everything he has not said.'

*François-Marie Arouet Voltaire
in a letter to M. Bertin de Rocheret*

Foreword

Perhaps no weapon ever produced had so many historical impacts in modern warfare, such as surface-to-air missiles produced in the Soviet Union. Originally designed to provide defense of the Soviet Union from attacks by American bombers during the Cold War, the first Soviet surface-to-air missiles decisively influenced the sequence of events, when they shot down the American U-2 reconnaissance airplanes over the USSR and Cuba. Soviet surface-to-air missiles were delivered to North Vietnam and played a significant role in the defense of North Vietnam inflicting a heavy toll upon US forces. A new generation of mobile surface-to-air missile during the October War of 1973 was a big surprise for the Israeli air force, which suffered considerable losses from these missiles. To this day, surface-to-air missiles manufactured in the Soviet Union and Russia are the backbone of the air defense for many countries. It is not surprising that a large number of surface-to-air missiles are still in use today, including the 2K12 Kub-M (SA-6 Gainful) self-propelled missile system.

Sergei Korolev conducted the first Soviet experiments with surface-to-air missiles before the outbreak of World War II. However, his further work on these experiments was cut short, due to the purges which brought Korolev in a gulag, under the accusation that he was undermining the Soviet government. During the war, the Red Army used unguided rockets nicknamed 'Katyusha' (officially designated as BM-13 Guards Mortar). One of the experiments with 'Katyusha' rockets was as barrage anti-aircraft missiles. After the great victory in World War II, Stalin ordered the German designers to be released and to form mixed teams for the production of ground-to-air missiles based on German technology, headed by Soviet designers. Soviet designer Isaiev led a team to develop a Soviet liquid-fueled rocket motor which technology was based on the German original. During the four-year development, it was determined that the development of missiles with German instructions has a lot of problems. Therefore, Stalin ordered his chief of the secret police Lavrenti Beria to carry out a 'ruthless solution to the problem' and enable Moscow to receive missiles for defense from the increasing American bombers as soon as possible. Beria, the head of the NKVD's secret Soviet police, was so rigorous in the exploitation of Russian engineers and German engineers prisoners of war, that the design bureau K-1 rapidly developed the S-25 Berkut in record time. This first missile was known in the west as the SAM-1 Guild. After Stalin's death, the development of Soviet surface-to-air missiles continues in several directions, which enabled the development of missile systems that entered into the Air Defense branch (PVO Protiv-Vazdushnaya Oborona - Против Воздушная Оборона) such as SA-75 Dvina (SAM-2A Guideline), S-75 Desna (SAM-2B Guideline B) S-75M Volkhov (SAM-2C Guideline C), S-75M Volga (SAM-2D Guideline D), S-125 Neva (SAM-3 Goa), S-200 Angara/Vega/Dubna (SAM-5 Gammon), as well as newer S-300 (SA-10 Grumble) and S-400 missile systems (SAM-21 Growler).

In parallel with the PVO, the Soviet ground forces got their own air defense mobile system 2K11 Krug (SA-4 Ganef). The 2K11 was followed by one of the most important surface-to-air missile systems in the Soviet Union production, a self-propelled missile system 2K12 Kub-M (SAM-6 Gainful) and successor 9K37 Buk (SA-11 Gadfly). This book is speaking about the 2K12, one of the most successful and the most proliferated air-defense missile system which is, after 50 years, still in use in many countries.

Organization of this Book

This book covers two main topics:
- K12 Kub/SA-6 Gainful missile system - design, development, versions, modifications, missile guidance, technical characteristics, and
- Personal accounts of the clashes between the air defense missile system and the fighter airplanes since the introduction until the present day.

In some sections, all of these topics are covered, as they often interact.

Chapter One provides an introduction and history of the 2K12 Kub/SA-6 Gainful air defense missile system development.

Chapter Two covers the implementation of the missile system in the Balkans.

Chapter Three covers missile system in wars - Arab - Israeli wars: Yom Kippur (October) War and Bekaa valley; Chad war, Angolan border war, Yemen civil war and Artsakh/Nagorno Karabakh war.

Chapter Four surveys the Kub engagement in the Yugoslav civil war.

Chapter Five addresses the NATO war against the Federal Republic of Yugoslavia and the aftermath.

Chapter Six covers K12 Kub/SA-6 modernization programs.

Chapter Seven describes the 2K12 Kub/SA-6 successor - 9K37 Buk missile system.

The Appendix covers the basic radar fundamentals, antiradiation missiles, towed decoys, field orientation, NATO codification system and contains a detailed glossary of potentially unfamiliar terms and abbreviations.

This book is based on the book "Nebeski Štit sa Zemlje" published in the Serbian language.

About the authors

Danko Borojević

Danko Borojević was born in 1973 in Sisak, Croatia. In secondary school, he specialized in electrical trades and computers. After high school, he also finished school for a non-commissioned officer, infantry branch, and associated courses for the command roles.

In the period from September 1991 to March 2008, he served in the armed forces of Republika Srpska and later in the armed forces of Bosnia and Herzegovina. During his military service, he performed different duties such as a platoon commander and company commander. He also performed administrative duties on the company and battalion levels. He finished military service in the rank of the senior sergeant 1st class (the western equivalent of warrant officer).

Danko authored the book 'Paklena Krila: Mlazni Avioni u ratu 1943-2004' (Hell's Wings: Jet Fighter Planes in the War from 1943-2004). Danko is also a co-author of the books 'Enciklopedija Mlaznih Aviona' (Encyclopedia of Jet Planes), 'Orlovi sa Vrbasa' (Eagles from Vrbas), 'Vojska Republike Srpske - 12 Maj 1992 - 31 Decembar 2005' (Army of Republika Srpska, 12 May 1992 - 31 December 2005), 'MiG-21, Legenda Hladnog Rata' (Mig-21, The Cold War Legend), 'Vazduhoplovne Snage Bivših Republika SFRJ 1992 - 2015' (Air Force of the Former Republics of SFRY, 1992-2015), 'MiG-29, Naša priča' (MiG-29, Our Story), 'Mlaznjak koji grmi, F-84G Thunderjet u JRV' (Thundering Jet, F-84G Thunderjet in JRV), 'Nebeske Sablje: F-86E/D Sabre u JRV' (Heavenly Sabres: F-86E/D Saber in JRV), '82. Avijacijska Brigada, od Benina do Mahovljana' (82. Aviation Brigade, from Benin to Mahovljan), and 'Nebeski štit sa Zemlje, Samohodni Raketni Sistem 2K12 Kub-M/kvadrat' (Skyshield from the Ground, Self-propelled Missile System 2K12 Kub-M/Kvadrat).

Danko was an associate of the Serbian military magazine 'Odbrana' (Defense), during 2010 and from 2014 to 2017. He published articles in the supplement to the military magazine 'Arsenal'. He also wrote for the aviation magazine 'Aeromagazin'. He also wrote articles for the portals 'www.vidovdan.com', 'www.tangosix.com', 'Military-Political Observer', 'www.ekspres.net', and 'www.patriot.rs'.

Danko cooperated with the publishing house 'Serbian Genealogical Center' from Belgrade, which publishes works related to anthropology and ethnology.

This book is his first book in the English language.

Mihajlo (Mike) Mihajlović MSc, PEng

Mihajlo (Michael) (Slobodan) Mihajlović was born in 1966, in Zrenjanin, Serbia. He finished high school - physics and natural sciences department. After the high school and enrollment to the University of Novi Sad he was drafted to the compulsory military service where he also finished officer training. His military posts were in army units in republics Bosnia & Herzegovina and Croatia. He specialized in air defense missile systems and artillery. After the graduation from the Faculty of Mechanical Engineering, Automation, and Computer Science branches, he worked as a teacher and lecturer at the technical college, teaching engineering subjects. He also worked in the consulting industry, advancing from junior to the chief engineer roles as well as in the defense industry. During the entire time after the regular military service, he also served as a reserve officer and was also engaged in military technical intelligence.

Since 2002 he lives and works in Toronto, Canada. Besides his graduate degree in engineering, he also has professional certifications which include a Canadian Professional Engineering license. His progressive engineering experience is in engineering design and technology for the defense industry where he designed light armored vehicles, weapon platforms, passive and active decoys, camouflage systems and ballistic protection. Other expertise includes engineering in civilian corporate and government sectors such as commercial, industrial, institutional, residential and government buildings, military bases, mining, metallurgy plants and smelters, project development, commissioning, technology development, technical courses, and lecturing.

Besides engineering, he is also a lifelong historian interested in particular in military history and technology. He is an author of three books covering the military subjects: 'Specijalne Snage Sveta' (World Special Forces) and 'Podmornice' (Submarines) published in the Serbian language, 'Missileers Against the Stealth: The First Downing of the Stealth Airplane in History', 'Shooting Down the Stealth Fighter: Eyewitness Accounts From Those Who Were There', and 'Jetliner Down: Tor-M1 Missile System which Downed Ukrainian Flight PS752' published in the English language. Besides the books, he is also the author of scientific and technical articles which includes both military and non-military subjects.

He also served in the Canadian Forces reserve as an officer in RC EME (Royal Canadian Electrical and Mechanical Engineers). His job provided him the opportunity to work all over the world, including tours with the Canadian Forces in Afghanistan (Kabul and Kandahar).

Mike is a contributor for BBC, CBC, BBC Persian, and Manoto TV. He appeared as a military expert in few documentary movies addressing the problems of air defense, missile systems, and the downing of the Ukrainian passenger airplane. He was also engaged by the UN investigative commission.

Zoran Vukosavljević

Zoran Vukosavljević was born in 1977 in Rijeka, Croatia. After high school, he enrolled in the specialist training for non-commissioned officers for the Air Defense forces in Sombor. After graduation in 1996, he was promoted to the rank of sergeant in the Light Anti Aircraft Artillery Systems.

His first place of service was the 60th Air Defense 2K12 Kub-M/SA-6 regiment in Danilovgrad, Montenegro. He was later sent for the missile launcher commanders' training course that was performed in the Air Defense Miltary Academy at the Batajnica military base. He spent two years as the commander of the 2K12 Kub/SA-6 2P25 missile launcher in the 3rd battery, 60th regiment. His next career step was as a commander of the P-15M target tracking and surveillance radar in fire control battery. In this role, he spent the 1999 war. His unit didn't have any irrevocable casualties during the war.

After the war, he got a citation by the then commander of the Air Defense Corps, Lieutenant General Branislav Petrović 'for the results achieved in building and strengthening the combat readiness of the Yugoslav Army'. After the war, at the end of 1999 at his request, he left the Yugoslav Army, as a sergeant 1st class and started civilian profession opening his own business in fire protection.

In recent years, he has been active in the study of the air defense and military systems, as well as in research activities related to the events of the 1999 war. In that sense, he was an active member of the most popular military-professional forums in Serbia (and wider in Southeast Europe) such as My City Military (www.macitymilitary.com) and Paluba Info (www.paluba.info), where he contributed to many military-professional topics, especially those related to the air war over the Yugoslavia in 1999.

On the publishing side, he is the co-author of the book 'Nebeski Štit sa Zemlje – Samohodni Raketni Sistem 2K12 Kub-M/Kvadrat' (Sky Shield from the Ground - Self-Propelled Missile System 2K12 Kub-M / Kvadrat). He also writes articles, analyzes, and columns for the largest aviation portal in Southeast Europe - Tango Six (www.tangosix.com) as well as for the Military Bookstore website (www.vojnaknjizara.com).

His texts, articles, analyzes, and opinions have often been cited by other electronic and printed media.

This book is his first book in the English language.

Table of contents

Foreword i
    Organization of the Book iii
    About the Authors iv
    Table of Contest vii

CHAPTER ONE 1
    Origins of 2K12 Kub (SA-6) missile system 1
    Development history 1
    Tests 7
    System components 11
        1S91 Straight Flush radar 12
        2P25 Self-propelled launcher 16
        3M9 guided missile 18
    Missile guidance method 23
    SA-6 in the Soviet Army 31
    SA-6 regiment and battery 35
    SA-6 regiment 35
        Fire control battery 35
        Command platoon 37
        Radar platoon 39
    SA-6 battery 42
        1S91 target tracking and fire control radar 42
        Transporter, erector and launcher 49
        T7M missile transporter and loader truck 50
    Missile technical battery 53

CHAPTER TWO 53
    SA-6 in the Balkans 53
    Beginning of the air defense missile forces 53
    Operational use 59

CHAPTER THREE 73
    2K12 (SA-6) in combat 73
    War of attrition and Yom Kippur war 73
    Bekaa Valley 89
    Other wars 89

Foreword

    Angolan border war 99
    Libya and Chad 99
    Iraq vs Iran 103
    Yemen 103
    Nagorno Karabakh 104

CHAPTER FOUR 107
    Yugoslav civil war 107
    Outbreak 107
    First blood 108
    SA-6 in the Army of Republika Srpska 110
    Basher Five-Two 117
    In defense of Republika Srpska 125
    SA-6 in Srpska Krajina 127
    From Republika Srpska to Bosnia and Herzegovina 131

CHAPTER FIVE 135
    2K12 Kvadrat in FR Yugoslavia army 135
    1999 - Prelude to war 135
    SA-6 Units situation in 1998 141
    Yugoslav Air defense order of battle 145
    USAF and NATO order of battle 151
    Attack 152
    Eyewitness accounts and controversies
    of the air war 1999 173
    2K12 against B-1B Lancer:
    Lightning or SAM strike?... 173
    2K12 against A-10A Thunderbolt 181
    2K12 against the drones 187
    Engaging NATO airplane over Podgorica 189
    The hardest night 192
    Aftermath 203
    Successful Deception Measures 205
    Fixed air defenses damaged but
    mobile air defenses survived 210

CHAPTER SIX 219
    2K12 Kub/Kvadrat modernization 219

ix

Ukrainian modernization 219
Lithuanian modernization 220
Iraqi missile modernization 222
Romanian modernization 223
Czech republic modernization 224
Polish and Hungarian modernization 227
Serbian modernization 229

CHAPTER SEVEN 231
2K12 successor - 9K37 Buk missile system 231
9K317M - Buk M3 234
Buk combat service 237

APPENDICES 239
APPENDIX A 241
Radar fundamentals 241
Radar system and radar range 241
The antenna 245
Radar displays 247
Radar classification 246
Basic radar functions 249
Military applications of radar systems 249
Radar cross section 252
APPENDIX B 253
Anti – Radiation Missile (ARM) Against the Radar ... 255
AGM-88 HARM 260
APPENDIX C 267
Towed decoys 267
APPENDIX D 271
Field orientation 271
APPENDIX E 280
Lighting strike and protection 280
APPENDIX F 280
NATO Codification System 283
Glossary and Abbreviations 285
References and Bibliography 303
Index 307

2P25 launcher with 3M9M3E missile.

Serbian 2P25 launcher blasting 3M9M3E missile.

Foreword

1S91 'Straight Flush' engagement and fire control radar.

CHAPTER ONE

Origins of 2K12 KUB (SA-6) missile system

Development history

During the 1950s introduction of the new battle tanks and troop transporters with the enhanced mobility and tactics development for the Soviet Army armored and mechanized forces yielded the new requirement for adequate protection against the enemy aerial threats. Armored and mechanized divisions long-range air defense was provided by the 2K11 Krug (SA-4 Ganef) missile system (Fig. 1-1). However, the question arose of what will happen if the long-range defense is not able to engage and stop all attacking airplanes, especially if they are performed at a low altitude. This situation dictated the new requirement: a need for a new missile system that can engage low-level airplanes at medium and short distances.

Figure 1-1: 2K11 'Круг' / 2K11 Krug/ SA-4 Ganef is a first Soviet Army mobile air defense missile system specifically designed for the use in the land forces. (Source: Wikipedia)

In the Soviet Union, armament production was highly centralized. In March 1953, after Stalin died, the Ministry of Armaments was combined with the Ministry of Aviation Industry to become the Ministry of Defense Industry, with Marshal Dimitry Ustinov assigned as head of this new ministry. Marshal Ustinov proposed the development of a new complex and sought the design bureau that will lead the development. The first choice was general designer Aleksandar Raspletin. The first 'General Designer' in the domestic radio industry, the founder of the scientific and technical direction for creating anti-aircraft missile weapons, one of the founders of the leading design bureau for the development of anti-aircraft missile air defense systems. After reviewing the technical requirements, Raspletin realized that solving the problem of hitting low-flying airplanes on rough terrain with the help of radio command guidance systems is a very difficult task, if not impossible. The missile of the future complex should be equipped with an autonomous homing head, which no one has ever done except some initial studies in KB-1[1]. Having worked out the task Raspletin rejected it.

Marshal Ustinov turned to Research Institute - 20 headed by General Designer Veniamin P. Efremov, who was SA-4 Ganef designer. Having studied the issue, Efremov also refused to take the task.

Both Raspletin and Evfremov believed that creating the required system on the existing element base is impossible. The three main reasons for the refusals to take the task were:

- it is impossible to discriminate the reflected signals from the target against the background noise (clutter) while exposed to active and passive interference,
- it is impossible to create a missile seeker with the required parameters, and
- it is impossible to place the radar on a self-propelled chassis.

Ustinov knew that both design bureaus were busy fulfilling orders of particular importance and are actually overloaded with work, so he did not insist and postponed the search for a solution. However, there were some dissatisfied members in the Central Committee of the Communist Party. Under the pressure of the Communist Party leadership, Ustinov called the Minister of Radio Industry Kalmykov and chief designer Raspletin and asked them to justify the refusal of the project. Both Kalmykov and Raspletin again firmly stated that the creation of a new missile system with given characteristics in the near future is impossible based on the current status of the Soviet technologies.

Continuing the search for a candidate to take the role of the chief designer, Ustinov drew attention to the aviation industry complex. After

---

1 KB is an abbreviation of the Russian initials of 'Конструкторское Бюро' – Konstruktorskoye Biro, meaning Design Bureau. During the Soviet era, KBs were closed institutions working on design and prototyping of advanced technology, usually for military applications. A bureau was officially identified by a number, and often semi-officially by the name of its lead designer.

Khrushchev proclaimed a course for the development of rocket and missile technology, orders for aircraft design bureaus decreased sharply, and their managers started looking for new orders, including non-core business.

Ustinov knew about this, as he also knew that, while dealing with aircraft weapons systems, aircraft designers have mastered dealing with every excess gram of weight and centimeter of length. At the end of 1957, Ustinov proposed the development of a new anti-aircraft missile system to the chief designer of the Zhukovsky OSKB-15 - Viktor Vasilyevich Tikhomirov (Fig. 1-2 left) and the chief designer of the Tushinsky experimental armament plant - Ivan Ivanovich Toropov (Fig. 1-2 right). After analysing the proposal, Tikhomirov initially agreed. Ustinov immediately reported his consent to the party Central Committee. The head of the Central Committee defense department, Ivan Dmitrievich Serbin, summoned Tikhomirov and 'carried out an interrogation'. Having firmly and convincingly answered all the questions of 'Ivan the Terrible' (as Serbin was called behind the back), Tikhomirov passed the 'cruel verbal exam' with flying colors.

Figure 1-2: Viktor Vasilyevich Tikhomirov   Ivan Ivanovich Toropov

Soon the news of Tikhomirov's decision spread throughout the industry, and ill-wishers immediately dubbed him as an 'adventurer'. But he was not an adventurer at all. Viktor Vasilyevich Tikhomirov was a real scientist and designer. He started work only when, after carefully considering the proposal, he gained one hundred percent confidence that the work is doable. Tikhomirov was very well known in the industry as he was the creator of the first Soviet aircraft radar 'Gneiss-2' and a number of other radar systems.

The lead developer of the complex was identified as OKB[2] -15

---

2   OKB is a transliteration of the Russian initials of 'Опытное конструкторское бюро' – Opytnoye Konstruktorskoye Biro, meaning Experimental Design Bureau.

GKAT³. Previously, it was a branch of the main developer of aircraft radars - NII⁴ -17 GKAT, located near the Flight Test Institute in Zhukovsky near Moscow. Soon, OKB-15 was transferred to the GKRE⁵, its name was changed several times and, finally, it was transformed into the Scientific Research Institute of Instrument Engineering (NIIP) of the Ministry of Radio Engineering Industry.

The development of the 2K12 'Kub' air defense system was set by the Decree of the Central Committee of the CPSU and the Council of Ministers of the USSR dated 18 July 1958. The 'Kub' complex was supposed to ensure the defeat of air targets flying at speeds of 420-600 m/s at altitudes from 100-200 m to 5-7 km at ranges up to 20 km with the probability of hitting the target with one missile no less than 0.7. At the same time, Soviet Air Defense (Protiv Vozdushnaya Oborona) had a similar requirement which is realized through the SA-3 Goa (S-125 Neva) system. Naturally, the design objectives were similar but more ambitious than those for the S-125/SA-3 Goa. The biggest difference was in the mobility and the short reaction time (Fig. 1-3).

Development was authorized in 1958, with the system design assigned to Tikhomirov, and the missile design to what is now Vympel⁶. The design was to be self- propelled and highly mobile, like the 2K11 Krug/SA-4 Ganef, but using a lightweight tracked chassis like the one that used by the ZSU-23/4P Shilka self-propelled antiaircraft gun.

Once when the requirements and the parameters were accepted, the sheer size of the task started to kick in. The system shall be operational by 1963 with the ability to defeat aerial targets from 100 m to 12,000 m altitude, at distances between 6-20 km and be ready for action in no more than 5 minutes. One of the engineers involved in the project commented with very simple words:

---

3   GKAT is Soviet abbreviation for the "State Committee for the Aviation Technologies - Государственный Комитет по Авиационной Технике ГКАТ).

4   NII is an abbreviation for Научно-Исследовательский Институт – Scientific and Research Institute.

5   GKRE - (State Committee for Radio Electronics)

6   An anti-aircraft guided missile for the complex was instructed to create a design bureau of plant No. 134 GKAT, which originally specialized in the field of aviation small arms and bomb weapons and had already accumulated some experience in the development of the K-7 air-to-air missile. Subsequently, this organization was transformed into GosMKB 'Vympel'. The development of the missile complex 'Kub' was started under the leadership of the chief designer I.I.Toropov.

'Guys, you are crazy!' [7]

The work on the system was supposed to ensure the beginning of the 2K12 (as the system was officially designated) missile system for joint tests in the second quarter of 1961. However, they dragged on and ended with an almost five-year delay from the planned date, two years behind the practically simultaneously started work on the 2K11 Krug/SA-4 Ganef complex. The evidence of the dramatic history of the creation of the Kub complex was the dismissal of the chief designers of both the complex as well as the missile included in it at the most intense moment of work.

The ambitious specifications and the use of immature technology, such as the Continuous Wave (CW) semi-active homing missile seeker, and solid propellant ramjet sustainer powerplant, resulted in a troublesome and protracted development process. Problems with the seeker and the powerplant resulted in numerous test failures, with the design only achieving

Figure 1-3: 2K12 Kub system in designated role - army air defense for motorized and armored units. (Source: Russian DoD)

---

7 'Ребято, ве сумашедшие!'. Source: Михаил Первов 'Рассказы о русских ракетах'; 'Столичная энциклопедия'.

certification in 1967-1968, a decade after the launch of the project.

Unlike the SA-4 complex, the SA-6 uses lighter chassis. One of the big differences is that all radio equipment was placed not on two machines, as in the SA-4 system, but on one platform and the launcher carry three missiles instead of two (Fig. 1-4).

Very difficult tasks were also solved when designing the missile. The supersonic ramjet rocket motor ran not on liquid, but on solid propellant. This excluded the possibility of adjusting propellant consumption in accordance with the speed and altitude of the missile. In addition, the missile was made without a booster - the charge of the starting motor was placed in the volume of the afterburner of the ramjet motor. For the first time on an anti-aircraft missile of a mobile complex, a semi-active Doppler radar homing head replaced the command radio control equipment.

Figure 1-4: 2K12 Kub/SA-6 concept: missile launcher and a central battery radar unit. (Source: authors)

The design concept was for a single self-propelled 1S91 fully mobile engagement and fire control radar system, with an integrated target tracking and acquisition radar, controlling a group of four 2P25 self-propelled series Transporter Erector Launcher (TEL) vehicles, each with three 3M9 series missile rounds mounted on the rotating platform. This generic battery structure would be supported by several 2T7 transloader/transporters, carried on the ZIL-157 trucks reloader (Fig. 1-5).

Figure 1-5: 2K12 Kub/SA-6 battery concept: battery radar and four missile launchers with a support missile loader/transporter. (Source: Russian DoD)

Tests

At the end of 1959, the first launcher was delivered to the Donguz test site, which made it possible at the same time to start air defense official tests. However, until July 1960, it was not possible to carry out a single successful missile launch with an operating sustainer stage. The bench tests examination revealed three burnouts of the chamber. NII-2, one of the leading scientific organizations of the GKAT, was involved in the analysis of the reasons for the failures. As a result, on the recommendation by NII-2, they abandoned the large-sized empennage[8], which was dropped at the end of the launch section of the missile flight (Fig. 1-6).

As a result of bench tests of the full-scale seeker, the insufficient power of its drive was revealed. In addition, the low-quality performance of the seeker fairing was identified, which caused significant signal distortions, generating synchronous interference, which led to instability of the stabilization loop. This was a common misfortune of many Russian missiles with first-generation radar homing heads. As a result, the designers switched to a pyro ceramic fairing. However, in addition to such relatively 'subtle' phenomena, during the tests, they encountered the destruction of the fairing in flight as a result of the structure aeroelastic vibrations.

Another significant drawback identified at an early stage of test-

---

8   The empennage is also known as the tail assembly. It is a structure at the rear of a missile that provides stability during flight.

Figure 1-6: 2K12 Kub/SA-6 during the winter exercise. Kub only served in the army air defense units.

2K12 Kub/SA-6 missile system

(Source: Russian DoD)

ing was the unsuccessful design of the air intakes. The formation of shock waves from the leading edge of the air intakes adversely affected the swing wings, creating large aerodynamic moments, irresistible for steering gears - the rudders (ailerons) were jammed in the extreme position. Based on the test results of full-scale models in wind tunnels, a suitable design solution was found - to lengthen the air intake by moving the front edges of the diffuser forward by 200 mm.

In 1961, tests also went with unsatisfactory results. It was not possible to achieve reliable operation of the seeker, no launches were carried out along the reference trajectory, there was no reliable data on the value of the second propellant consumption. It was not possible to develop a technology for reliable deposition of the inner surface heat-protective coating on the afterburner titanium housing, which was exposed to the combustion products erosion effect of the main engine gas generator containing aluminum and magnesium oxides. Later, steel was used instead of titanium.

So-called 'organizational restructuring' followed: In August 1961 Toropov was replaced by Lyapin, in January 1962 Figurovsky took the place of, a three times Stalin Prize winner Tikhomirov. But time gave a fair assessment of the work of the designers who determined the technical appearance of the system. The former OKB-15 today bears the name of Viktor Tikhomirov.

The dismissal of the development pioneers did not lead to the acceleration of work. By the beginning of 1963, out of 83 launched missiles, only 11 were equipped with a seeker. At the same time, only 3 launches were successfully completed. The missiles were tested only with the experimental seeker, because the delivery of the standard ones has not yet begun. The reliability of the seeker was such that in September 1963, after 13 unsuccessful launches with the rejection of the seeker, flight tests had to be interrupted. The tests of the missile main motor were also not completed.

In 1964, missile launches were carried out in a standard design, but the missile systems had not yet been equipped with communication equipment, linking individual positions. By mid-April 1964, the first successful launch of a missile equipped with a warhead was carried out. Testers managed to shoot down a target – remotely controlled IL-28 flying at medium altitude. The following tests were successful, and the accuracy of the missile guidance system to the target simply delighted the test participants.

After the successful completion of the tests and by the decree of the

Central Committee and the Council of Ministers of the USSR of 23 January 1967, the complex was adopted by the Army Air Defense Forces (Fig. 1-6 and 1-7).

Figure 1-7: 2K12 Kub concept: missile launcher during the military parade in mid-eighties. (Source: Russian DoD)

System components

The main combat assets of the system are:
- self-propelled unit having fire control and engagement radar 1S91 (SURN[9]) with NATO codification name 'Straight Flush'
- self-propelled launcher (SPU[10]) 2P25, and
- 3M9 missiles.

---

9   Russian abbreviation for Samohodnaya Ustanovka Razvedki i Navedenia (Самоходная установка разведки и наведения) - Self-propelled Reconnaissance and Guidance Unit, In Yugoslavia it was named RStON for Radarska Stanica Osmatranja i Navodjenja (for radar station for surveillance and guidance).
10 Samohodna Puskovaya Ustanovka – Self-propelled Launcher.

1S91 self-propelled fire control and engagement unit

The 1S91 self-propelled fire control and engagement unit, NATO name 'Straight Flush', consists of two radar stations - the 1S11 air target detection and targeting radar and the 1S31 precision target tracking and illumination radar for semi-active missile homing guidance, as well as means for target identification, navigation, topography, relative orientation, radio-telecode communication with self-propelled launchers, a television-optical sight, an autonomous power supply (a gas turbine electric generator was used), antenna lifting and leveling systems (Fig. 1-8 and 1-11).

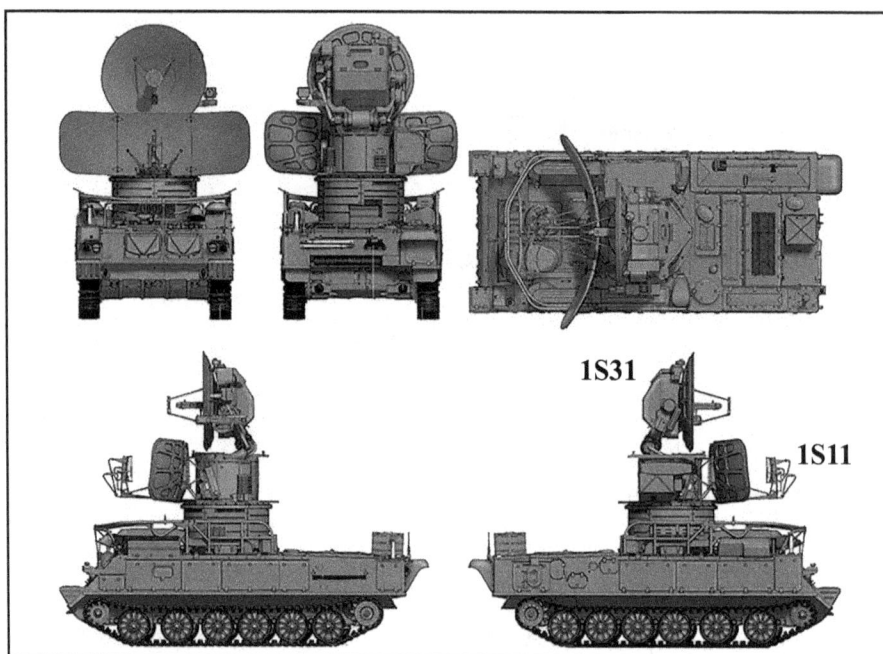

Figure 1-8: 1S91 'Straight Flush' engagement and fire control radar is indeed two radars 1S11 and 1S31 mounted independently. (Source: authors)

The radar antennas were mounted in two tiers above each other - 1S31 as a top antenna, and 1S11 paraboloid section antenna as a bottom antenna. Both antennas can rotate independently. To reduce the height of the self-propelled vehicle on the march, the cylindrical base of the antenna devices is retracted inside the body of the vehicle, and the 1S31 antenna was flipped down and positioned behind the antenna of the 1S11 station.

Based on the intention to provide the required range with a limited power supply and considering the overall and mass restrictions on the antennas, the 1S31 station adopted a coherent-pulse radar scheme. However, when illuminating the target for stable operation of the seeker during low-altitude flight under clutter from the ground, the continuous radiation mode was implemented (Fig. 1-9).

Figure 1-9: 1S11 target acquisition and tracking radar is a coherent pulse radar and has a parabolic antenna that can rotate 360⁰. (Source: authors)

The 1S11 station is a coherent[11] pulse centimetric wavelength radar with a rotation of 15 rpm in early variants which were later increased to 20 rpm. 1S11 has two independent waveguides transmitting and receiving channels operating at separated carrier frequencies and the emitters installed in the focal plane of a single antenna mirror. It is able to detect, identify and designate the target at ranges from 3 - 70 km and at altitudes from 30 – 7,000 m with a pulse radiation pick power of 600 kW on a discrete operating frequency. Cited PRF[12] is 2.0 kHz with a 0.5 microsecond pulse width. The receiver sensitivity is in the order of 10^{-13} Watts. The beam

---

11   In a pulse radar system, coherence describes the phase relationships between the transmitted and the received pulses. Oscillations and electromagnetic waves are described as coherent if their phase relationships are constant.

12   PRF is an abbreviation of the pulse repetition frequency. PRF is the number of pulses of a repeating signal in a specific time unit, normally measured in pulses per second.

width along the azimuth is approximately 1⁰ and the total field of view in elevation is 20⁰ meaning that the main lobe[13] can be elevated through 20⁰.

To ensure the station noise immunity, the following was provided:

- moving target indicator (MTI) and suppression of asynchronous impulse noise;
- receiving channels manual gain control;
- pulse repetition rate modulation, and
- transmitters frequency tuning.

1S31 station also has two channels with emitters installed in the single antenna parabolic reflector focal plane for precision target tracking and target illumination for semi-active missile homing guidance. On the

Figure 1-10: 1S31 is a precise tracking and target illumination radar for semi-active missile homing guidance. (Source: authors)

---

13   In a radio antenna's radiation pattern, the main lobe, or main beam, is the lobe containing the higher power. This is the lobe that exhibits the greater field strength. More information can be found in the glossary.

target tracking channel, the station had a pulse power of 270 kW, a receiver sensitivity of about 10^{-13} W, and a beamwidth of about 1°. The root-mean-square error (RME) of target tracking in angular coordinates is about 0.5°, and about 10 m in range. Two 270 kW peak power channels are used to perform fine tracking and terminal CW[14] illumination for the 3M9/9M9 SAM seeker. The app. 1.0° main lobe can be steered independently of the 1S11. Cited maximum antenna slew rate is 20°/sec and elevation rate of 10°/sec. The station could capture an F-4 Phantom II or similar size airplane for auto-tracking with a probability of 0.9 at a distance of up to 50 km. Protection against passive interference and reflections from the ground was carried out by the SDC[15] system with a programmed change in the pulse repetition rate, from active interference - using the method of mono-pulse direction finding of targets, an interference indication system and tuning the operating frequency of the station. In the event that the 1S31 station is still suppressed by interference, it was possible to track the target in angular coordinates using a television optical sight (TOV) and receive information about the range from the 1S11 radar. The station is capable of low-level targets stable tracking (Fig. 1-10 and 1-11).

1S91 also have installed a 9Sh33 optical tracker which uses a TV camera for visual angle tracking of targets (Fig. 1-33 and 5-11). A 1S51 identification friend or foe (IFF) system is integrated. A 1S61 digital data-link terminal is carried and the purpose is to communicate with 1S61 terminals on the 2P25 mobile missile launchers and transfers target location to cue the launcher and drive elevation and azimuth inputs for the launcher missile platforms.

All equipment is located on the GM-568 chassis. The mass of the self-propelled reconnaissance and guidance unit with a combat crew of 4 people is 20.3 tons.

In the Yugoslav People's Army 1S91 was designated as RStON 'Radarska Stanica Osmatranja i Navodjenja' which is an abbreviation for the translated meaning of 'Radar Station for Surveillance and Guidance'.[16]

---

14   In a radio antenna's radiation pattern, the main lobe, or main beam, is the lobe containing the higher power. This is the lobe that exhibits the greater field strength. More information can be found in the Appendix.

15   SDC is an abbreviation for Surface Deformation and Change.

16   RTsON is an interchangeable term with 1S91 and will be used during the entire book, especially when describing the Kub employment in the Balkans.

Figure 1-11: 1S91 'Straight Flush' station in the combat position (both antennas are risen and extended). (Source: Czech DoD)

2P25 self-propelled launcher

2P25 self-propelled launcher (TEL – Transporter Erector Launcher) is placed on the GM-578 chassis with the rail guides platform which can accommodate three missiles. The launcher has electric power tracking drives, a computing device, navigation equipment, orientation and topography devices, communication equipment, missiles prelaunch control, and an autonomous gas turbine electric unit (Fig. 1-12).

The missile control during positioning and docking on the guides is executed by the two umbilical connectors (electrical connectors). These are used to initialise the missile and power the seeker prelaunch and monitor missile status and condition During the missile launch phase, these umbilicals are cut off with the help of special rods as the missile starts moving along the guide beam. The prelaunch missiles positioning in the direction of the anticipated interception point is carried out with the aim of the carriage drives, which processed the data from the 1S91 self-propelled fire control and engagement radar, which were fed to the self-propelled launcher via the radio-communication link 1S61 (Fig. 1-13).

Figure 1-12: 2P25 missile transporter erector and launcher (TEL) with erected 3M9 missiles in one of the static museum exhibitions. (Source: authors)

In the transport position, the missiles are positioned with the tail section facing forward along the vehicle centerline - the 'guns go backwards to battle'.

The weight of a self-propelled launcher with three missiles and a combat crew of three is about 19.5 tons.

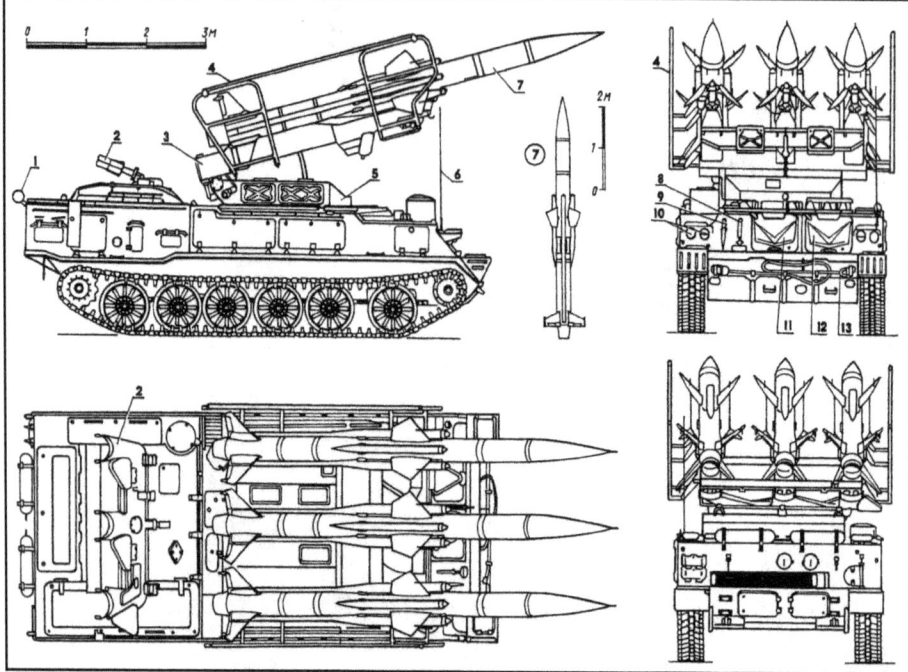

Figure 1-13: 2P25 transporter, erector, launcher: 1 - compressed air tanks; 2 - missile mounting brackets; 3 - guiding beams; 4 - railing; 5 - swivel base; 6 - radio antenna; 7 - missiles; 8,9 - tools; 10 - headlights; 11 - operator's hatch; 12 - driver's hatch; 13 - towing cable.

3M9 guided missile

While the long-range ramjet missile system 2K11 Krug/SA-4 Ganef has direct western equivalents in the contemporary ramjet Bendix RIM-8 Talos, Bristol Bloodhound and Armstrong Whitworth SeaSlug, no such equivalent exists for the 2K12 Kub/SA-6 Gainful system. In terms of airframe and propulsion configuration, the nearest equivalents are the 3M80 Moskit/Sunburn and Kh-31 Krypton supersonic anti-ship missile. The 3M9 missile design introduced the first solid-propellant ramjet engine in Soviet missiles, resulting in a missile with superior range performance to its conventional solid rocket competitors, as the missile did not need to carry the mass of the full oxidiser component of the propellant[17].

Figure 1-14: 3M9ME-UR (Uchebno-Razreznaya) cutaway training missile. Note the ramjet inlet structures and the compressed air-lines. (Source: Miroslav Gyűrösi)

An overall look of the 3M9 missile from the SA-6 system in comparison with the 3M8 missile of the SA-4 'Krug' system amazes with the

---

17   Dr Carlo Kopp https://www.ausairpower.net/APA-2K12-Kvadrat.html.

elegance of its outlines (Fog. 1-14, Fig. 1-15 and Fig. 1-16).

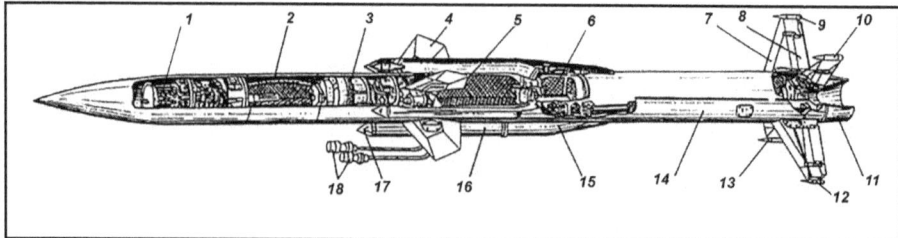

Figure 1-15: 1 - 1SB4M CW monopulse semi-active homing seeker with Doppler closure rate capability; 2 - 3N12 57 kg blast-fragmentation warhead 3 - 1SB6M Autopilot; 4 - wings; 5 - ramjet motor; 6 - 9D16K sustainer solid gas generator charge (67 kg LK-6TM reducing propellant); 7 - stabilizer; 8 - rudder 9 - encoder; 10 - fairing; 11 - nozzle; 12 - encoder; 13 - carrier with adjuster; 14 - missile housing; 15 - air intake canal to missile body transition; 16 - ramjet air intake canal; 17 - cover for ramjet air intake canal; 18 - shear connector.

Figure 1-16: 3M9ME-UR (Uchebno-Razreznaya - Учебно-Разрезная) cutaway training missile. (Source: Miroslav Gyűrösi)

Like the 3M8 (in SA-4 missile system), the 3M9 missile is made according to the 'rotary wing' scheme. However, unlike the 3M8, the 3M9 missile rudders, which are located on the stabilizers, were additionally used for control. As a result of the implementation of this scheme, it was possible to reduce the size of the rotary fins, reduce the required power of the steering gears and use a lighter pneumatic drive instead of a hydraulic one.

The nose of the missile houses the Agat designed 1SB4M CW semi-active homing coherent dual-plane mono-pulse seeker, which employs a parabolic section reflector antenna that produces mono-pulse sum and pitch/yaw difference signals. The seeker also uses the difference in Doppler between the illuminator carrier frequency and backscatter from the target to estimate the closure rate between the missile and target. An adaptive tunable narrowband filter is claimed to be used to reject clutter. The seeker is analogue and in addition to producing pitch/yaw commands for the autopilot, it activates the proximity fuse (Fig. 1-17).

Figure 1-17: Agat 1SB4ME monopulse CW SARH seeker. The polarisation screen is positioned over the reflector and the unique feed arrangement with matching stubs. (Source: Miroslav Gyűrösi)

Early variants of the 1SB4 seeker would acquire the target while the missile was on the rail, but the later 2K12M3/3M9M3 seeker could acquire the target post-launch, permitting the missile to be launched before CW illumination is initiated. A variant of the 'P-nav' control law is employed. Due to the absence of seeker cooling, the missile seeker can be powered up on the launch rail for 5 to 10 minutes before it overheats and must be powered down to cool off. Training emulator rounds have characteristic cooling fins on the seeker section for this reason[18].

As mentioned previously, the missile is equipped with a combined propulsion system. In the front section of the motor is the gas generator

---
18   Ibid.

chamber with the charge of the 9D16K marching (second) stage motor. For a solid propellant gas generator, it is impossible to regulate the propellant consumption in accordance with the actual flight conditions, so the choice of the form of charge is carried out on the basis of a conventional typical trajectory, which in those years the developers considered the most probable in the combat use of the missile. The nominal duration of operation slightly exceeded 20 seconds, the mass of the fuel charge (760 mm long) was about 67 kg. The composition of the LK-6TM propellant developed by NII-862 was characterized by a large excess of propellant in relation to the oxidizer. The combustion products of the gas generator charge entered the afterburner, where the remaining propellant was burned in the airflow entering through 4 air intakes. The inlet devices of the air intakes, designed for supersonic working conditions, are equipped with conical central bodies. At the launch site, before the propulsion engine was turned on, the exits of the air intake channels to the afterburner were closed with fiberglass plugs, entering through 4 air intakes (Fig. 1-18).

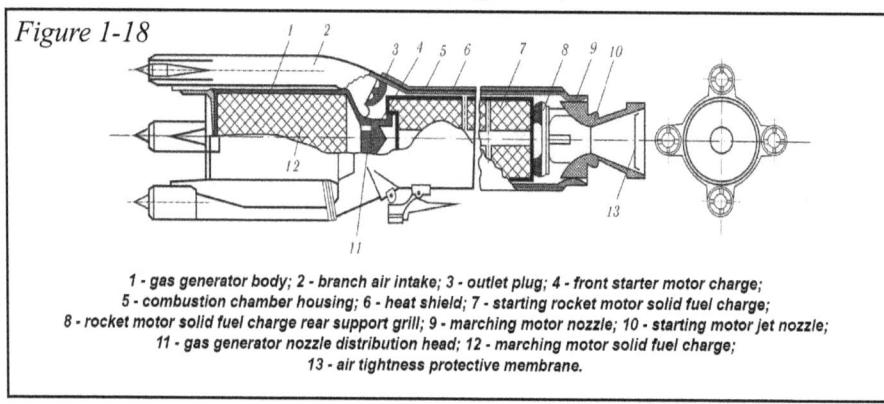

Figure 1-18

1 - gas generator body; 2 - branch air intake; 3 - outlet plug; 4 - front starter motor charge;
5 - combustion chamber housing; 6 - heat shield; 7 - starting rocket motor solid fuel charge;
8 - rocket motor solid fuel charge rear support grill; 9 - marching motor nozzle; 10 - starting motor jet nozzle;
11 - gas generator nozzle distribution head; 12 - marching motor solid fuel charge;
13 - air tightness protective membrane.

The centre and aft sections of the missile fuselage are mostly occupied with the solid propellant charges for the propulsion system. The afterburner houses a solid propellant charge of the launch stage - an ordinary checker with armored ends (1.7 m long and 290 mm in diameter, with a cylindrical channel 54 mm in diameter) made of VIK-2 propellant weighing 172 kg. The igniter initiates a burn along the central 54 mm diameter cavity. The engine has a burn duration of about 3 to 6 seconds and accelerates the missile from 0 to ~ Mach 1.5. Once the booster has burned out, it becomes the combustion chamber/nozzle for the solid propellant rocket ramjet. Four symmetrically placed air inlets feed into this chamber. Frangible fibreglass covers are used to prevent air ingestion prior to sustainer ignition.

It should be noted that the 3M9 missile is the first in the world missile with this kind of design formally put into the serial production and acceptance into service. Later, after the Israeli forces captured several undamaged 3M9 missiles, the Soviet design served as a base for the creation of a number of anti-aircraft and anti-ship missiles.

The use of a ramjet engine ensured the maintenance of the high speed of the 3M9 missile along the entire trajectory, which contributed to the provision of high maneuverability. During training and control-serial missile launches, a direct hit on the target was systematically achieved, which happened extremely rarely when using other relatively large anti-aircraft missiles.

The detonation of a high-explosive fragmentation warhead 3N12 weighing 57 kg (developed by NII-24) was carried out at the command of the autodyne two-channel continuous-radiation 3E27 radio fuse, created at NII-571. The 3E27 CW two-channel radio proximity fuse will nominally trigger at a 30 m distance from the target, using antennas on the sides of the missile fuselage.

The 3N12 57 kg blast-fragmentation warhead is mounted behind the fuse (Fig. 1-19).

Figure 1-19: The 3N12 series fragmentation warhead on the training missile. For the 3M9 missile, the warhead has the preformed casing: (Source: Miroslav Gyűrösi)

The missile ensured the defeat of targets maneuvering with an overload of up to 8 units (8g), but at the same time the probability of hitting such targets, depending on various conditions, was reduced to 0.2-0.55, while the probability of hitting non-maneuvering targets was within 0.4 - 0, 75.

The length of the missile is about 5.8 m with a diameter of 330 mm. To ensure the transportation of the assembled missile in the 9Ya266 transport and storage container, the left and right stabilizer consoles were folded towards each other (Fig. 2-14).

Missile guidance

The design of a guided missile is a substantial undertaking requiring the effort of many engineers with expertise in aerodynamics, flight control, structures, and propulsion, to mention just a few. The different design groups must work together to produce the most efficient weapon at the lowest possible cost (Fig. 1-20).

Guided missile (also known as guided munitions) systems contain a guidance package that attempts to keep the missile on a course that will eventually lead to an intercept with the target. Most guidance SAMs or air defense systems employ either homing or command guidance to intercept the target. At this point, it is appropriate to note that short-range, shoulder fired SAMs using IR guidance has been developed by various nations.

Two of the most used guidance methods are:

- the homing guidance system, which guides the interceptor missile to the target by means of a target seeker and an onboard computer; homing guidance can be modeled;
- command guidance, which relies on missile guidance commands calculated at the ground launching (controlling) site and transmitted to the missile.

Electromagnetic radiation is the most popular form of energy detected by homing systems. Radar can be the primary sensor for any of the three classes of homing guidance systems, but it is best suited for semi-active and active homing. Currently, the use of electromagnetic radiation via radar in a target seeker is foremost in effectiveness. Radar is little restricted by weather or visibility but is susceptible to enemy jamming. Heat (infrared radiation) is best used with a passive seeker. It is difficult to mislead or decoy heat-seeking systems when they are used against aerial targets because the heat emitted by engines and rockets of the aerial targets is difficult to shield. With a sufficiently sensitive detector, the infrared system is very effective. Light is also useful in a passive seeker system. However, both weather and visibility restrict its use. Such a system is quite susceptible to countermeasure techniques.

Various flight paths or trajectories may be deployed with respect to fixed targets, but for moving targets special requirements must be met. In homing systems, sensing elements must be sharply directional to perceive small angular displacements between a missile and its target. Surface to air missile systems typically uses command and other type of guidance.

The optical tracking method also allows engagements to altitudes below that where the radar can track targets.

Surface to air missile guidance is generally divided into three distinct phases:

1. Boost or launch,
2. Midcourse, and
3. Terminal.

The boost phase lasts from the time the missile leaves the launcher until the booster burns all of its fuel. The missile may or may not be actively guided during this phase. The midcourse phase, when it has a distinct existence, is usually the longest in terms of both distance and time. During this phase, guidance may or may not be explicitly required to bring the missile onto the desired course and to make certain it stays on course until it enters a zone (in parametric space) from which terminal guidance can successfully take over. The terminal phase is the last phase of guidance and must have high accuracy and fast reactions to ensure an intercept with the target. In this phase, the guidance seeker (if one is used) is locked onto the target, permitting the missile to be guided all the way to the target. Therefore, proper functioning of the guidance system during the terminal phase, when the missile is approaching its target, is of critical importance. Much work has been done to develop extremely accurate equipment for use in terminal-phase guidance (Fig. 1-21, Fig. 1-22).

There are several guided systems that fall into this category. The

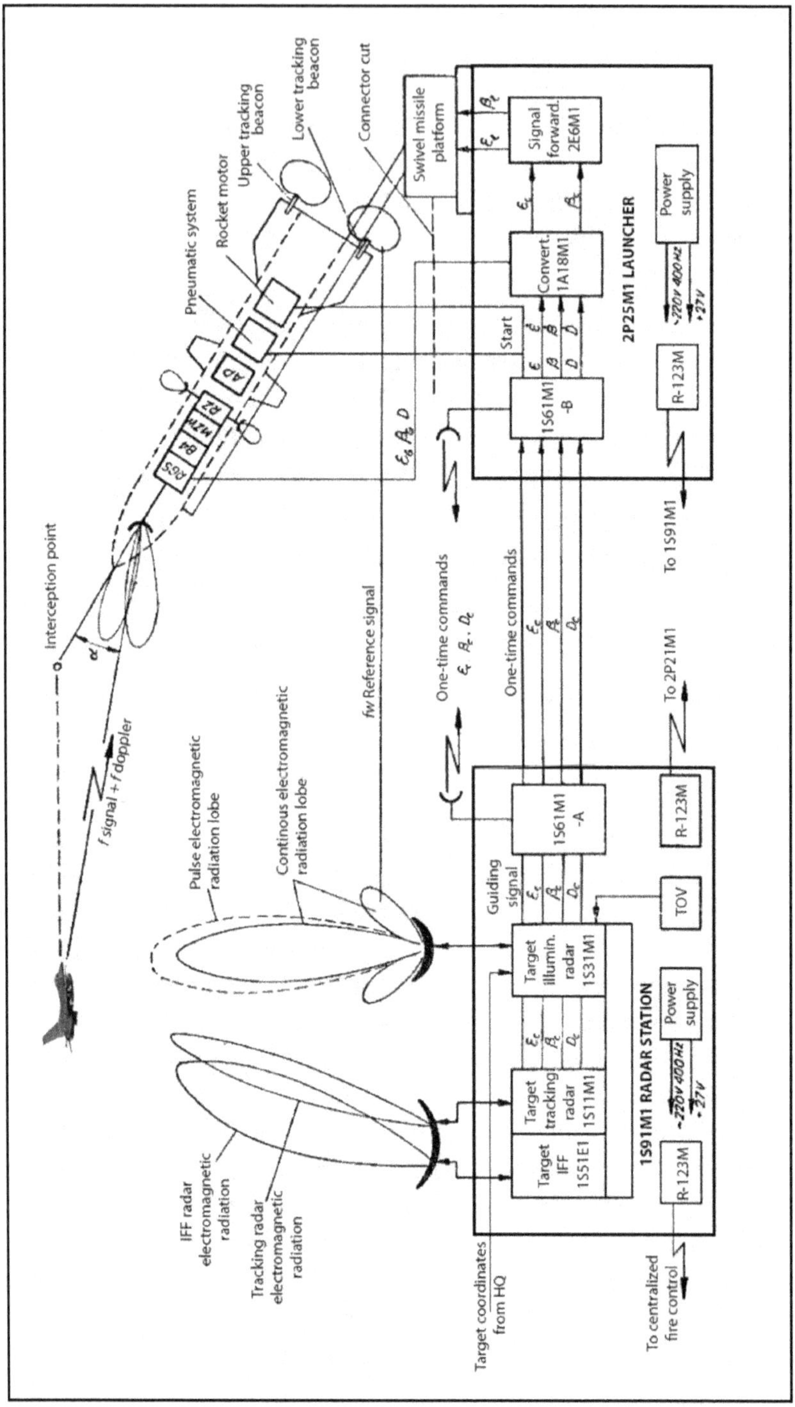

*Figure 1-20: 2K12 Kub simplified functional diagram.
(Source: authors)*

most common ones are the short-range homing systems and some types of inertial system. These terminal systems may also be the only guidance systems used in short-range missiles. Pre-launch aiming errors must be minimized because these errors tend to translate directly into miss distance. Subsequent to launch, the missile has certain requirements. First, the missile needs a target signal. For example, in the case of a semi-active guided missile, the target signal is the result of energy reflected from the target. The source of this energy is the interceptor, which in turn receives energy from the illuminator. Thus, subsequent to launch, the missile requires that the target be continuously illuminated. Target illumination by itself does not require that the interceptor track the target, although this may occur.

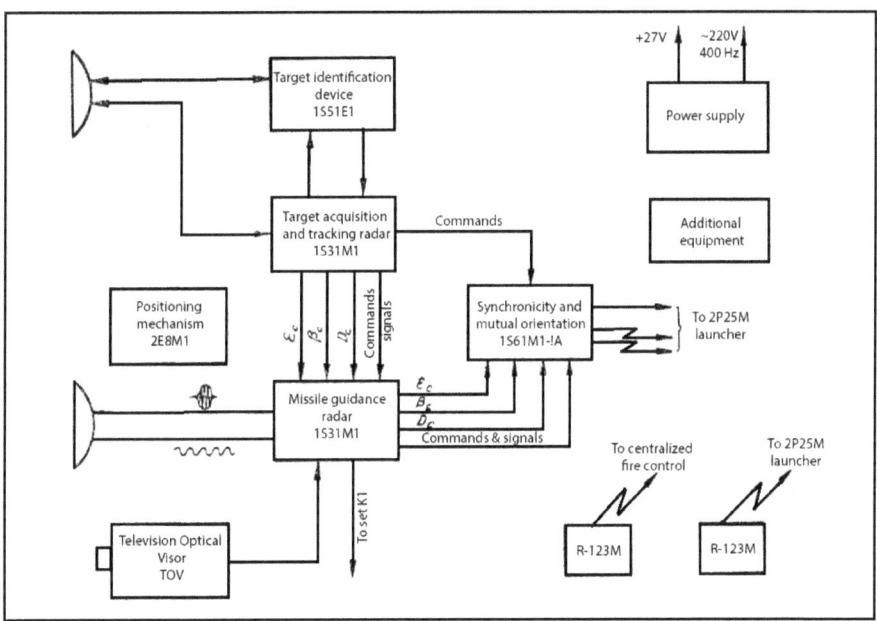

Figure 1-21: 1S91 tracking and fire control radar block diagram. (Source: authors)

In addition, the missile requires the presence of certain modulations on the target return, which are conveniently impressed on the illuminating signal itself. Typically, this is an 85 Hz FM ranging signal, which the missile uses to select the target from clutter or noise.

Guidance techniques, as well as other command/homing methods which are part of the post-launch phase, can be affected in a number of ways, the more prominent of which are listed as follow:

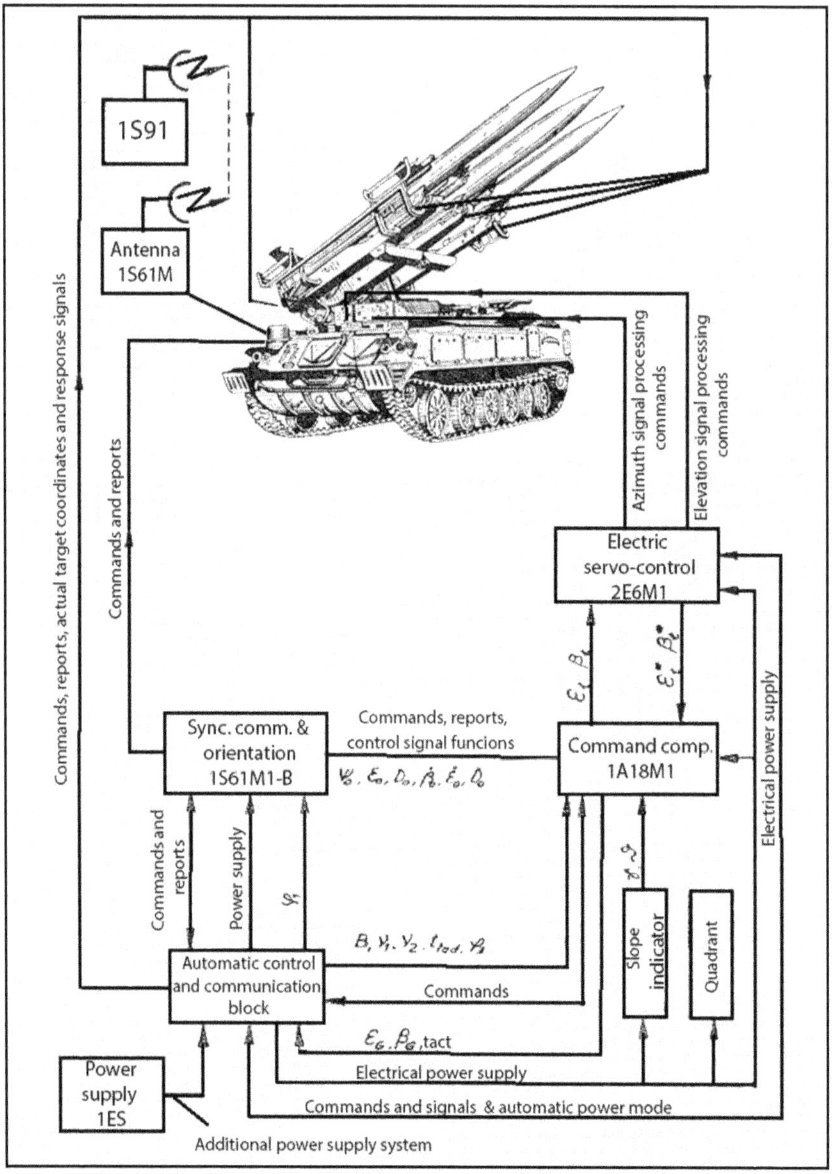

Figure 1-22: 2P25 launcher simplified functional diagram. (Source: authors)

<u>Command Guidance</u>: Command guided missiles are missiles whose guidance instructions or commands come from sources outside the missile. In this type of guidance, a tracking system that is separated from the missile is used to track both the missile and the target. Therefore, a missile seeker is not required in command guidance. The tracking system may consist of two separate tracking units, one for the missile and one for the target

aircraft, or it may consist of one tracking unit that tracks both vehicles. Tracking can be accomplished using radar, optical, laser, or infrared systems. A radar beacon or infrared flare on the tail of the missile can be used to provide information to the tracking system on the location of the missile.

The target and missile ranges, elevations, and bearings are fed to a computer. Consequently, using the position and position rate information (i.e. range and range rate), the computer determines the flight path the interceptor missile should take that will result in a collision with the target. The computer at the launch point determines whether the interceptor missile is on the proper trajectory to intercept the target. If it is not, steering commands are generated by the ground computer and transmitted to the in-flight missile. Furthermore, the computer compares this computed flight path with the predicted flight path of the missile based on current tracking information and determines the correction signals required to move the missile control surfaces to change the current flight path to the new one. These signals are the command guidance and are sent to the missile receiver via either the missile tracking system or a separate command link, such as radio. In addition to the steering instructions, the command link may be required to transfer other instructions to the missile, such as fuse arming, receiver gain setting, and warhead detonation. Finally, in command guidance, the launch point commands the missile.

Command to Line of Sight (CLOS): A particular type of command guidance and navigation where the missile is always to be commanded in the line of sight (LOS) between the tracking unit and the aircraft is known as 'command to line of sight' (CLOS) or three-point guidance. The missile is controlled to stay as close as possible on the LOS to the target after missile capture. In CLOS guidance an up-link is used to transmit guidance signals from a ground controller to the missile. More specifically, if the beam acceleration is taken into account and added to the nominal acceleration generated by the beam-rider equations, then CLOS guidance results. Thus, the beam rider acceleration command is modified to include an extra term. The beam-riding performance described above can thus be significantly improved by taking the beam motion into account. CLOS guidance is used mostly in short range air defense and anti-tank systems.

Pure command guidance is not normally used in modern SAM systems since it is too inaccurate during the terminal phase (when the missile is about to intercept the target). This is because the ground-based radars are distant from the target and the returned signal lacks resolution. However, it is still quite practical to use it to guide the missile to a location near the target, and then use another more accurate guidance method to actually intercept the target. Almost any type of terminal guidance can be used, but the most common are <u>semi-active radar homing (SARH)</u> or <u>active radar homing</u>.

The 3M9 missile is command guided with terminal semi-active radar homing (SARH) from the startup, with target illumination provided by the 1S91 'Straight Flush' radar. Detonation is via either the impact or proximity fuse. The newer 3M9M3(E) missile is possible to launch before the lock-on is established – Lock-on After Launch (LOAL). The missile is launched into the projected target interception point and after 3-4.5 seconds, after the command 'forbidden lock-on' is removed the seeker starts to search for the target by frequency (velocity and Doppler) and for that, it is available 2.5-3 seconds. The first 3-4.5 is inertial guidance and following 2.5-3 seconds by inertial-memory guidance.

On the latest models, this carrier is also fitted with an optical tracking system that allows engagement without the use of the radar (for active RF emissions stealth reasons, or due to heavy ECM jamming) in which case the effective altitude is limited to 14 km/46,000 ft.

SARH missiles require tracking radar to acquire the target, and a more narrowly focused illuminator radar to 'light up' the target in order for the missile to lock on to the radar return reflected off the target. The target must remain illuminated for the entire duration of the missile's flight. This could leave the launch platform vulnerable to counterattack, as well as giving the target's electronic warning systems time to detect the attack and engage countermeasures. Because most SARH missiles require guidance during their entire flight, older radars are limited to one target per radar emitter at a time.

The maximum range of a SARH system is determined by the energy density of the transmitter. Increasing transmit power can increase energy density. Reducing the noise bandwidth of the transmitter can also increase energy density. Spectral density matched to the receive radar detection bandwidth is the limiting factor for maximum range.

SA-6/Kub in the Soviet army

The operational air defense unit in the Soviet Army (land forces) was the anti-aircraft missile regiment equipped and armed with the 2K12 Kub/SA - 6 systems. Each regiment consisted of a regiment command post, five anti-aircraft missile batteries, a fire control battery and a technical battery. Each missile battery included one self-propelled reconnaissance and guidance unit 1S91, four self-propelled launchers 2P25 with three 3M9 missiles on each, as well as two 2T7 transport-loading vehicles on the ZIL-157 chassis and, if necessary, was able to independently perform combat mission (Fig. 1-5 and 1-21).

Figure 1-23: 2P25 missile launcher from one of the Soviet army air defense units. After the disintegration of the Soviet Union, 2K12 passed to the succeeding countries. (Source: Russian DoD)

Under centralized control, combat control commands and target designation data for the batteries came from the regiment's command post (from the KBU - the combat control cabin of the automated command and control complex 'Crab' (K-1) with the surveillance radar attached to it. This information is received on the KPTs battery - the target designation receiving cabin of the K-1 complex, and from it was transmitted to the self-propelled reconnaissance and guidance unit of the battery. The technical battery of the regiment included 9T22 transport vehicles, 2V7 control and measuring stations, 2V8 control and test mobile stations, 9T14 technological trolleys, repair machines and other equipment.

Production and export

SA-6 serial production of all modifications was organized with the multiple factories and enterprises:

- self-propelled reconnaissance and guidance installations - at the Ulyanovsk mechanical plant of the Ministry of Radio Industry,

- self-propelled launchers - at the Sverdlovsk machine-building plant named after M.I. Kalinin - Minaviaprom (MAP),

- missiles - at the Dolgoprudny machine-building plant.

In the course of SA-6 all modifications serial production from 1967 to 1983, more than 500 air defense systems, and tens of thousands of missiles were produced for the Soviet army. More than 4000 missile launches were carried out during tests and exercises.

In addition to the Soviet Union, from 1971 to 1985 the SA-6 Kub version for export, designated as 'Kvadrat; missile system was also delivered to the following countries: Algeria, Angola, Bulgaria, Czechoslovakia, Egypt, Ethiopia, India, Iraq, Yugoslavia (SFRY), GDR Yemen (South Yemen), GDR Korea (North Korea), Cuba, Kuwait, Libya, Hungary, DR Germany (East Germany), Poland, Romania, Syria and Vietnam.

SA-6 missile system today is in the arsenal of the following countries: Algeria, Angola, Bosnia and Herzegovina, Bulgaria, Egypt, Ethiopia, India, Iran, Armenia, Kazakhstan, Cuba, Hungary, Poland, Romania, Russia, Syria, Serbia and Vietnam.

Soviet Modernization

Characteristics of SA-6 system variants:

	Kub	Kub-M1	Kub-M3	Kub-M4
Engagement envelope, km				
- by range	6-8 ... 22	4 ... 23	4 ... 25	4 ... 24 **
- in height	0.1 ... 7 (12 *)	0.08 ... 8 (12 *)	0.02 ... 8 (12 *)	0.03 ... 14 *
- by parameter	up to 15	up to 15	before 18	before 18
Kill probability				
- fighter using single SAM	0.7	0.8 ... 0.95	0.8 ... 0.95	0.8 ... 0.9
- helicopter	-	-	-	0.3 ... 0.6
- cruise missile	-	-	-	0.25 ... 0.5
Max. target speed, m/s	600	600	600	600 **
Reaction time, s	26 ... 28	22 ... 24	22 ... 24	24 **
SAM velocity, m/s	600	600	700	700 **
Missile mass, kg	630	630	630	630 **
Warhead mass, kg	57	57	57	57 **
Engagement concurrency (number of channels)	1	1	1	2
Missile concurrency (number of missile channels)	2 ... 3	2 ... 3	2 ... 3	until 3
Deployment (stow) time, min	five	five	five	five
The number of missiles on a combat vehicle	3	3	3	3
Year of adoption	1967	1973	1976	1978

* if used with the K-1 'Krab' (9S44) system for the automatic fire control

** with the 3M9M3 missile. When using SAM 9M38 characteristics are analog to SA-11 Gadfly (9K37 Buk).

Kub-M1

In the Soviet practice, as the system is fielded in the Army, the work on modernization started based on the testing and field experiences. In accordance with the recommendations of the state commission, the SA-6 modernization began in 1967. As a result of improvements, its combat capabilities were increased.

The first of these was the 2K12M Kub M1, which included a greater engagement envelope, a missile seeker with better ability to defeat deceiving countermeasures, the capability to interrupt radar emissions in order to evade AGM-45 Shrike anti-radiation missiles (ARM), and support for an ARM decoy. In 1972, the modernized complex was tested at the Embensky proving ground under the leadership of a commission headed by the head of the proving ground Kirichenko and in January 1973 it was put into service under the code "Kub-M1".

Naval Kub M-22

Since 1970, work has been carried out to create an M-22 anti-aircraft complex for the Navy using the 3M9 family of missiles, but after 1972 this air defense system was developed for the 9M38 missile that replaced the Kub with a new Buk missile system.

Kub-M3

The next modernization of the 2K12 Kub/SA-6 complex was carried out from 1974 to 1976. As a result, the combat capabilities of the air defense system were further increased:

- the range is extended;
- the ability to engage departing targets with speeds up to 300 m/s, and at stationary targets at altitudes above 1000 m;
- the average flight speed of missiles was increased from 600 to 700 m/s;
- capability to the defeat of aircraft maneuvering with overloads of up to 8g;
- improved noise immunity of the seeker;
- the probability of hitting maneuvering targets is increased by 10-15%;
- improved reliability of combat ground-based air defense systems and its operational characteristics.

Joint tests of the air defense missile system took place in early 1976 at the Embensky test site (head of the test site was B.I. Vashchenko) under the leadership of a commission headed by O.V. Kuprevich, and by the end of the year, it was put into service under the code 'Kub-M3'.

Aerial Target 3M20M3

In recent years, another modification of the missile defense system has been presented at international aerospace exhibitions - a 3M20M3 target converted from a combat missile, designed to simulate air targets with an RCS of 0.7-5 m^2 flying at an altitude of 6-7 km along a route up to 20 km.

Kub-M4

The final 2K12 designated as a Kub M4 variant was a hybridized 1978 design, with the 1S91M3 radar system being capable of controlling the 2P25M3 and SA-11 9A38 TELs and guiding the 3M9 and 9K37 Buk/SA-

2K12 Kub/SA-6 missile system

11 9M38 missiles. The 9A38 TEL variant was also capable of carrying the 3M9 missile and providing terminal tracking and illumination using the 9S35 Fire Dome radar on the TEL.

A missile battery is a basic tactical unit that can operate independently or within the higher units. For the typical SA-6 missile regiment, this book will be described Yugoslavian/Serbian SA-6 formation.

SA-6 Regiment and Battery

Roles and duties in an SA-6 missile battery/battalion/regiment are defined and regulated through the operation and service manuals issued by the Ministry of Defense and Air Defense Branch of the Army. It is essentially based on the general Soviet military doctrine with some minor local modifications. The subjects of these manuals are not much different from those of their western counterparts: combat service, organization, system equipment, communication, safety, etc.

To have a fully trained and functional missile system combat crew, years of training and exercising are necessary. For example, for an officer direct from the military academy, to be fully familiar with every component of the system, a minimum of five years on the designated system is necessary. For a commander, ten years of work on the system is a necessary minimum.

As previously mentioned, SA-6 regiment consists of up to five batteries but that may vary from country to country. There is no universal rule on how the regiment shall be organized.

SA-6 Regiment

Each air defense missile regiment consists of the following components (Fig. 1-24):

Fire control battery

Fire control battery consists of the following subcomponents:

- Command platoon with the 9S416M command and control section, transportation section and communication section. 9S416M is a Serbian version that includes a 9S417 radio relay van.

- Radar platoon – P-40/1S12 (1RL-128-D1 Bronya[19]) mobile radar section (NATO code name is 'Long Track'); PRV-16B 'Thin Skin' height finder section; P-15M 'Flat Face' surveillance and target acquisition radar section and transportation section with the FAP-2026 truck with mounted power generation PES-100.

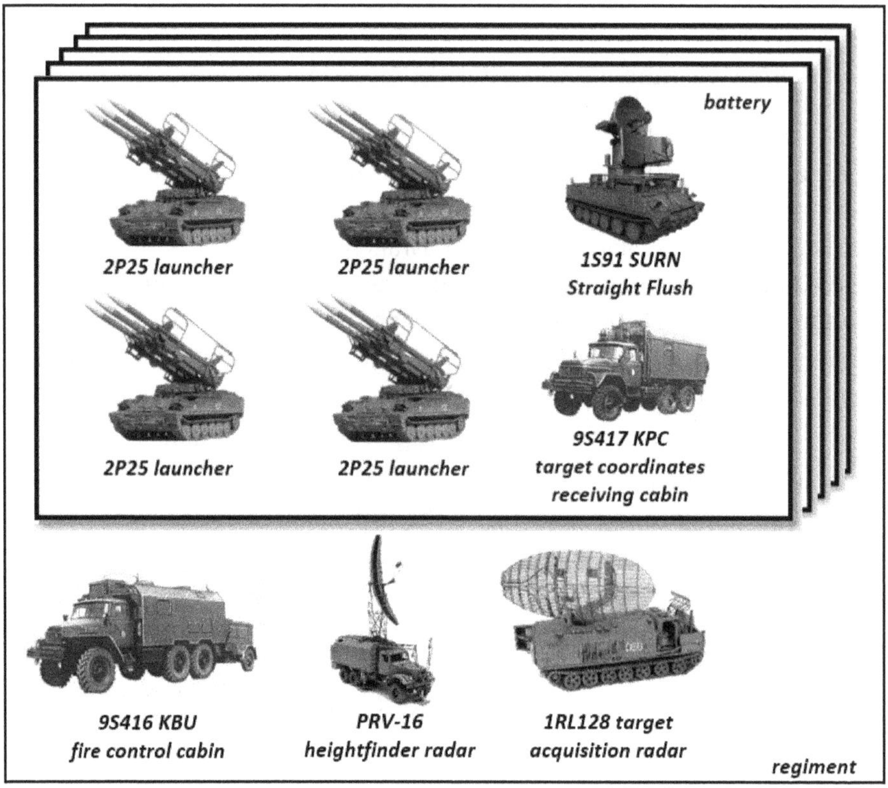

Figure 1-24: Typical 2K12/SA-6 regiment. (Source: Pinterest)

Missile regiment equipment components:

Component	Qty.	Function	Vehicle
1S91 (Straight Flush)	1	Self Propelled Engagement Radar	GM-578
2P25	4	Transporter Erector Launcher	GM-578

---

19 'Bronya' is Russian word for armor. 'Bear' is the local nickname name for 1RL-128-D1 radar used in Yugoslav armed forces. The term is used in the part describing Kub system employment in the Balkans.

2T7/2T7M	2	Transporter/Transloader	ZIL-131
9T227	2	Towed 6 Round Semi-Trailer Transporter	ZiL-157
BTR-60PB or BRDM-2	1	Site Survey Vehicle	BTR-60 or BRDM-2
P-40/1S12 Long Track	1	Self Propelled Acquisition Radar	AT
9S417	1	Radio and data relay (transfer) van	ZiL-157
2V8M1E	1	Missile Repair/Test Station	ZiL-131
MS1760/1761	2	Missile Preparation/Assembly Station	ZiL-131
9G22M1-9	1	Compressed Air Tanker	ZiL-131
UKS-400	1	Mobile Air Compressor	ZiL-157
2V7M2	1	1S91/2P25 Repair/Test Station	ZiL-131
Repair Station	1	P-15, P-18, P-19, P-40 Radar Repair/Test Station	ZiL-131
Repair Station	1	GM567/568, AT, BTR-60P Repair/Test Station	Ural-375
Vympel 3M9ME	48	Missile Warstock Deployed	9T22

Additional components:

System	Qty.	Function	Vehicle
P-15M Squat Eye	1	UHF-Band Low Level Acquisition Radar	Ural-375
P-15/19 Flat Face	1	UHF-Band Acquisition Radar	Zil-157/Ural-375
1L22 Parol 4/75E6 Parol 3	1	IFF Interrogator	KrAZ-255
PRV-16 Thin Skin	1	Altitude Finding Radar	SP

Command platoon

The role of the command platoon is to perform command and control of the subordinate units, perform the centralized asset management for airspace surveillance, acquisition, selection and distribution of targets, and the submission of guidance data by medium self-propelled missile batteries and observation of shooting results.

The main purpose of the 9S416M is to determine the targets and transfer the assigned target to the individual batteries fire control radars without turning on those radars. The information to the device large screen comes from the P-40 radar and the information about the target altitudes comes from the PRV-16 or PRV-9 radars. The crew of 9S416M consist of the regiment commander and chief of the staff which seat by the large round display. The other workstations are for the fire control battery commander, station commander and the crew with the manual plotter board (Fig. 1-25).

The crew of 9S416M[20] provides the following:

- guiding the altitude measurement radar,
- semiautomatic data collection for up to 10 targets and their computing in the digital computer,
- target distribution and transfer of the coordinates and parameters to the target transfer device,
- report receptions from the target transfer devices,
- computing the target interception points, and
- equipment automatic functionality checks.

Centralized command system K-1M consists of 9S416M, P-40 (1RL128D, PRV-16 (PRV-9 in reserve), and P-15M. 9S416M can track the situation in the airspace at the distance of up to 600 km. One of the abilities of this system is to get the target coordinates (for the maximum speed of 1,000 m/s and altitude of 30,000 m) in semiautomatic mode at distances from 20-200 km. The maximum number of target direction is eight with the interception point of two. The maximum number of the transferred command is ten, based on the target distances and the radio command distance of 20 km.

9S416M has a geodetic direction calculator based on the work by the recorder connected with the movement of the radar swipe.

To get the proper positioning of the missile battery with the regiment command post the proper orientation shall be performed. One of the steps is to introduce the parallax which is actually the difference between the standing points and that is executed by the equipment of 9S416M.

---

20   The local Yugoslav designation for the Fire Command and Control device the UKUV (Uredjaj za Komandovanje i Upravljanje Vatrom). Designations 9S416M and UKUV are interchangeable.

Figure 1-25: Command and control system (UKUV) 9S416M of upgraded 2K12 Kub/Kvadrat-M Soviet-made mobile surface-to-air missile system of Serbian Army on display at Partner 2019 military fair. (Source: Srđan Popović)

One of the negative sides of 9S416M is a sensitivity to jamming. Because of this reason, during the 1999 war almost all communication with the subordinate batteries was performed through the wired communication. For example, to connect the fire control battery with the four subordinate SA-6 batteries, more than 80 km of cables were needed.

Radar platoon

The main purpose of the radar platoon is to operate the battery surveillance and target tracking equipment. Some of the task that platoon member performs are:

- perform the surveillance, acquisition, tracking and identification of the detected targets in the surrounding airspace,
- automatic control for the altitude (height) measurement radar,
- determining the target coordinates (azimuth and distance) and information transfer to the combat unit, and
- surrounding airspace information data transfer through 9S417.

P-40 radar section:

One of the key components in the radar platoon equipment is the P-40 radar (in Yugoslavia/Serbia known as a 'Bear' when combined with height finder PRV-16). This radar had been considered very reliable and resistant to jamming (Fig. 1-26).

*Figure 1-26: RL128D long-range 'Long Track' surveillance radar.
(Source: Vitaly Kuzmin)*

If the radar receiver is tuned up properly and if the protocols for the working frequencies are kept secret meaning that in peacetime only one frequency is used, then in the time of combat engagement with the changes of the remaining 'secret' frequencies, the radar can be pretty efficient. The radar has 8 working frequencies and only one is used during the peacetime and the rest 7 are kept in the safe and it is forbidden to use them in peacetime or without the special order from the higher command. The reason is simple: deny the potential opponent to detect and record frequencies. In war conditions, frequencies can be changed manually according to the situation and the time base. Frequencies can be changed automatically as well with every antenna revolution with the timing program for the frequencies 'jumping' changes. With this application, the program is changed every 15 minutes.

The durability of P-40 radars was proven during the 1999 NATO aggression on Yugoslavia when 4 radars were hit by the anti-radar missiles, but they were repaired and returned to the service in the shortest period of time.

PRV-16B radar section

The main purpose of this radar is to determine the altitude of the target. This task can be executed either by the information from the acquisition radars or through the semiautomatic data transfer system. This radar can determine the altitude, angular distance and azimuth. One of the abilities of this radar is to determine the angle of the active jamming sources (Fig. 1-27).

Figure 1-27: P-16B 'Thin Skin' height finder radar. (Source: authors)

P-15M target acquisition (surveillance) radar section

The P-15 is a high mobility radar with the high ability to detect low altitude flying targets. With the antenna mounted directly on the single truck (Zil-157) used for transport, the system could be deployed and taken down in no more than 10 minutes. The P-15 uses two open frames elliptical parabolic antenna accomplishing both transmission and reception, each antenna being fed by a single antenna feed. The radar can rapidly shift its frequency to one of four pre-set frequencies to avoid active interference, with passive interference being removed by a coherent Doppler filter. Azimuth was determined by mechanical scanning with an associated accompanying PRV-11 (NATO reporting name 'Side Net') used to determine elevation. A secondary radar for identification friend-or-foe (IFF)is used in conjunction with the P-15, generally the 1L22 'Parol' (Fig. 5-23 and 5-29).

The radar works in decimetric waveband with frequencies range from 830-882 MHz. This radar has an ability to raise the antennas with the mast AMU-15 (Unzha) which increases the detection distance of the low-level flying targets by 25%. The radar has jamming protection and 15 working frequencies grouped in three programs.

What the radar crew need to do is to choose the proper position, at the relatively flat surface with a clean, unobstructed radius not leas than 1,500 m. In the mountainous regions, it can be positioned on a relatively flat surface with the radius not less than 500 m. For additional safety, the radar can be connected with a detached indicator which provides the crew ability to work remotely. An interesting fact for this radar is that is widely present in both Air Defense Forces, as well in the Army Air Defense units.

During the war in 1999, this radar was relatively easy jammed and couldn't survive direct hit with the antiradiation missile.

SA-6 Battery

This basic tactical independent combat unit is a battery. Each battery of a modernized Kub/SA-6 systems, as a minimum, consists of:

- target tracking and fire control radar 1S91M 'Straight Flush'
- self-propelled launcher 2K25 with three 3M9M missiles and
- 9S417 radio and data transfer van

Fig. 1-28 presents an illustration of the typical 2K12 battery:

1S91 Target Acquisition and Tracking radar RStON

1S91 has a crew of four:

- commander,
- first operator (target tracking 1S11 radar),

2K12 Kub/SA-6 missile system

- second operator (precise tracking and illumination 1S31 radar),
- driver.

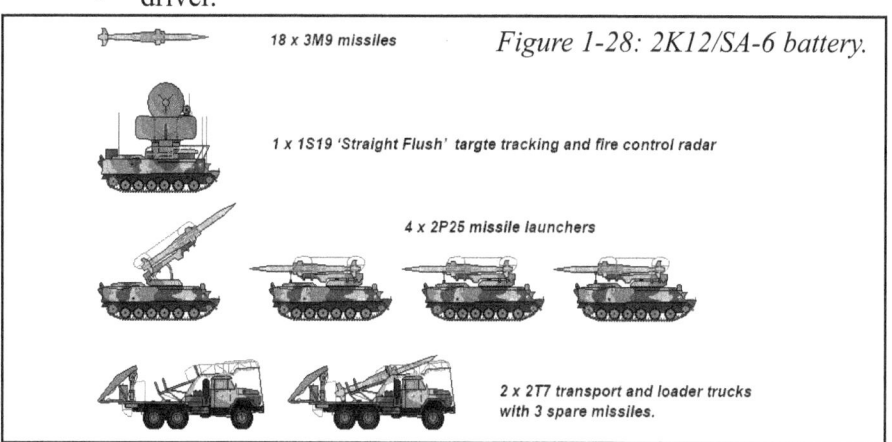

Figure 1-28: 2K12/SA-6 battery.

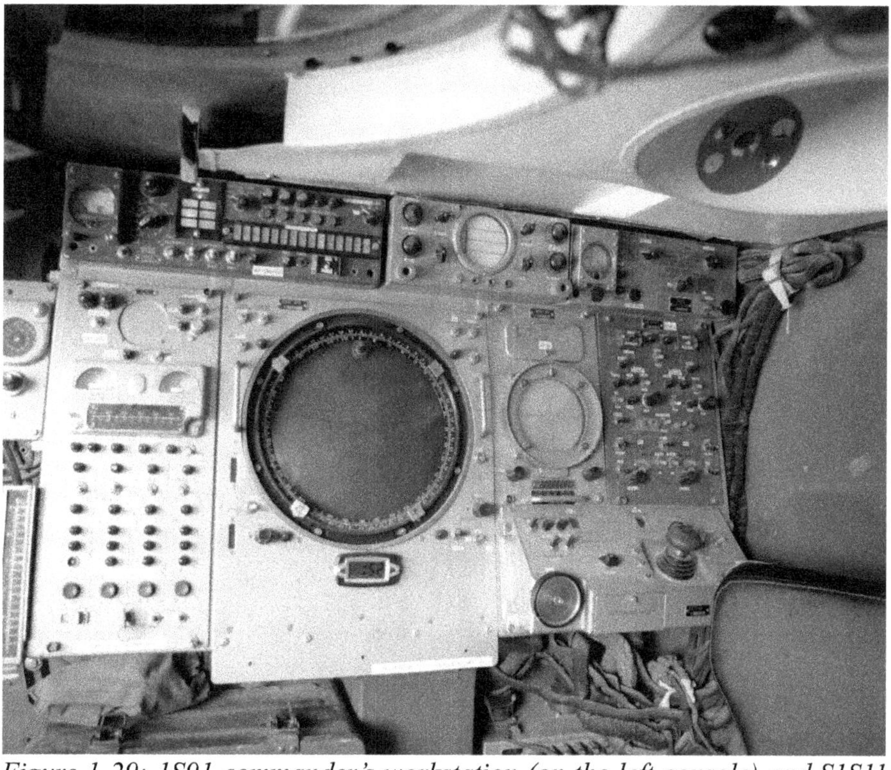

Figure 1-29: 1S91 commander's workstation (on the left console) and S1S11 operator station (on the right) with large and small circular displays. (Source: Wikimedia)

Commander workstation

Looking at the commanders' working station from left to the right (Fig. 1-29 and Fig. 1-30) there are speed and altitude indicators. In the second raw below of these two indicators, there are individual launcher light indicators (green color) which indicates individual missile launcher marked with the Roman numerals I - IV. Below these indicators, there are switches 'Target' that are turned on by the commander when the target is assigned to one of the launchers. Below these 'target assigned' switches there are the light indicators 'Readiness' (green color) indicating that the individual launchers inform the 1S91 commander that the missiles (one or two) are ready for launch. When the missiles are ready for launch, besides the green light indicator 'Readiness', one, two or all three indicators representing individual missiles will be illuminated with a red light. At the bottom of the panel, there are circular shaped press switches marked as a 'Pusk' (Launch) to launch the missiles. Which of the missiles will be launched first, is de-

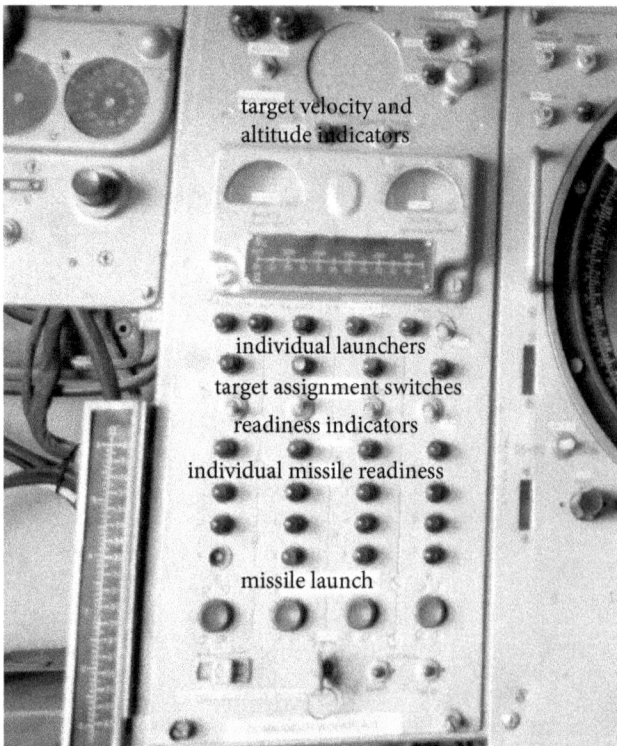

Figure 1-30: 1S91 commander's workstation missile readiness and launch indicators and switches. (Source: Wikimedia, modified by authors)

fined in the individual launcher through the AKR[21] - analog command computer and typically the first missile that will be launched is the one that is on the right-hand side viewing from the front of the vehicle.

Target tracking radar operator on 1S11

The central position of the first operator – target acquisition radar console is occupied by the large circular indicator (Fig. 1-31). This indicator screen has marks that show the distances. The azimuth marks are on the azimuth indicator circle around the indicator. On the screen, there is a yellow line that represents the time base. This line with the center of the indicator constantly rotates and sweeps the screen. Targets that are swept will be shown in the form of blips. Besides the targets in the air all other objects such as natural formations, clutter and noise may be shown as well. After the commander determines which target will be engaged, the tracking radar operator marks up the target by turning the azimuth and distance wheels on his console. After the target is marked, the operator transfers the target (to

Figure 1-31: 1S11 operator's workstation with large circular display (on the left) and a small display on the right) with manipulating handle and wheel. (Source: Wikimedia, modified by authors)

---

21   AKR – Analogni Komandni Računar – Analog Command Computer

the smaller screen for precise tracking. This indicator s called ITC[22]. The purpose of this indicator is to increase the efficiency of the tracking system by azimuth. The screen is showing the target in a Cartesian (rectangular) coordinate system. This system is limited in comparison to the circular indicator (IKO)[23] screen in the +/- 20^0 by azimuth and +/- 10 km by distance. ITC screen also receives the signal from the guidance radar and forms the double search raster.

At the small indicator, the target blip is shown, and the precise coordinates can be determined by azimuth and distance. The altitude can be only estimated based on the target appearance in the upper or lower search radar main lobe by height and the marker is shown on the IKO screen with one or two labels. Based on this, the tracking radar operator, manipulating the corresponding switches, will position the antenna under a certain angle by height. At that moment the fire control 1S31 radar antenna starts to turn toward the target. The missile platforms on the individual launchers will also turn toward the target.

The tracking radar operator manipulates the azimuth and distance wheels and guides the fire control radar on his ITC screen. He also uses a manipulating stick while pressing the button on the stick. When the target is positioned between the boundary lines, he transfers the target to the fire control radar operator.

In the mode 'IIC' which means the second target tracking, the system provides the ability to mark up the second target while automatically tracking the first one with the control system by the fire control radar. In this way it was possible to shorten the time of targeting the second target after the first target is engaged.

Fire control (guidance) radar operator on 1S31

This radar operator operates target tracking and illumination radar. When the target acquisition and tracking radar operator transfer the target to the precise tracking and illuminating radar which is actually a fire control radar, the antenna is already positioned by azimuth, distance and approximately by height (Fig. 1-32 and 1-34).

At the operator console, there are two indicators: the left-hand side indicator for positioning antenna onto the target by angles and the right-hand side indicator for positioning antenna by distances. On the left

---

22   ITC – Indicator Precizne Oznake – Precise Marking Indicator.
23   IKO – Idikator Kruznog Osmatranja – Circular Surveillance Indicator.

guiding indicator screen there are two parallel lines which are positioned

Figure 1-32: 1S31 fire control radar operator's workstation. (Source: Wikimedia)

Figure 1-33: Video signal VPU-55 receiver and manipulating stick. TOV 9Sh38 consists of TV camera KT-101 paired with 1S91 radar (beside antenna) and VPU-55 receiver, middle block PB-107 and spare parts. (Source: Wikimedia)

5 cm above and below the screen center horizontal line. The operator manipulates the wheels and guide the antenna to bring the target between the indicator's lines. When the target is tracked by distance and angle (named mode 'Poisk I[24]') or by distance and azimuth (mode 'Poisk II') the target is between those two lines, there is no deviation by angles and the

Figure 34: 1S31 indicator for positioning antenna onto the target by angles (left screen) and the indicator for positioning antenna by distances (right). This is the first version.
(Source: still from documentary movie 'Zdelano v SSSR')

---

24   'Poisk', or Russian Cyrillic 'поиск' meaning search.

tracking is by the distance between these two horizontal lines. When the target is captured by angles and distance and when the automatic tracking is established, the operator turns the illuminating transmitter and reports to the commander. After this, the commander can launch the missile after the indicator light is illuminated on his screen indicating that the missile is ready for launch. The operator is also handling the TOV system (Fig. 1-33 and 5-11)

On the right-hand side distance indicator, the tracking is performed through the two scanning distances – rough up to 60 km and precise up to 2 km. The amplitude (missile pulse) is shown at the terminal guidance phase. When the missile amplitude reaches the target amplitude it is considered that the target is hit. The hit is also reflected by the target velocity and altitude at the operator's indicators. This is very important in the after-engagement analysis.

Transporter, erector, launcher (TEL) 2P25M2

2P25M2 missile launcher has a crew of three:

- launcher commander
- operator
- driver

The launcher section commander is responsible for the launcher positioning and communication with the battery radar 1S91. Together with the rest of the crew, he participates in the missile loading, checking and camouflaging. He is positioned in the middle of the vehicle. The driver is on his left-hand side and the system operator on the right-hand side. Under his command, the operator releases the missile for the lock-down position and perform the functionality check. After the functionality check, the launcher commander informs the battery commander in 1S91 (RStON) about the readiness. The battery commander then orders the functionality check No. 2 to all four launchers in the battery. On this way, all components and missiles are checked and the battery commander can inform the upper command on the regimental level about the battery combat readiness. The launcher commander and operator observe the instruments and indicators on the control panels during the engagements. On these indicators, they can see the elevation and azimuth of the missile ramp. Light indicators also show the situation with the target lock-on and readiness for the launch (Fig. 1-35).

An important indicator is the 'Svyaz'[25] (communication link) light which indicates the communication functionality between the launcher and 1S91 RStON. In the case that the lamp is not illuminated, the commander must check immediately the cable. If this is not functioning, the launcher is not in the combat regime. The communication link can be also a radio telecoded link but for that, it is necessary to have the line of sight to the RStON.

Figure 1-35: Driver's position (right seat) and launcher commander's position (left seat). Partially is visible operator's seat (on the left). (Source: Wikimedia)

In the case that any of the missiles catch the fire (for example flammable composition of the missile fuel consisted of natrium-nitrate, magnesium and naphthalin), it will be immediately registered on the control panel and the launcher commander, upon the approval by the battery commander, forcibly launch the missile.

What is important to mention is that some of these buttons and switches are actually designed to activate only upon considerable finger pressure and pushed twice. The reason for this is to avoid any unintentional

---

25 Svyaz or in Cyrillic 'связь' is a Russian word for communication.

activation (Fig. 1-36 and Fig. 1-37).

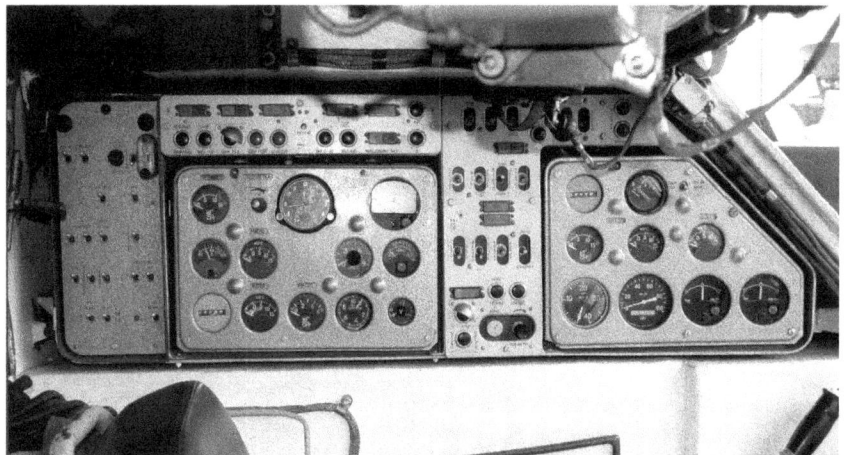

Figure 1-36: Left-hand side looking from the driver seat. (Source: authors)

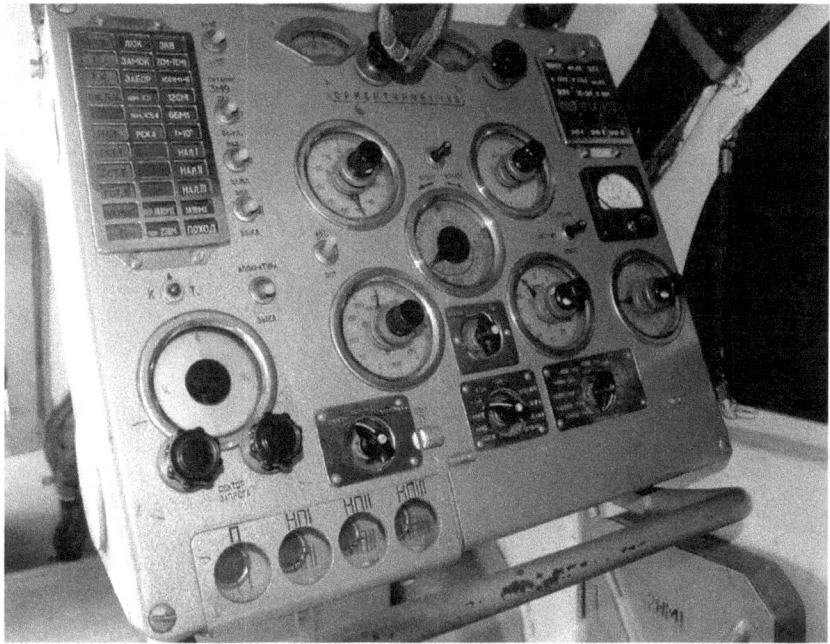

Figure 1-37: 2P25 launcher alignment and orientation console. (Source: authors)

Figure 1-38: 2T7M truck with the integrated crane during the missile transfer from the loader to the 2T7M launcher. (Source: Serbian DoD)

Figure 1-39: Missile transfer from the loader to the 2T7M launcher. (Source: Serbian DoD)

2T7M missile transporter and loader truck

The missile transporter and loader are an important component. Without this truck, it is not possible to transport the missiles from the missile technical battery to the combat position and transfer them on the launcher. The truck has a crew of four – section commander, two operators and two drivers (Fig. 1-38 and 1-39).

Missile Technical Battery

Missile technical battery is an integral part of every 2K12 Kub./SA-6 regiment. It is not a combat unit but without this component, combat units would not be able to function for an extended period of time (Fig 1-40 and Fig. 1-41).

Figure 1-40: Field missile preparation - offloading the missile transport and storage containers.
(Source: Still from the documentary movie 'Zdelano v SSSR')

This unit has multiple platoons tasked for transportation, maintenance, equipment check-up and logistics. Depend on the size and structure of the armed forces, members of the support units may be trained as combat systems operators so that they can take turns. It is not their primary specialty, but keep the additional manpower trained for the combat duties.

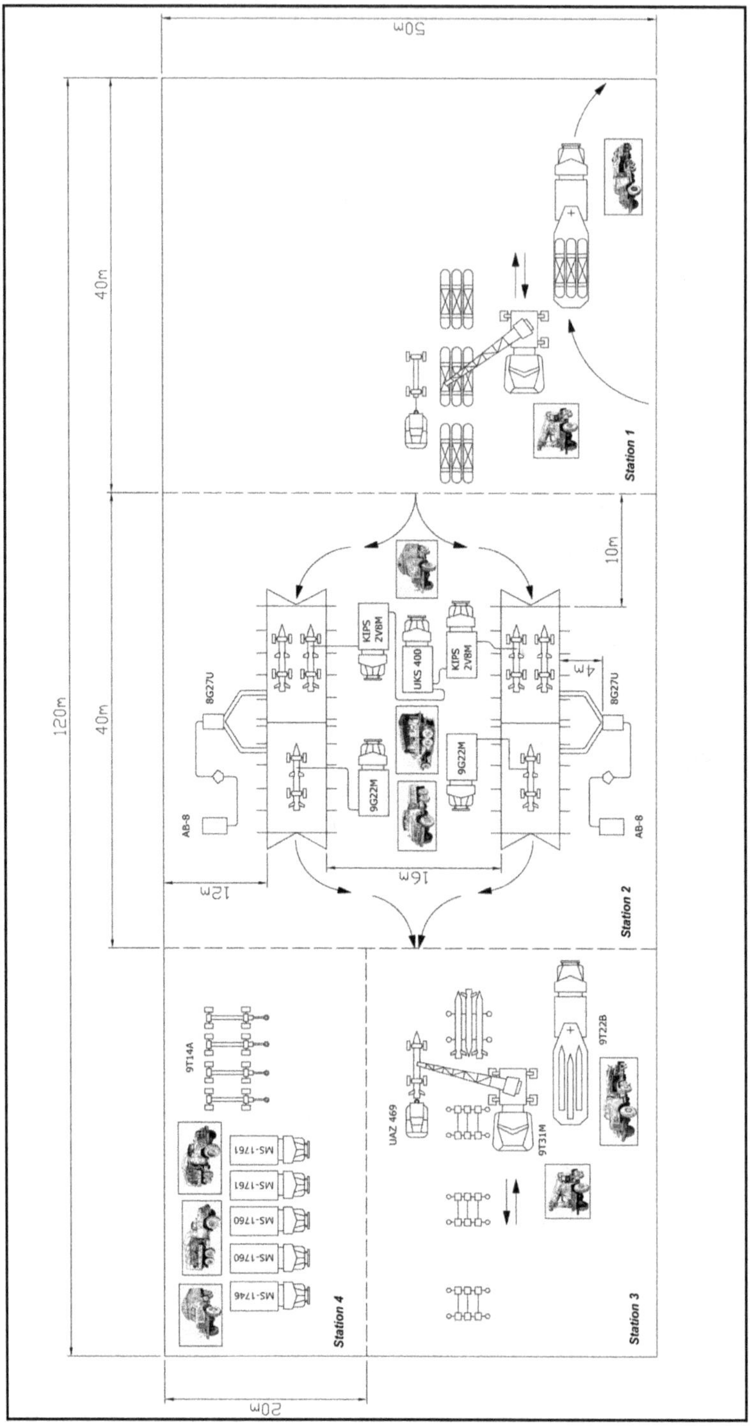

Figure 1-41: Missile technical battery deployment layout.
(Source: authors)

CHAPTER TWO

SA-6 in the Balkans

Beginning of the air defense missile forces

Downing of an American pilot Gary Powers (who was flying for CIA on a reconnaissance mission in a secretive U-2 spy plane at a very high altitude above the Soviet Union, by the S-75 Dvina missile (in NATO terminology designated as SAM-2 Guideline) was one of the turning points in contemplating air defense at the zenith of the Cold War.

Guided surface-to-air missiles became a very significant new weapon, with high expectations in the air space defense of a particular country.

Yugoslav military leadership was also very impressed with this event which happened right at a time when it was needed - to modernize the air defense system, which already was significantly inferior in comparison with the surrounding Warsaw Pact and NATO countries.

In 1961 the decision to procure one missile regiment for the territory air defense passed through the political and military circles.[26]

In early 1961 Yugoslav Air Force Technical Directorate requested through Yugoslav diplomatic missions from the governments of the United States, Britain, France, Switzerland, and Japan an offer for the sale of guided missiles. The request was formed based on the earlier analyzes of guided missiles and the basic tactical and technical requirements of the armed forces.

Only one offer arrived from the British firm 'English Electric' for the sale of the guided Thunderbird[27] missile system (English Electric Thunderbird Mk.1). From 7-10 March 1961, the company representative officially visited Belgrade and on 20 May 1961, the Yugoslav delegation started the visit to the potential supplier. During the meetings, the hosts in detail explained the technical capabilities and operation of the Thunderbird system. One missile regiment consists of two batteries. Each battery has eight launchers with a number of radars and support vehicles. The Thunderbird

---

26   Bojan B. Dimitrijević, Jugoslovensko Ratno vazduhoplovstvo i Protivvazdušna odbrana, ISI, Beograd 2017, page 201-204.
27   Ibid

missile has a solid fuel motor-main motor and four start motors-boosters, semi-active homing, start mass of 2000 kg, maximum speed of 2.5 Mach, maximum height 20 km, and maximum horizontal range of 36 km (Fig. 2-1).

Figure 2-1: English Electric Thunderbird Mk. 1 which was offered to Yugoslavia. (Source: Adrian Pingstone)

At the same time, the previously tense relationship with the Soviet Union started to warm up and the procurement of the military hardware shifted from the western supplier to the eastern one meaning that Thunderbird never entered into the Yugoslav service.

The first air defense system that the Socialist Federative Republic of Yugoslavia procured was the Soviet S-75 Dvina. The missile component of the air defense started with the forming of the 250th missile regiment. As per the top-secret order No. 423, the first missile regiment was formed on 24 September 1962. The first procured missiles systems were S-75 Dvina (SA-2A), then S-75M Volkov (SA-2C) which was followed by S-125 Neva (SA-3 Goa) at the beginning of the seventies (Fig. 2-2 and Fig. 2-3).

At the beginning of the seventies, the air defense doctrine evaluated with the redesigned component of the territorial defense with the advantages with the fire-power but also with the disadvantages regarding the mobility and sensitivity to the jamming. To mitigate these disadvantages, the

Figure 2-2: S-75 Dvina (SA-2A) was the first air defense missile system procured by Yugoslavia. S-75M (SA-2C) Volkov followed. (Source: authors)

Figure 2-3: S-125 Neva (SA-3 Goa) was the second air defense missile system procured by Yugoslavia. Like S-75, it was distributed within the Air Forces branch. (Source: authors)

decision was made to purchase the mobile missile systems 2K12 Kub M.

After the outstanding performances that the 2K12 Kub missile system achieved during the 1973 Yom Kippur, military executives in SFRY decided to procure that system for the JNA[28]. Unlike previous missiles systems that are included in the composition of Air Forces and Air defense Forces (Ratno Vazduhoplovstvo i Protiv Vazdušna Odbrana) as territorial air defense, the 2K12 Kub/Kvadrat-M missile system shall be distributed as part of the Army Air defense component.[29]

Figure 2-4: *First Yugoslav SA-6 from 149th regiment during JNA military parade in 1975. (Source: Still from the JNA Victory Day military parade held in 1975 - Youtube movie)*

---

28   JNA – Jugoslovenska Natrodna Armija – Yugoslav People's Army

29   Members of these units equipped with the Kub-M system always considered themselves as an 'infantry', and this became especially pronounced when Kub-M was removed from the Army Forces and included in the Air Force and Air Defense Corps. In the JNA they wear olive drab army uniforms which were very different compared to other missileers in the Air Force corps who wear a blue uniform. The army air defense approach to training was much closer to the training that was initially carried out in the army. Today, all 'Kub men' like to say that they are the only 'infantry' in the Air Force and Air Defense corps.

In the period 1975-77, the Soviet Union delivered in total 16 batteries. By 1983, the Yugoslav People's Army got 26 batteries. The first regiment that received the new system was the 146th regiment, established in March 1975 with the home base at Pleso airport, near Zagreb. This regiment had 4 batteries. This regiment participated in the Victory Day parade 1975 for the first time with the new equipment (Fig 2-4).

After the 149th regiment, the 60th regiment was formed in the Artillery and Missile School Center in Šepurine near Zadar. The next one was the 230th regiment with the base in Niš (2nd Army) followed by the 240th regiment (7th Army) in Lukavica near Sarajevo. The characteristic of all of these regiments is that they all head 4 batteries as well as a certain number of reserve launchers, radars and other support equipment.

In 1982, the 1st Army formed the 310th regiment in Kragujevac and later that year, the 3rd Army formed the 311th regiment in Skopje. The main difference between the last two regiments and the others was that the last two had 5 batteries each.

The main task for these regiments was the protection of the large industrial and political centers and in the case of aggression to absorb the initial impact. According to the estimates, in the case of war, the life expectancy of the missile battery was approximately ten days taking into the consideration quantity of available missiles and the probability that launchers and radars may be damaged or destroyed. In the peacetime conditions, the major task was deterrence and control of the airspace around the designated areas. The only two republics of former Yugoslavia that didn't have any of the SA-6 regiments were Slovenia and Montenegro. The reason was topographical configuration.

Operational use

During peacetime, every SA-6 regiment consisted of the two components:

- the professional component of 100-120 regular military personnel (officers and NCOs) and permanently employed civilians, and
- enlisted component of 220 – 240 servicemen on the compulsory military service.

The civilian component consisted of a highly skilled technical staff

in the technical maintenance company. All enlisted servicemen, except the vehicle drivers that came from the automotive training center, came to the military service directly from civilian life. There was also a reserve officers candidates' component which came from the reserve officer training centers. The reader can notice that for the majority of enlisted troops there were no recruits' depots like in some western countries, rather they were trained from the beginning in the assigned units (Fig. 2-3 and 2-12).

Each regiment consisted of the headquarter, fire control battery, missile equipment maintenance company and 4-5 batteries and one missile-technical battery. Each regiment has one 1RL-128D-1/1S12 nicknamed 'the Bear' which can detect the aerial target up to 600 km. This radar, in the case of need, can act also as a command center and when worked in conjunction with the altitude finder (height finder) radar PRV-9 or PRV-16 it formed the radar station known as a P-40 (Fig. 2-5). These two radars were connected to the fire control center with the data transfer cables. Every battery within the regiment had its own radar 1S91M2 (Straight Flush) for target tracking and fire control up to the 70 km range. Every 1S91M2 radar is connected through the radio link or cables with four 2P25M launchers (TEL). Every regiment in the startup has available between 48 to 60 3M9M3 (3M9ME) missiles positioned on the TEL ramps. Six regiments had more than 300 missiles available for action (without the replenishments) in the case of the war outbreak.

Figure 2-5: PRV-16B height finder (left) and 1RL-128D-1/1S12 nicknamed the 'Bear' (right) when paired make P-40 system. (Source: authors)

Each regiment also included two self-propelled anti-aircraft artillery (AAA) batteries equipped with M53/59/70 Praga (Fig. 2-6), with a dual 30 mm cannons for the close defense of each headquarter. A platoon of military police equipped with Strela - 2M MANPADs could also be added as a point defense. Each regiment also has a set of ZIL trucks for missile transport and reloading which belongs to the transport and reloading battery.

Figure 2-6: In Yugoslavian use, M53/59 Praga self-propelled dual anti-aircraft 30 mm cannon was used for the close protection of regimental position. (Source: authors)

Target long-range acquisition and tracking radar, P-40 Bear, was already previously described. In JNA it had a crew of commander, driver, signalman and two operators. The transformation from the marching into the combat-ready position, including the orientation and target acquisition with the shortening of the electronic preparation, took approximately 9 minutes. In JNA there was a record of deployment that still is not broken in any armed forces that have this radar – 4 minutes and 5 seconds. The same crew also has second place with 4 minutes and 25 seconds. The radar had its own power generation units – two airplane engines out of which one always worked and the second was the reserve one. These engines had a fuel consumption of 100 liters per hour. The radar could be also powered from the electrical grid or from the diesel aggregates mounted on the vans.

The radar for the altitude measurements PRV-16[30] was the only one set up on the wheeled platform. The rest were on the tracks.

Each 1S91 'Straight Flush' radar was able, under clear weather conditions, to do visual tracking through the TV optical system. This was particularly important under the heavy jamming conditions. This system can be used in a combination with a short radar 'burst' which will illuminate the target for a short period of time so that the reflected electromagnetic waves can be detected by the missile while on the TEL so that the launching can be executed. Once launched, the missile can be guided optically. Each 1S91M has a crew of three – commander, driver and operator. Each 2P25M TEL has a crew of three of as well – commander & operator, driver and power system operator.

Each 3M9 missile has a radar for self-guidance with the proximity fuse that can be activated at 0-100 m distance from the target. In the case of a miss, the missile will drop to the ground like a log. In the case of fell under the specific, so-called, risk angle, the warhead can be activated even without the proximity fuse. Missiles with a gray (blue) colored cone are one of the older types and could engage the target only in approaching direction. In the contrary, missiles with the white cones could engage bot approaching and departing targets.

The training of the conscripts in units were extensive. For example, the crane operators for the missile transfers from the reloader to the launcher were considered fully trained if they can do a transfer of a bucket filled with water from the truck to the launcher without spilling anything of the contest.

Both RL128D and altitude finder radar PRV-16B with the command center were typically positioned around 20 km from the Straight Flush radars and corresponding launchers, and the batteries were positioned around 20 km from each other in the circle or some other pattern around the command center. The distance and pattern greatly depended on the terrain configuration and estimated direction of the potential enemy (Fig. 2-7).

Each 2P25 launcher has three launching beams and it can launch individual missiles with a time delay. Two different launchers can simultaneously launch missiles with a launch interval of 3 seconds. The missile is an "intelligent" one and the reason for this is that before it can be launched it shall signalize to the operator that the target is acquired (visible to the

---

30 In the local terminology, it was known as "Visinac" or height-finder.

missile radar), in the engagement zone and that it is ready to be launched. After the launch, the missile electronics will calculate the interception point and it will fly to that point, not to the target directly. The launch can be also performed with a delay – the launch button is staying "inactive" at the first push. This provided additional security so that the missile can't be launched if somebody pushes the button by mistake.

Figure 2-7: Regimental command post: 9S416M fire control & command, PRV-16B, power supply PES-100 and 1RL128D 'Bear'. (Source: authors)

Figure 2-8: 9S416M or locally called UKUV. (Source: Srđan Popović)

The fire control of each regiment is performed through the command center 9S416M, locally called UKUV (Fig. 2-8). All communication is through radio links. In the case that UKUV is out of service - damaged or destroyed, the 'Bear' can take over command and control acting as a command radar.

Figure 2-9: 1RL128D 'Bear' indicators (top and bottom). (Source: authors)

In the role of the command radar, the Bear have three panoramic indicators in her cabin and the communication will be executed through the laryngophones among the crew and the radio communication with all assigned batteries. The crew can also communicate with the friendly air force pilots and guide the airplanes to their targets. To do this, the vehicle has a telescopic antenna that can be automatically erected in the working position. The communication is always recorded with the "black box" located in the cabin operational space. All information about the target altitudes will come from the altitude finder radar which antenna directions can be directed with the handle located at the operator's console (Fig. 2-9).

The 'Bear' has the ability to do the identification, friend-or-foe, for the aerial targets and for that it uses a numerical filter which is set up for the particular hour and operational time coordinated with the air force base in the area of responsibility. The 'Bear' also have an antenna called 'Jagi', to receive the signals from the airplane in case if the airplane is in danger.

The 'Bear' has an advantage in use on her displays/indicators which is represented in the ability to move the "time base" (every indicator independently) and sector scans with the ability to expand the time base providing that the target reflection and the blip on the screen can be larger on the screen. The operator can perform the aerial space scan in four different zones. The scan can be performed in either automatic mode or manual mode. Every antenna revolution can scan 1-3 zones or 1-4 zones that are overlapping (Fig. 2-10).

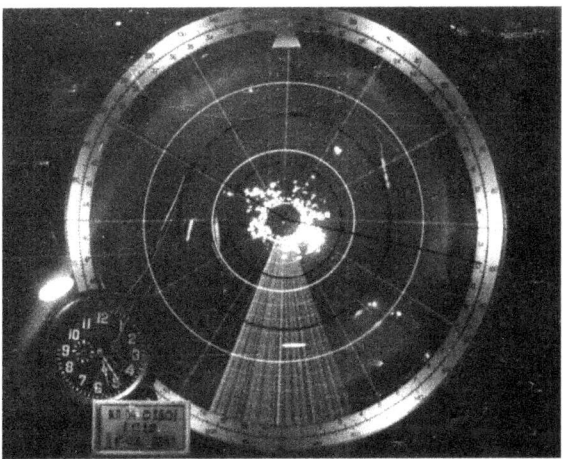

Figure 2-10: A screen-shot of one of the RL128D 'Bear' circular indicators.

One of the 'Bear' characteristics is that the time base on the screen is rotating counterclockwise. The antenna can rotate 6, 12 or 18 times per minute. The other performances of the radar such as frequencies and range are dependable on the antenna rotation speed.

The electromagnetic wave power for the emitted signal is from 1.8 – 2.2 MW. The return signal to the receiver is less than 0.1-12 W and as that the signal is filtered through the moving target indicator (noise filtration) where it further loses the strength, but the 'Bear' was still able to detect it.

The nickname 'Bear' was given because of the robust look that somehow associates to the bear look. The design was so strong that in the case of nuclear war it could protect the crew if the onboard over-pressure system is activated. The shear strength of the output signal caused some precaution and safety measure while working with the system. The 'Bear' has the ability to choose the emitter strength in five amplifier levels and it was almost never used below the first two levels because it affects the quality of the received picture and the radar range (Fig. 2-11).

Figure 2-11: 1S12/RL128D 'Bear'. (Source: authors)

When all five levels are turned on (first level CPT tube with a progressive wave) and second, third, fourth and fifth with amplitron[31] the out-

---

31   Amplitron is a Crossed-Field Amplifier (CFA), is a broadband microwave amplifier that can also be used as an oscillator (stabilotron). It is a so-called 'velocity-modulated tube'. The CFA is similar in operation to the magnetron and is capable of providing relatively large amounts of power with high efficiency. In contrast to the magnetron, the CFA have an odd number of resonant cavities coupled with each other. These resonant cavities work to as a slow-wave structure: an oscillating resonant cavity excites the next cavity. The actual oscillation will be lead from the input waveguide

put power and range were the highest ones. The radar wave is partially formed with the reflection from the ground which dictated that the maximum allowable time of any person within the radius of 130 m from the radar should not exceed 120 minutes for every 24 hours. The maximum allowable time at the distance from 130 m to 350 m is to up 15 min for every 24 hours. The maximum time allowed to be in the emitter department inside the vehicle (in the case of taking some reading and measures) is also limited up to 15 min for every 24 hours. These measures were introduced because they were concerns for human health, especially vision, hearing, nerve system and reproductive organs.

The 'Bear' can also work in the "equivalent"[32] mode but in that case, there are no target indications on the screens. To release the high frequency energy in the space, the mode "equivalent" shall be changed into the "antenna" mode.

Figure 2-12: Loading of 3M9M3E missile (white cone) in 311th missile regiment, 1986. (Source: authors)

---

to the output waveguide.
32   Equivalent – means that the energy is encapsulated into the system when the switch is selected - turn off the high frequency energy emission into the space, but not turn off the radar.

In the former Yugoslavia, the maintenance and overhaul of all missile systems were performed in the Airspace Technical Center 'Kosmos' in Banja Luka in today's Republika Srpska (Fig. 2-13, 2-14 and 2-15). The technical center employed a large number of world-class experts in radar and missiles technologies and often performed the services and maintenance to other countries such as Libya, Iraq and Iran. Representatives from those countries were often visitors. One event is of particular interest - the visit performed at the same time by Iraqis and Iranian representatives in the mid-eighties (Iraq and Iran were at war that time). Both teams were at

Figure 2-13: Technical center 'Kosmos' Banja Luka. The main military maintenance and repair center for the air defense Equipment in Former Yugoslavia. (Source: 'Kosmos' Banja Luka)

Figure 2-14: 3M9ME missile in the transport & storage container. (Source: 'Kosmos' Banja Luka)

the center at the same time, and at distance of 10 m, but never noticed each other.

Each regiment had its own maintenance company for the equipment maintenance at the first and second level. The requirement for the maintenance was that the radars shall not be disassembled in the stage that can't be put together within two hours in the case of any emergency. The third level of maintenance and overhaul was performed in 'Kosmos' (Fig. 2-13, 2-14 and 2-15).

In the case of major repairs, it was not always possible to correctly estimate the repair time or how long the radar will be out of service.

Figure 2-15: 3M9ME missile. In the front plan, left-hand side is a 3N12 fragmentation warhead. Behind her is a two-channel 3E27 CW (continuous wave) proximity fuse. (Source: 'Kosmos' Banja Luka)

It is interesting to say that the Soviet Union sold the overhauled Bears as a new one. Those radars were delivered to the 210th and 311th regiments. How these radars were determined that they were not the new ones? In the transmitter section, the paint on the blocks barely covered the nameplates and abbreviations on the blocks and there were new marks over the old one corresponding to the modified versions. These radars from time to time caused some problem for the users.

After multiple complaints to the supplier, in 1986 the Soviets finally sent a team of experts to personally exam and investigate radars. One of the chief radar designers was in the team as well. Because of the sheer numbers of Bears, the Soviets had a practice for the narrow specialization of the technical personnel meaning that they have, for example, experts for the emitters, experts for the receivers, experts for the displays and indicators etc. In JNA the practice was different – one person shall know all of these systems. To be fully technically proficient with a Bear radar, it was necessary to spend six years at the system.

Procurement of the SA-6 system from the Soviet Union also included technical support meaning that the Soviet experts spent two years in JNA units during the duration of the warranty. The reason for this was that the representatives can right on the spot examine and correct all deficiencies. These experts were also trained intelligence officers and also interested in tactical information and readiness levels of the specific air defense units. Because of these reasons, the freedom of their movement was somehow restricted. In the majority cases, the representatives recognized the problems with the particular radars and other equipment.

In the Soviet Union, technical centers for the maintenance and overhaul of the 2K12 systems and associated equipment were huge which associate with how many radars and missile systems were in that country and other Warsaw Pact allies.

JNA performed different courses every two years so that a large number of people can be trained in different specialties and 'jump' to other tasks if necessary (Fig. 2-16). The majority of the technical maintenance people were high school educated technicians with a certain number of engineering specialists in electronics, telecommunications, missile technology and mechanical engineering. Technical support was always provided by the civilian employees as well.

In the former Yugoslavia, diesel fuel (D2) was the basic fuel for military vehicles. The quality of the fuel was not as per the western standards and sometimes caused problems. It appears that the equipment manufacturers also counted with the lower fuel quality, so the systems were actually designed and optimized for that meaning often the design overkill in some components.

After the last regiment is delivered in 1983, the authorities started with the analyses of the procurement of the 3D radars and 2K12 successor

– the 'Buk'. As the new procurement is not month to month business, the decision dragged for a while and in the end, the decision to procure the new system never materialized.

Figure 2-16: 2K12 Kub/SA-6 2P25 self propelled launcher of the Yugoslav People's Army. (Source: authors)

Development of computer technology and software engineering were supported in some of the units and in 1986 the 311th Regiment introduced a computer animation that suggested the commander in the fire control center which battery is in the best position to engage the target. From today's viewpoint, this looks archaic and funny, but we shall not forget that in the mid-eighties the software development was at the beginning. In

some of the military units, the new ideas for the software were accepted, supported and encouraged while in other these ideas didn't find the "fertile environment". For example, Mike Mihajlovic, one of the authors of this book, developed programs to calculate the ballistic trajectories, maintenance records and a missile launch simulation but these ideas were suppressed because the "old school" commanders that sometimes didn't have the "ear" for the new things.

Almost every air defense missile unit in the former Yugoslavia performed the live launch at the position called Kamenjak, near Pula. Usually, once a year each regiment played a host and different situations were exercised including shooting at the static and moving targets and testing the combat readiness of the radar and missile crews.

During the mid-eighties, one of the exercises was performed and the subject was the missile regiment operations in the electronic warfare saturated space. The initiator was one colonel which this exercise was the final exam for the general rank. Almost all EW assets of the JNA were involved in these exercises. What was noted is that the K-1M system can be jammed without difficulties. For SA-6 to working in the K-1M environment, it was ordered that the two batteries be connected through the wired communication lines. About 40 km of wire was used and it took almost all night to put the wires between batteries but that annulated the wireless communication jamming.

CHAPTER THREE

2K12 (SA-6) in combat

2K12 (SA-6) export version, designated as a Kvadrat[33], through foreign economic channels was supplied to the armed forces of more than 20 countries (Algeria, Angola, Bulgaria, Cuba, Czechoslovakia, Egypt, Ethiopia, Guinea, Hungary, India, Kuwait, Libya, Mozambique, Poland, Romania, Yemen, Syria, Tanzania, Vietnam, Somalia, Yugoslavia, etc.).

The SA-6 complex has been successfully used in almost all military conflicts in the Middle East.

War of Attrition and Yom Kippur War

In the 'Six Day War' 1967, the Israelis gained a military victory and new territories, but they did not win the peace. Soviet resupply of Arab clients led to a drawn-out land and air war of attrition along the Suez Canal, the new border between Egypt and Israel. In summary, according to the Israeli information, between July 1967 and January 1970, the IAF lost 15 aircraft (13 to ground fire), while it claimed 74 Egyptian and Syrian aircraft. In September–October 1969, the IAF took out the Egyptian SAMs along the canal. In January 1970, the Israelis received US ECM pods and, within three months, neutralized the Egyptian air defense system by destroying three-fourths of its early warning radar. The offensive was again successful.[34]

The operation exacted a tremendous cost in lives, both military and civilian, and was accomplished under the worst imaginable conditions. The Soviets countered in early 1970 by sending more missiles, including the SA-3, to Egypt. The missiles became operational in April 1970, and by the end of June, the Egyptians had 55 SAM batteries. Soviet technicians and operators bolstered the Egyptian air defenses

---

33   Kvadrat is the Russian word for Square. Export versions are more or less different comparing to the system designated for use in the Soviet Army.
34   Kenneth P. Werrell - Archie to Sam: A Short Operational History of Ground-Based Air Defense (2005, Air University Press) 148-173

During the War of Attrition, SA-6 was not engaged in a large number. The brunt of air defense fell on SA-2 and SA-3. The first SA-3/S-125 engagement was bloody. On the night of 14/15 March 1970, a Soviet missile crew made its 'debut' by shooting down an Egyptian Il-28 which entered the zone of destruction of the SA-3/S-125 air defense system at an altitude of 200 meters. The 'Friend-or-Foe' transmitter on the Il-38 was out so the missile crew had no chance to check the origins of the plane. Alongside the Soviet officers at the guiding station, some Egyptian officers were there as a liaison. They assured the Soviet missile crew that there was no friendly aircraft in the zone of fire. The combat crew engaged the target and launched the two missiles that struck the plane (Fig. 3-1 and, 3-2).

Figure 3-1: ZSU 23/4 Shilka manned by the Soviet crew somewhere in Egypt, in the 1970s. (Source: Russian MOD)

Three days later a second incident happened when one of the shoulder-launched Strela-2 operators fired upon an Egyptian airplane, this time an Antonov An-24. Fortunately, the passenger plane managed to land safely despite missing an engine. The incident was first reported as an 'inglorious end of the Israeli aggressor', but it was obvious that coordination between the Soviet crews and the Egyptian liaison was not working properly.

In a few weeks came an engagement with the real enemy. At first, they were unsuccessful. Israeli pilots were briefed on the main location of the missile batteries and they tried to bypass the zones of the destruction of the SAMs deployed in their defensive structures. Israeli pilots fired on enemy aircraft on the far edge of the launch zone, and then turned around and escaped.

It was clearly necessary to correct and adjust the SAM tactics. The missile system complexes were withdrawn from the permanent areas well known to the Israeli pilots, to 'ambush' positions on unprepared locations which were hard to detect. Because of the desert terrain, however, it was just a matter of time until Israeli reconnaissance airplanes pinpointed the new locations. Missile launches were carried out at targets ranges up to 15 km – not from the furthest range, so that the target did not have time to counter the missile.

As a result, on 30 June 1970, Captain V.P. Malauki's battalion managed to bring down the first Phantom, and five days later the battalion of S.K. Zaversnitsky shot down the second F-4E.

This was followed by retaliatory attacks by the Israelis and in the course of a fierce battle on 18 July eight men from V.M. Tolokonnikov's battalion were killed. The Israelis lost four Phantoms.

Figure 3-2: Egyptian SA-3 dual launcher on the firing position. (Source: Egyptian War Museum)

Three more Israeli planes were shot down by the battalion of Kutyntsev on 3 August, and a few days later an agreement was reached to cease hostilities in the Suez Canal zone.

The previous is based on the memories of participants in the events published in the 2001 collections 'Then in Egypt' and 'Internationalists'. According to the commander of the Soviet air defense battalion, Lieutenant General A.G. Smirnov, the effectiveness of the SA-3/S-125 air defense system from June to August 1970 is shown by the nine shot down and three damaged enemy aircraft. According to some estimates, the SAMs achieved twenty-one victories. The Israelis however confirmed the loss of only five of their F-4E aircraft shot down by the SA-3/S-125 systems. Casualties on

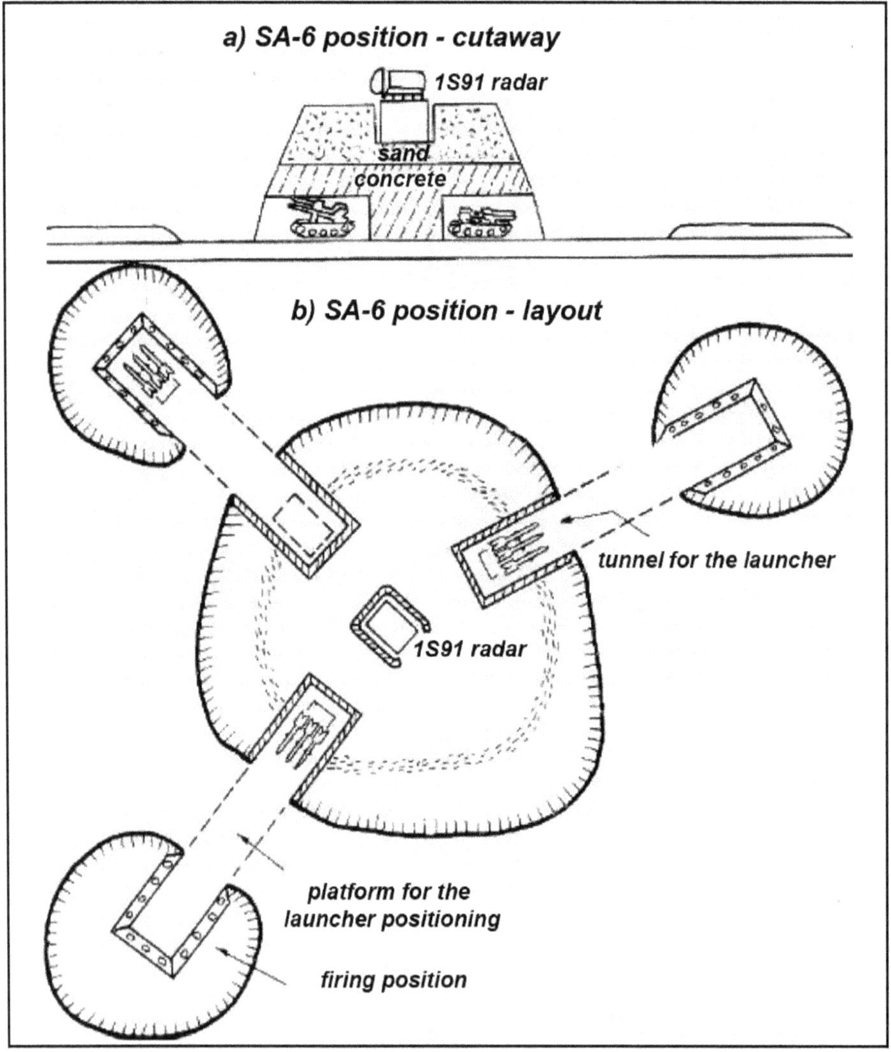

Figure 3-3: Typical layout of the 2K12/SA-6 combat position during the Yom Kippur War 1973. (Source: JNA HQ, First Directorate)

the Soviet side were never published, but western estimates are that several battalions were hit with equipment and human losses. The SA-3/S-125 systems were instrumental in forcing Israel to accept a UN ceasefire.[35]

Before the Yom Kippur War in October 1973, the Egyptian commander, Field marshal Ismail Ali, ordered his commanders and staff to study the lessons of past combat experiences, especially the use of air defense against the powerful Israeli Air Force. Field marshal Ali recognized that the Israeli Air Force had achieved air superiority. The Israelis were using the F-4 Phantom and the A-4 Skyhawk, provided by the US. These aircraft were equipped with a dazzling array of sophisticated weaponry and electronics which defended them against surface-to-air missiles. They carried television guided bombs and thermal guided rockets. They also had state-of-the-art radar jamming equipment, SAM evasion electronics and electronic countermeasures with which to defeat SAMs. Ismail Ali determined that Egypt would have to establish a sophisticated, modernized air defense umbrella using SAMs and anti-aircraft guns (Fig. 3-3 and 3-4).

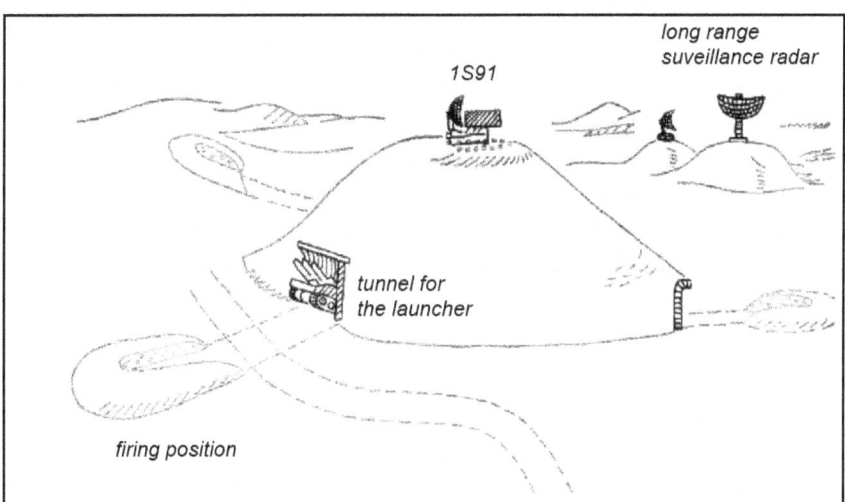

Figure 3-4: General look of the 2K12/SA-6 combat position. (Source: JNA HQ, First Directorate)

The Egyptians installed an interlocking SAM system over the Suez Canal to protect their rear areas and airfields. They learned their lessons well from the 1967 war. They updated their system from the SA-2 to the SA-3, SA-6 and SA-7, all supplied by the Soviet Union. These were state-

---

35 Mike Mihajlović & Djordje Aničić, Shooting Down the Stealth Fighter: Eyewitness accounts from Those Who Were There. Pen and Sword, 2021.

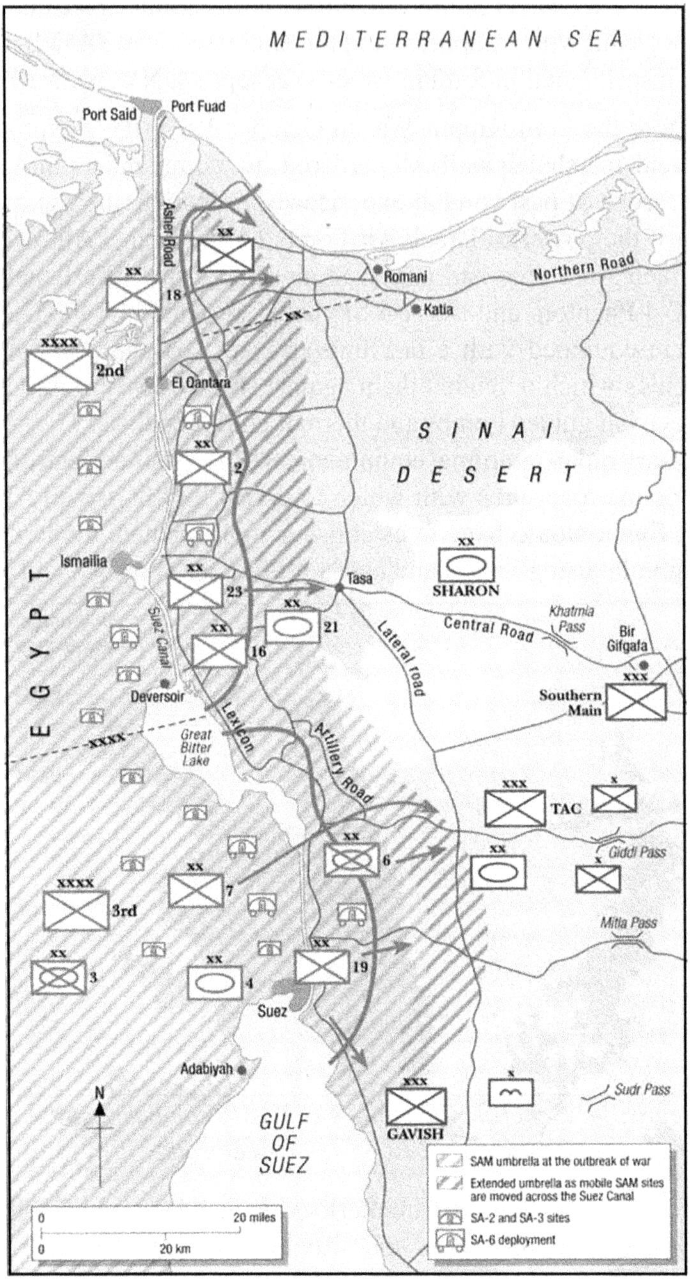

Figure 3-5: The Suez Canal crossing and Egyptian air defense umbrella on 14 October 1973. (Source: The Yom Kippur 1973 (2), Osprey Campaign 126)

of-the-art SAM systems in use by the Soviets. Additionally, SAM batteries were moved in the echelon from Cairo to the Suez Canal, which would be the line of departure for the Arab assault forces. Slowly moving the batteries forward enabled the Egyptians to build up their umbrella without the Israelis realizing it. By June 1970 there were four echelons of SAM batteries between the Egyptian capital and the Suez Canal (Figure 3-5 and 3-6).

Figure 3-6: Egyptian 2K12 Kvadrat/SA-6 2P25 launcher with 3M9ME missiles during the military parade 1974, a year after the 1973 Yom Kippur (also often called the October War). (Source: US DoD)

The Egyptians planned to launch their offensive on a very broad front across the Suez, attempting to deny the Israelis the opportunity of using interior lines and preventing them from concentrating their firepower against a flank. The Egyptian high command ordered their troops to attack on a 170-kilometer front across the Suez. They planned to send unsupported infantry across the Canal and have them establish a bridgehead with a depth of ten to fifteen kilometers. Once bridges were built across the Suez, armor support would come across, reinforce the infantry, and allow the drive to continue into the Sinai. The Egyptians planned on using forward deployed air defense assets to protect exposed infantry from Israeli air attacks (Fig. 3-5).

Massed formations of Egyptian armor and infantry, backed by artillery and air strikes, assaulted across the Suez Canal in the afternoon of

6 October 1973. Simultaneously, Syrian forces – later supported by Iraqi and limited Jordanian detachments – attacked Israeli positions on the Golan Heights. The Israeli Air Force scrambled aircraft to support embattled ground forces, however, Egypt and Syria had received huge shipments of Soviet air defense equipment since the end of the War of Attrition and dense SAM 'umbrellas' shielded Arab forces from Israeli Air Force attacks on both fronts. By 8 October, Arab forces had made consolidated gains in both the Golan and the Sinai (Fig. 3-5).

Figure 3-7: Egyptian 2P25 missile launcher crew. (Source: Egyptian DoD)

This air defense umbrella above the Arab armies was massive, mixed, and mobile. The Egyptians emphasized their surface-based air defense force (formed as a separate service in 1968) that had three times as many personnel as did their air force and made up one-fourth of their total armed forces. The Syrian air defense was smaller but denser because of the smaller battlefield. The Syrians manned nearly 47 SAM batteries (32–35 SA-6s and the rest SA-2s and SA-3s), while the Egyptians operated 150 batteries, of which 46 were SA-6s (Fig. 3-6, 3-7 and 3-8).[36]

The Israelis' greatest mistake before the 1973 war was that they

---

36   Kenneth P. Werrell - Archie to Sam: A Short Operational History of Ground-Based Air Defense (2005, Air University Press) 148-173

underestimated the Egyptians. They had been proclaiming to the world for years that the Egyptian army was inefficient, unimaginative, and lacking in the will to fight. The problem began when the Israelis believed their own propaganda. They relied on the Suez Canal to protect them from invasion, as well as a series of fortresses on the Sinai Peninsula thought to be invulnerable. On 6 October 1973, the myth of Israeli invincibility was shattered. The Israeli Air Force flew 446 daytime sorties and 262-night missions. Because of the efficiency of the Egyptian air defense umbrella, all the missions failed to reach their targets. The accuracy and deadly effect of the air defense system devastated the Israeli Air Force.

Figure 3-8: 1S91 'Straight Flush' self-propelled engagement and fire control radar in the Egyptian forces. (Source: Egyptian DoD)

One of the crucial things that contributed to the initial Egyptian success was the Egyptians were able to successfully jam Israeli UHF/VHF radio frequencies with Soviet-made equipment which resulted in almost complete disruption of the Israelis' air to ground communications.

The first days of the air campaign were therefore traumatic for the Israeli Air Force. In the southern sector, the Israelis lost fourteen strike aircraft in the first three hours of the war alone. The Israelis launched an operation against Egyptian air defenses on 7 October, 'Operation Tagar', but this was compromised by the coincident need to attack Egyptian ground formations. Moreover, only the first phase of 'Tagar', focused on the suppression of Egyptian airfields and some AAA sites, could be completed before the air force was diverted to support operations in the north. Egyp-

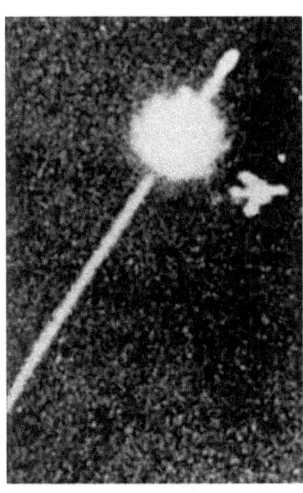

Figure 3-9: Proximity explosion of the missile near the Israeli Dassault Super Mister. The aircraft crashed after being hit.

tian SAM sites were, therefore, left untouched. For many senior Israeli Air Force officers, the incomplete execution of Tagar was the most critical mistake of the war. (Fig. 3-9, 3-10 and -11).

How it looked like to the Israeli Air Force at the first hours of the war[37]:

Finally, at four o'clock Israeli jets took off. They came in over the dunes, saw the ground level off beneath them, and crossed over the Suez Canal. It was a hasty, thrown-together mission. There were no assignments, no attack coordinates. The orders were to acquire targets visually, and open fire.

The SAM-6s slammed into the jets as soon as they neared the west bank. There was no warning. The electronic counter

Figure 3-10: Israeli Phantom II crash-landed, probably after damaged by Egyptian or Syrian missile hit. (Source: Israeli DoD)

---

37   Howard Blum, The Eve of Destruction: The Untold Story of the Yom Kippur War, Harper Collins Books, 2004

measure pods on the jets' underbelly were not tuned to the SAM-6 signal. The pilots never heard the shrill "Sam Song" that usually sounded in the cockpit when the ground radar locked on. Their only hope was to spot the puff of white smoke that signaled a missile launch. With the rocket's sensors relentlessly homing in on the exhaust from the jet's engines, the pilots had forty-two seconds before impact. Forty-two seconds to twist and turn frantically, to climb and dive across the sky. Twelve Phantoms were shot down before the mission was scrapped.

Figure 3-11: Destroyed Israeli airplane. No confirmed cause but most likely during the 1973 war. (Source: Israeli DoD)

Early failure was equally stark in the northern sector. One hundred and twenty-nine sorties were flown against ground targets in the first thirty hours of fighting and Israeli aircraft losses were high. The potency of Syrian SAM defenses in these early hours of the war was evident in the fate of a close air support mission attempted at dawn on 7 October. An entire four-ship of A-4 Skyhawks called in by infantry commander Lieutenant Colonel Oded Erez was shot down by Syrian missiles. The second flight of Skyhawks lost two of its number to further missiles as appalled Israeli ground troops watched. Given such losses, Erez quietly 'declined to call for any more air support'. The Israeli Air Force attempted to prosecute a preplanned operation against the northern Syrian defenses later on 7 October, 'Operation Dugman'. As in the south, the operation was a failure. The Israelis lacked updated positions for mobile SA-6 systems, and electronic warfare helicopters had been transferred to the Egyptian sector and could not be repositioned in time. Desperate calls for close air support by ground forces engaged on the Golan Heights further compromised Israeli Air Force efforts to focus on the counter-SAM mission. As a result, the 'Dugman' attacks against Syrian missile sites resulted in the destruction of only a single SAM battery – and the loss of six Phantoms, with another ten heavily damaged. Israeli Air Force confidence was shaken, and the air force remained committed to close air support missions without having achieved control of the air. By the end of 7 October, the Israeli Air Force had lost 14 aircraft in 272 strike sorties in the Golan (Fig. 3-9, 3-10, 3-11 and 3-12).

Figure 3-12: A portion of SAM-6 missile somewhere at the Golan Heights, 12 October 1973. (Source: National photo collection by David Rubinger)

In the south, the Israeli Air Force achieved freedom from ground threats only when Egyptian forces attacked beyond the coverage of their SAM 'umbrella' on 14 October. The results were decisive: the Egyptians lost 260 tanks to Israeli ground and air attack in the largest tank battle since the Battle of Kursk in 1943. This Egyptian reverse was followed by an Israeli armored raid across the Suez Canal on 16 October during which Israeli forces destroyed a number of SAM positions.

The partial collapse of the Egyptian SAM 'umbrella' allowed the Israeli Air Force to provide effective close air support to Israeli troops in the canal zone. Attrition rates fell. The Air Force lost only four aircraft in 2,261 strike sorties in the Sinai zone between the canal crossing on 16 October and the end of the war on 24 October.

Syrian air defenses were never truly degraded in the northern zone. Echoing the experience in the south, the Israeli Air Force enjoyed the freedom of action only when the ground battle moved beyond the range of Syrian SAMs. The Israelis were here assisted by the deployment of the Syrian air defense system well to the east and the reluctance of Syrian commanders to redeploy SA-6 systems to support early gains. Arab formations that maneuvered beyond the extent of their air defense coverage were decimated by Israeli ground and air forces, just as in the south. However, a combination of the persistent air defense 'shield' and heavily fortified rear positions ultimately created a stalemate in the Golan.

Figure 3-13: Egyptian ZSU-23/4 Shilka of the Egyptian army somewhere in the Sinai peninsula. (Source: Egyptian DoD)

Overall, Israeli Air Force support to ground forces had been compromised by dense Arab air defenses, especially in the early part of the war. However, the Israeli Air Force was not totally ineffective, and it achieved significant successes in other roles. The Israelis still maintained clear dominance in air-to-air combat.

It was the difficulties experienced by the Israeli Air Force, and especially their struggles against Soviet-supplied Arab air defenses, that attracted most analysis in the war's aftermath. The Israeli Air Force lost approximately 100 aircraft in less than three weeks of fighting and struggled to impose itself on the ground battle. As the war ended, it appeared that the future of tactical air power was in doubt. It seemed that the 'missile bent the aircraft's wing'. For the US Air Force, the uncomfortable view was of Soviet missiles bending American and French-supplied wings.

The Israelis also learned a hard lesson in radio security. During the opening phase of the war, the Israeli air commander broadcast an attack order to his pilots over a radio channel that was monitored by the Egyptians. As a result, the SAM batteries were waiting for the Israelis.

According to the Soviets, Arab defenses using a combination of SA-6, ZSU-23/4 Shilka (Figure 3-13) and SA-7 (Strela-2) MANPADS are responsible for 88 Israeli aircraft shot down of which 64 we downed by SA-6 with expanded 95 3M9 missiles. 12 other were downed by S-125 and 15 in air-to-air combat. According to Israeli estimates, six of their planes were shot down by the Arab SA-3/S-125 air defense system during the 1973 October war. As expected, Israeli and Arab/Soviet sources are not matching. In any case, losing 100 modern frontline aircraft against air defense for Israeli is devastating statistics.

The SA-6 proved especially effective by destroying a sizable proportion of IAF aircraft and indirectly by forcing Israeli aircraft into Arab AAA fire. The SAM's rapid speed and its new and changing frequencies were difficult to counter. The overconfidence of the Israelis, their neglect of ECM (at one point, the IAF stripped ECM from their aircraft for greater economy, speed, and maneuverability), and US restrictions on ECM sales left the IAF in a serious bind. The result was that "The IAF could go anywhere except near the Golan Heights and the Suez fronts, where it was needed most. As they had begun to do three years earlier, the Soviet missiles successfully redefined the nature of modern war." In response, Israeli improvisation was speedy and effective, yet costly. [38]

The IAF used a variety of means to deal with the SAM threat. To defeat heat-seeking missiles, it employed violent maneuvers, turning toward the missile to present the IR seeker a "cold side," and maneuvering aircraft to cross in the sky creating a "hot spot." In addition, Israeli airmen dropped flares, even jettisoned fuel, and then ignited it to decoy the heat-seeking missiles. Spotters in helicopters warned pilots of missile launches. The IAF also used chaff, first carried in speed brakes, later in a more conventional manner; improved American ECM pods; and standoff jammers operating from the ground, helicopters, and transports. [39]

In his book 'Loud and Clear' Brigadier General Iftach Spector describes how it looks like to attack the SA-6 position[40]:

38   Ibid.
39   Ibid.
40   Loud and clear: the memoir of an Israeli fighter pilot by Iftach Spector; translated by Samuel Gorvine. Zenith Press.

The SAM arrays we were familiar with until then, types SAM-2 and SAM-3, were stationary batteries. That is, the enemy could move them from one place to another, but very slowly; it took days. In this situation we had no difficulty finding out where they were at any given time. Enough time to photograph the area—the Fighting First did it regularly—and the new SAM deployment was there on film. The locations of the batteries were fixed for the rest of the day. Under such conditions you could plan attacks on them. Although stationary arrays could kill you, too, attacking them was still a reasonable option. You flew to the target and bombed the hell out of it. Braving enemy fire and taking the hill is part of a soldier's job, isn't it?

But the situation is very different when the threats are mobile, and you enter the enemy killing zone without any notion of where that hill is. You can photograph, but even while you look at the pictures the deployment has changed. The SAM-6 mobile missile batteries were mounted on vehicles, and could move from one location to another in a short time. With such batteries, the area becomes an unknown array of threats. In short, if there really were SAM-6 batteries, all our current doctrine—which was based on the lessons of the War of Attrition—had become obsolete. Defy and Model would be thrown to the winds with all the investment in time and energy. All our plans had to be rewritten, training changed, and more. Everyone in the room knew that.

...

The squadron took off formation after formation, and I, after some management duty, happened to be the last leader from our squadron to take off, leading a three-ship section; we lacked a fourth ship. We entered the missile array from behind, as planned. As I had anticipated, nobody expected us to come in that way, and everything was quiet. No one shot at us, but we found nothing where our SAM-6 battery was supposed to be. The place was empty. The battery, like most of its kind, had deployed forward with the attacking Syrian Army, in the direction of the Hula Valley in Israel.

All I saw around were columns of armored infantry. I found myself in the heart of the Syrian ground forces. Groups of

vehicles were driving west, and antiaircraft farted smoke balls shooting west. I flew over there, and the Syrian soldiers looked up at me; my target was nowhere to be seen, and I felt like an uninvited guest at a party. So I pulled up and made another, higher circle, searching, hoping to find that battery somehow.

This was the moment when the Baboons began paying off on that investment—I was not at a loss. In their trials they had analyzed techniques of tempting missile batteries and threatening them to make them launch a missile and expose themselves. It was totally clear to me that circling around in easy radar range and in the heart of the fire zone, my navigator and I were juicy bait, and I hoped the idea would work. And at last somebody nearby woke up and launched a missile at us. The missile's fire and trail of smoke exposed his location. But I was not just bait but also a threat, carrying eleven half-ton high-explosive bombs. As soon as the missile took off - Erel saw it first and pointed it out—I rolled down and dived right on its source. My wingmen, who had seen the SAM the same time we did, pulled up from ground level and came in after me. And indeed when I put my gunsight there, I could see a group of vehicles comprising an SAM-6 battery there. They shot another, smaller missile at us. We needed no extra assurance that this was indeed our target. All three aircraft unloaded all our ordnance on the site, blowing it to kingdom come. Then we turned back and went home very satisfied with ourselves.

And only when we landed, overjoyed to see that all our pilots were back safely from the Golan, were we stunned to hear that all was not well. Not only had the air force missed most of the SAM batteries and bombed vacant land, it also had lost seven Phantoms in this operation. The Syrian SAM-6 array—except for the minute part that we probably took out—was essentially untouched. Operation Model, which was planned to deal with the fixed SAM batteries, failed miserably when it met the mobile array.

In addition, the Israelis directly assaulted the SA-6s. The SA-6's low initial trajectory encouraged the IAF to dive-bomb the SAMs from very steep angles - desperate measures improvised for a desperate situation. The IAF also fired Shrike antiradiation missiles[41]. Israelis managed to stop Syrians in Golan, then eliminate the air defense units with coordinated attacks. Syrians expended almost all of their 3M9 missile in the first few days and without them, their batteries were not effective. The Israeli attack on the air defense command further degraded the efficiency of the Syrian systems.

During the land operations, Israelis were able to capture few destroyed SA-6 launchers and 1S91 radars, but this is not officially confirmed. It is estimated that these examples are thoroughly studied and the results, as well as captured samples, were shared with the US.

It is worth saying that SA-6 was not only deadly to Israeli aircraft. Because of the poor coordination between Egyptian and Syrian air defense and air forces and without proper information about their own air force actions, often Egyptian and Syrian aircraft were engaged by their own air defenses. Due to the friendly fire, Syria lost 20 airplanes. The situation with Egyptians was even worst – they lost 40 aircraft downed with SA-6. Israeli inflicted casualties on SA-6 units as well: 5 batteries on the Golan heights and 4 batteries in the Suez Canal area.

During this war, Israeli pilots gave a notorious nickname to the system: "Three Fingers of Death". For them it was deadly – an estimate is that 55 Israeli pilots were killed and 44 were able to eject.

The high efficiency of the Kvadrat air defense missile system was also confirmed in the period from 8 March to 30 May 1974, when the launches of 8 missiles destroyed 6 aircraft.

In the following years, a set of countermeasures equipment and tactics were developed with the sole role to encounter SA-6 menace.

Bekaa Valley[42]

One of the greatest air defense suppression engagements after the Yom Kippur War was the Bekaa valley battle (Operation Mole Cricket 19), fought on 9 June 1982 between Syrian air defense and the Israeli Air Force. The more modern and mobile KUB (SA-6) system was engaged and this battle

---

41   Ibid.
42   Mike Mihajlović & Djordje Aničić, Shooting Down the Stealth Fighter: Eyewitness accounts from Those Who Were There. Pen and Sword, UK, 2021.

cemented the future of air suppression and air defense tactics for the wars to come (Fig. 3-14). This is also the first engagement in which remotely piloted vehicles (RPV) were used, later known as unmanned aerial vehicles (UAV) or drones.

The IDF (Israeli Defense Forces) attack against nineteen Syrian SA-6 sites was the execution of a highly orchestrated, combined arms plan that involved planning, intelligence, training, surprise, command, control, communications, and countless elements of electronic combat in a three-phased attack.

The plan for the suppression of enemy air defenses was designed to take advantage of two Syrian air defense mistakes. The most fundamental mistake was the lack of movement by the missile batteries. The SA-6 was designed as a mobile SAM system, yet the Syrians had had their SA-6 batteries dug in for over a year in the Bekaa valley clearly visible to Israeli air reconnaissance (Fig. 3-15 and 3-16). The second mistake was the lack of radar emission control by the Syrian SAM operators. The Syrians turned their radars on frequently and often used more radars than required when practicing engagements. This allowed the Israelis to fingerprint or identify the exact frequencies used by the Syrians. The fingerprinting allowed for jamming operations and the targeting of anti-radiation missiles. Most of this information was the direct result of the Israeli prewar intelligence effort. For an extended period of time before the Lebanon invasion, Israeli drones overflew the area defended by the Syrian SAMs and collected intelligence for the attack plan. The two workhorses of this effort were the UAVs Mastiff and the Scout (Fig. 3-19). The Mastiffs contained a gyro-stabilized television and a high-resolution panoramic camera which proved extremely effective in photo-reconnaissance. The Scouts were configured for electronic intelligence and picked up the radar emissions which enabled the fingerprinting of the SAM radars. Both RPVs were capable of relaying their information to ground and airborne command posts for immediate analysis. But good intelligence and a good plan must be followed by training.

The Israeli Defense Forces conducted extensive northern border training exercises which were actually rehearsals for the upcoming invasion. These exercises, which took place over thirteen months, included rehearsal sorties against simulated SA-6 sites in the Negev desert. Countless rehearsals eliminated many of the problem areas that planners do not always foresee in coordinating an integrated plan. They also achieved planned desensitization of the PLO and Syrians. Fearing that a real invasion was underway, the PLO and Syrians reacted to the first five northern border exercises, but to the rest, little or nothing, nor to the real thing.

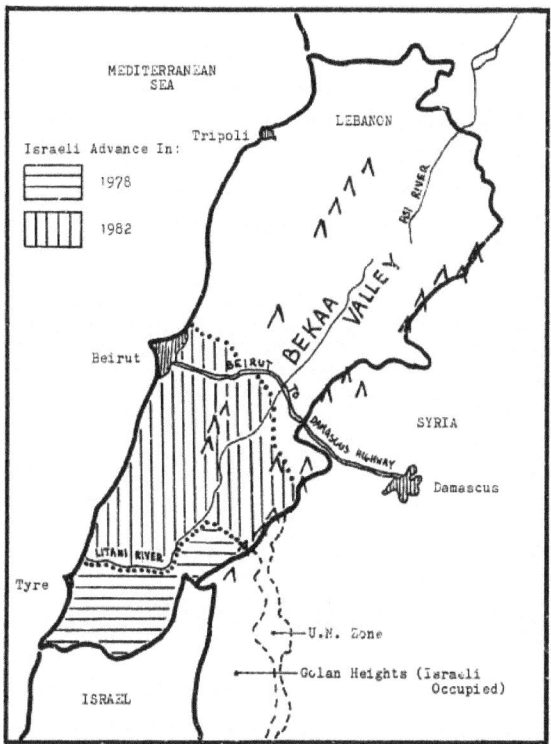

Figure 3-14: Israeli advance during the 1982 invasion of Lebanon.

Israel was able to achieve real surprise in their invasion because of Palestinian 'alert fatigue' or 'cry wolf' syndrome (Fig. 3-17 and 3-18).

A second reason for their surprise was that the PLO assumed they had a real deterrent to invasion. They incorrectly assumed their threatened massive rocket attacks against northern Israeli settlements and the threat of Syrian military reaction would deter.

And finally, with the devastating success of the SA-6 against Israeli aircraft in the 1973 war, Syrians concluded the Israelis would consider an attack against the SAM sites too risky. With the element of surprise in hand, along with a good plan, precise intelligence, and with extensive training completed, Israel now looked to her military commanders to conduct

Figure 3-15: Syrian 2P25 missile launcher commander during the TV interview in 1982. The location of this launcher was not specified but it can be assumed that is somewhere in Lebanon. (Source: Syrian TV)

Figure 3-16: Syrian 2K12 Kvadrat/SA-6 position near the Beirut - Damascus highway in Bekaa Valey at the beginning of 1982. The missiles are still in a "locked" position indicating that the battery is not in combat mode. (Source: US DoD)

the fight. They actually invaded on their ninth exercise and found no real resistance.

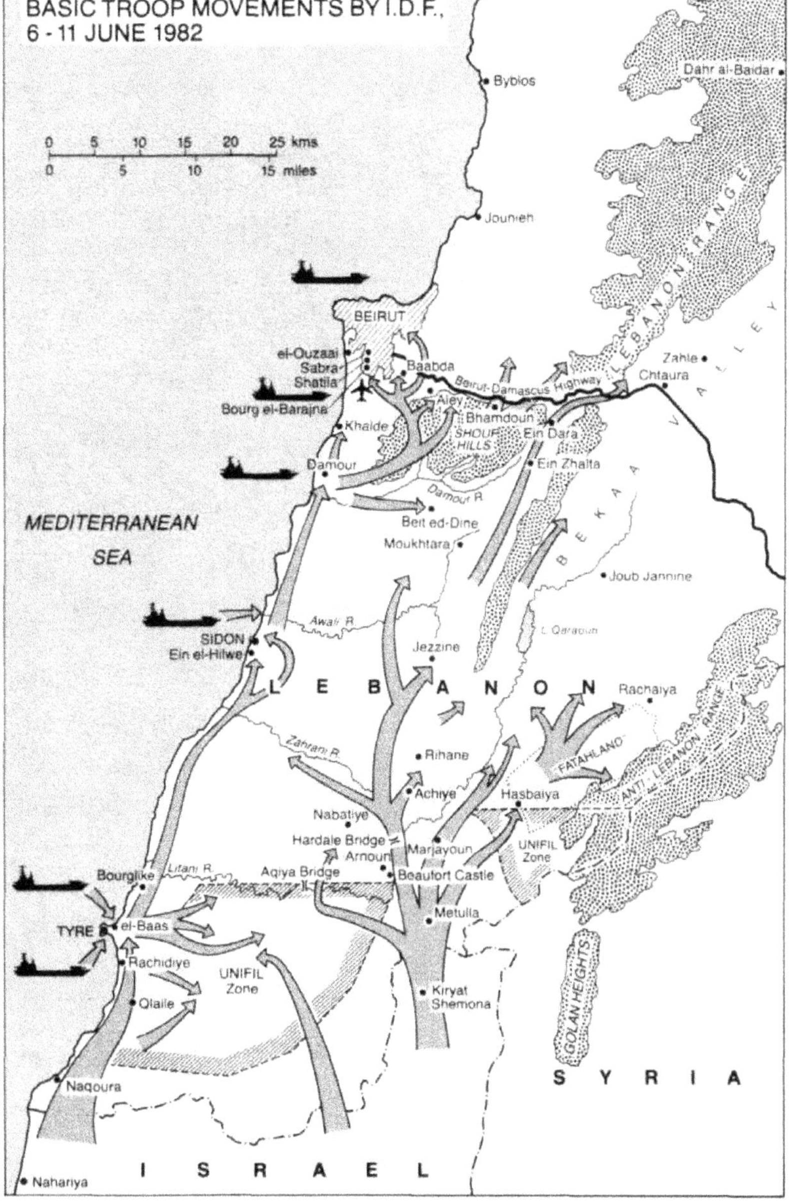

Figure 3-17: Direction of the main Israeli advance during the June 1982 invasion of Lebanon.
(Source: The War of Desperation, Lebanon 1982-85, page 60)

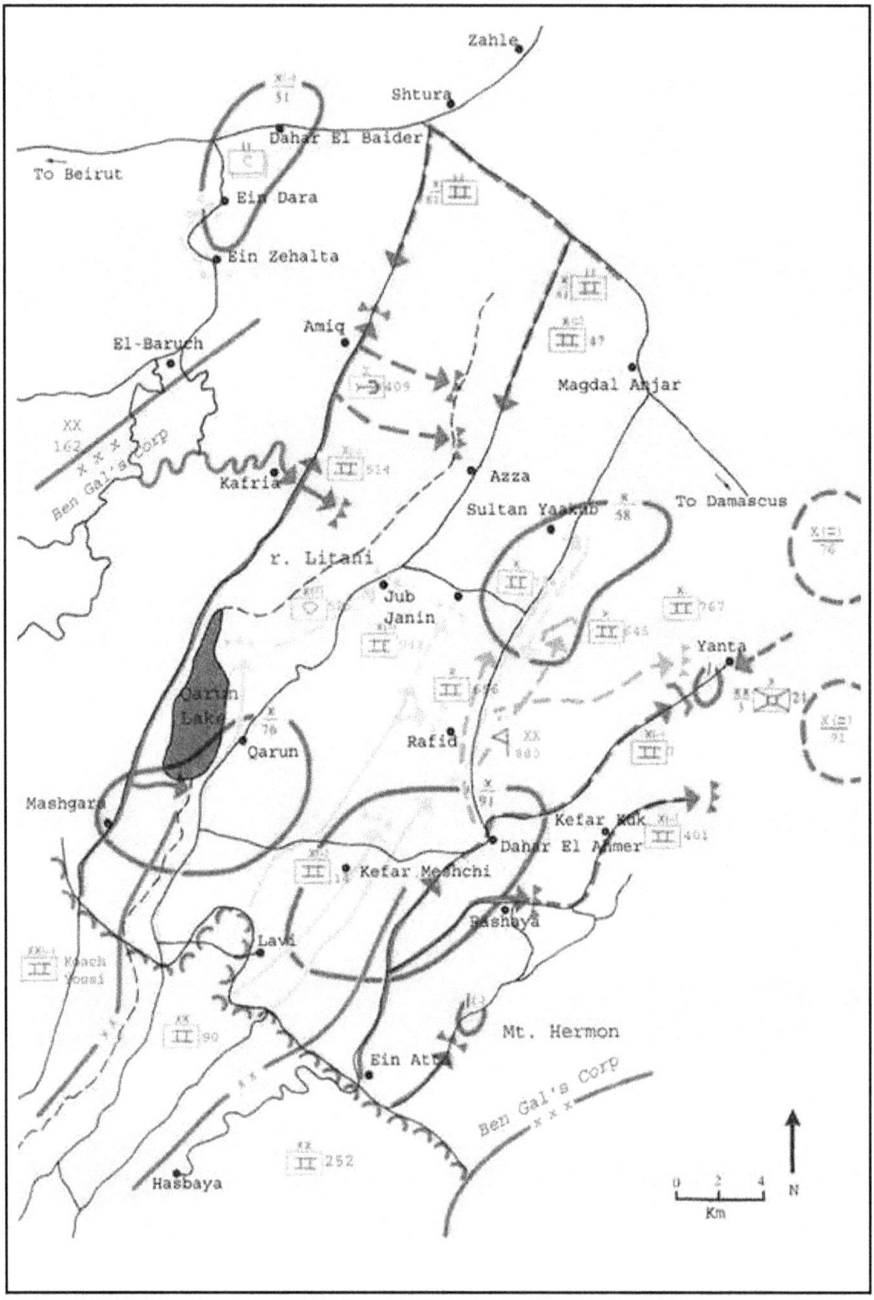

Figure 3-18: Combat in the Bekaa Valley region. (Illustration source: Jerusalem Post)

Israeli commanders proved that an effective command, control, and communications (C3) system is the essential ingredient to a successful combined arms effort and denial of C3 to the enemy. C3 is the nerve system of a modern military force and the tactical commander is the brain. In the Israeli SEAD effort, the tactical commander received most of his information through an Israeli version of the Boeing 707 and from E-2C aircraft. The 707 served primarily as electronic support measures (ESM) and electronic countermeasures (ECM) platform. ESM involves the gathering of communication and electronic intelligence. ECM primarily involves the jamming and deception of enemy communications. The E-2C served primarily as an airborne command post. With the facilities aboard these aircraft, the tactical commander was able to process real-time intelligence, develop a picture of the tactical situation, coordinate his offensive assets with the proper timing, monitor the attack in progress, and then immediately assess the effectiveness of the attack. Furthermore, the tactical commander was also able to coordinate the jamming and deception that so effectively disrupted Syrian defenses. On the afternoon of 9 June 1982, the commanders commenced their attack.

Figure 3-19: Israeli Scout UAV, a key component in pinpointing locations of the Syrian air defense systems. (Source: Israeli Air Force Museum)

The first phase, deception, involved the stimulation of the Syrian radar systems. The initial drones over the target were probably a combination of 'Mastiffs' and 'Scouts'. These drones reverified the locations of the SAM sites and their radar frequencies, and also served to stimulate the radars into activity. The slow speed of the 'Mastiffs' and 'Scouts' probably did not generate any more than the usual amount of disinterest shown over the previous year. The large force of air-launched 'Samson's' and ground-launched 'Dalilah's', though, did receive their full attention. These decoy drones more closely resemble the speed and appearance of attacking aircraft when viewed on a radar screen. The direction of the attack placed the afternoon sun directly behind the incoming drones, degrading Syrian optical guidance systems on the SAMs. This forced greater reliance on their radar and increased vulnerability to anti-radiation missiles. The Syrians took the bait as expected. They showed poor target discrimination and firing discipline. They launched most of their available SAMs against the incoming drones. When the Boeing 707's ESM sensors confirmed the Syrian radars were fully activated and the SAM batteries were in their first reload cycle, the next phase of the attack was initiated. During this phase, Syrian missiles destroyed a number of drones.

Figure 3-20: Israeli Phantom F-4E crew after the completed mission. (Source: Israeli DoD)

The second phase of the attack integrated many activities into extremely effective harassment and suppression effort. The 707 now used its ECM capabilities and began to jam Syrian radar frequencies, blinding their missiles. The 707 was augmented with ground-based jammers and with other airborne jammers located on CH-53 helicopters and on the attacking aircraft. Artillery fire, with their aim adjusted by the TV pictures from the Mastiff, now harassed the SAM operators. The sites were shelled with 155 mm howitzer rounds and with Ze'ev missiles carrying terminally guided cluster munitions. Chaff-dispensing rockets further obscured the radar picture for the Syrian radar operators. With radar screens blinded by jamming and chaff and operators harassed by artillery fire, the Israeli Air Force went to work. F-4s launched their 'Shrike' and 'Standard' anti-radiation missiles which homed in on the radar signals emitted by the SAM radars, destroying the radar antennas. After this attack, the tactical commander was able to determine how many and exactly which SAM sites remained effective. Armed with the information fed to him via RPV television pictures and the ESM assets aboard the 707, he then commenced the final phase of the attack (Fig. 3-20, 3-21 and 3-22).

The final phase destroyed the remaining pieces of the Syrian SAM sites in the Bekaa valley. The E-2C airborne warning and control aircraft now guided Israeli Air Force F-16s, A-4s, and Kfir C-2s. The E-2C vectored them through the undefended areas for the follow-on attacks against the surviving radar vans and SA-6 missile launchers. Using standoff munitions, cluster bomb units, and general-purpose bombs, the Israeli aircraft simultaneously attacked from multiple directions after a low-level ingress. The Syrians continued to launch missiles from the now radarless sites in a futile effort to defend themselves. Lacking acquisition and target tracking

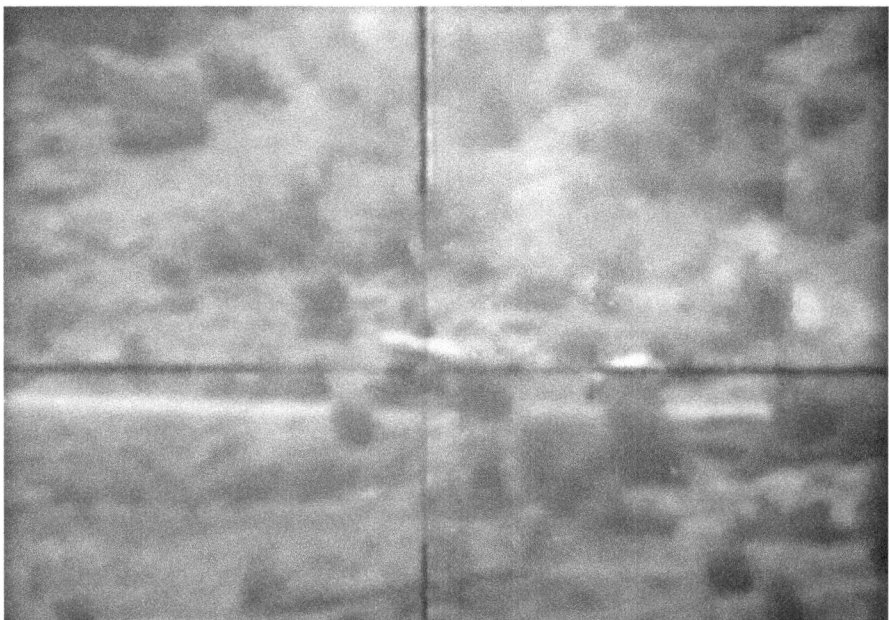

Figure 3-21: Syrian 2K12/SA-6 targeted by the Israelis in Bekaa Valley. (Source: still from the documentary movie "Lebanon 1982")

capability without their radars, the missiles were ineffective against the maneuvering aircraft. The Syrians tried to obscure the SAM sites with smoke to prevent the use of laser guided weapons by the Israelis, but the fires were started too late to create enough smoke. In fact this tactic only made target acquisition easier. Finally, the Syrian operators turned the remaining radars off to avoid destruction, the ultimate act of futility.

Losing the battle on the ground, the Syrians launched about a hundred Mig-21 and Mig-23 aircraft to repel Israeli aircraft. Selective airborne communications jamming disrupted the airwaves for the MiG-21s and MiG-23s and cut them off from ground control, making them vulnerable to AWACS-directed attacks from the Israeli F-15s and F-16s.

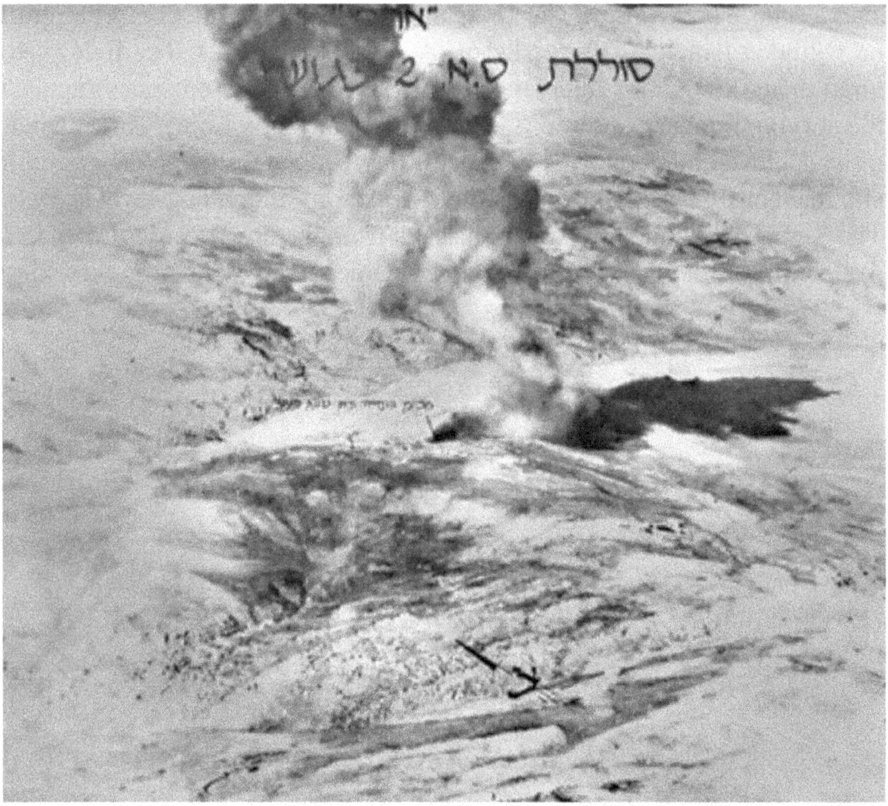

Figure 3-22: Position of the Syrian 2K12/SA-6 batteries ponded by the Israeli Air Force attacks. The Hebrew text on the photo means "hit at the second battery. (Source: Israeli DoD)

The IAF positioned RPVs over three major airfields in Syria to report when and how many Syrian aircraft were taking off. The data was transmitted to the E-2Cs. The IAF took advantage of the fact that the MiGs had only nose and tail alert radar systems and no side warnings or look-up and look-down systems, by jamming the GCI communications net. E-2Cs guided the Israeli aircraft into positions that enabled them to attack the Syrian aircraft from the side, where the latter would have no warning. Because of the jamming, the Syrian GCI controllers could not direct their pilots towards the incoming Israeli aircraft. Sparrow missiles attacked at speeds of Mach 3.5 at ranges of 22 to 40 km, outside the Syrians' radar range. The Sidewinders' 'head-on' capabilities at close range gave the Israelis a further firepower advantage. At nearly 16:00, with fourteen SAM batteries destroyed and an hour left until dark, the Israelis decided to call off the operation, assuming the optimal result had been achieved.

Head of the Soviet delegation in Syria, general Grigoriy Yashkin, reported to the Soviet minister of defense, Marshal Dmitri Ustinov, that the Syrian air defense missile units, air force and units for electronic and radio warfare had done as much as they can to perform their duties but the equipment that they used is not on the same level and a bit inferior comparing to the equipment used by Israelis and USA. Besides the equipment, significant mistakes were made in the Syrian armed forces command decisions.[43]

Other wars

Angolan border war

During the South African border war with Angola, there were numerous engagements of South African air forces attacking Angolan and Cuban positions. The Angolan forces with the help of Soviet instructors developed an extensive anti-aircraft system over time, which included guns and a full range of surface-to-air missiles. The latter included the SA-7, SA-14 and SA-16 shoulder-launched missiles; SA-9 and SA-13 infra-red homing missiles mounted on armored vehicles; the self-propelled SA-8 medium-range system (the first used outside the major Warsaw Pact forces); and the longer-ranged mobile SA-6 and semi-mobile SA-3. The weapons were backed up by a comprehensive radar system. All in all the Angolan air defense

---

43 Grigoriy Yashkin: Beneath the Hot Sun of Syria, Journal of Military History/Voenno-Istoricheskii Zhurnal no. 4, 1998; Vladimir Voronov, The Syrian Nemesis, Russia Studies Center, January 2017.

system in the second half of the 1980s was very similar to that encountered by the allied forces in Iraq in 1991. The SAAF (South African Air Force) was, however, generally able to continue to operate effectively, bypassing the air defenses or conducting air defense suppression strikes. Several aircraft were lost to SAMs. Most of the SAAF's aircraft losses, however, were suffered by helicopters and Impalas (light trainer and attack aircraft) flying low, and most of them were lost to light anti-aircraft guns.

During the fifteen years of bush war between 1979 and 1989, the SAAF lost a total of twenty-two aircraft to enemy action. Also, many airplanes were struck by enemy fire but landed safely. Most of these were hit by either SA-3, SA-7 or SA-9, some by small arms. A pilot, Arthur Piercy, suffered a hit by an AA-8 (R-60) missile launched from a Mig-23.

According to the Cuban information, SA-6 manned by the Cuban crew shot down a South African Impala Mk II.

Libya & Chad

Libyans have their SA-6 systems engaged in the war in Chad to combat threat from the French aviation. On 7 January 1987 French Jaguars and Mirages successfully hit the position of one Libyan battery.

I was at that time head of the detachment of Jaguars," pilot André Carbon remembered. *'France had decided to take military action against Libya. There were two options — fire a missile against the radar of the airbase of Ouadi Doum or attack an airfield near Aouzou. The missile shot was preferred, but to do this it was necessary that the radar emit.'*

French intelligence services indicated that Aouzou and Maaten-Sahra air bases were buzzing with activity, making them prime targets. At 08:00 in the morning on 7 January 1987, the Atlantic patrol plane headed for the 16th parallel. The Jaguar pilots waited on the ground.

Both missions were ready to take off. I was leading eight Jaguars armed with rocket launchers - and were only waiting for the green light from the Breguet Atlantic which 'tickled' the 16th parallel, awaiting the good will of the Libyans switching on their radars," Carbon recalled.

It was almost 09:20 and the crew of the Atlantic still had not detected anything. The crew of the C-135F in charge of refueling the two air-defense Mirage F.1Cs announced that it had no more fuel to deliver to the fighters. The Mirages returned to N'Djamena, leaving Peccavy's Atlantic undefended.

> *At the time limit, still not sensing any signal, the Breguet Atlantic should have given me the green light at the expense of my comrades from EC 3,* Carbon said, *but the air commander on board* [the Atlantic] *... decided to make one last run ... because it was his birthday.*

It was during this last pass - at 09:30 in the morning - that the P-15 'Flat Face' (as per French estimate) air-defense radar at Ouadi Doum finally began to emit. The French force had a target. But they wanted more.

It was 11:00 when the two pilots of the EC33, Goutx and Dischly, climbed into their Mirages. It fell to them to tickle the radar at Faya-Largeau in order to trigger more radars at Ouadi Doum. Their rendezvous with a C-135F tanker was scheduled for noon.

Once they'd filled their tanks, the Mirage F.1CR pilots flew into the radar coverage zone of Faya-Largeau. Meanwhile, the missile-armed Jaguars accompanied their C-135FR tanker 160 nautical miles south of Wadi Doum in order to readjust their navigation systems.

At around 12:50, the two Mirage pilots reached their preplanned turning point northwest of Faya-Largeau. They were flying at 300 feet and 450 knots. They angled 90 degrees to the right and climbed to 6,000 feet.

The 'Flat Face' at Faya-Largeau detected them, as they had intended. On board the Atlantic, sensor operators picked up increased emissions on the frequencies between Ouadi Doum and Faya-Largeau. The Libyans had panicked.

The 'Flat Face' at Ouadi Doum began to emit continuously. The time to attack was now. The Jaguars were 50 miles south of their objective, flying at 500 knots and 200 feet. Pilots Lebourg and Wurtz were in the lead. At a distance of 35 miles from Ouadi Doum, Wurtz's AS-37 missile detected the 'Flat Face signal. Wurtz then climbed to 300 feet to facilitate radar lock. He fired his missile at 13:00.

The AS-37 struck its target.[44]

A Libyan source claimed that the radar the French pilots targeted

---

44 https://medium.com/war-is-boring/in-1987-the-french-air-force-staged-a-daring-raid-on-libyan-defenses-4f8c6fa6f119

wasn't actually a 'Flat Face'. Rather, it was a 'Straight Flush' fire-control system belonging to one of the SA-6 sites at Ouadi Doum. Another source insisted that the missile actually failed to hit any radar antenna, and instead struck a nearby vehicle that had reflected the radar emissions (Fig. 3-23).

Figure 3-23: Libyan 1S91 'Straight Flush' radar during the transport. (Source: French DoD)

Figure 3-24: Captured Libyan 2P25 launcher by the Chadian forces. Quadi Doum, Chad, 1987. (Source: Rivista Italiana Difesa/CIA)

In any event, the French had proved they could tease, target and strike Libyan defenses.

The second pair of Jaguars flown by Saussier and Guy failed to achieve lock. The four Jaguars turned around at a very low altitude. At the same time, the two F.1CR pilots were flying between 400 and 500 feet above the ground 12 miles west of Faya Largeau. A fire-control radar, probably from a ZSU-23/4 anti-aircraft gun, locked onto Dischly's Mirage.

Both Mirage pilots descended to 100 feet and accelerated to 570 knots and raced away for a distance of 125 miles. South of the 17th parallel, the two Mirages climbed to 15,000 feet for refueling. They then ascended to 30,000 feet and returned to N'Djamena, landing just behind the Jaguars and Mirage F.1Cs.

Goutx and Dischly soon met the crew of the Atlantic, which told the fighter pilots that at the same time they were dodging the apparent ZSU-23/4, a Libyan MiG-23 had pursued them, as well. The MiG followed the two French fliers for around 60 miles before turning around, probably owing to a lack of fuel.

The French mission was a success - and apparently helped to restrain Libyan ambitions in Chad.

In March of the same year, the Chadian fighters take over one of the Libyan airports (the Chadian airport used by the Libyan air force). They managed to capture several SA-6 batteries. Some of the vehicles and launchers were handed over to the USA and France and the rest were included in the service with the Chadian army (Fig. 3-24).

On 8 August 1987 one Libyan Tu-22B (Tu-22B Blinder-A) bomber became a victim of that system when attacking an abandoned Libyan base.

Iraq vs Iran

During the Iran-Iraq war (1980-1988) Iraqis SA-6 were able to shoot down several Iranian F-4E, F-5E and F-14A.

In the operation 'Desert storm' in 1991, the Iraqis succeeded to damage one USAF B-52 bomber and shoot down one F-16C fighter (serial number 87-0228). The pilot, Captain Harry 'Mike' Roberts was captured.

During the US invasion of Iraq in 2003, as per available information, Iraqi SA-6 acted without results.

Yemen

SA-6 resurrect during the ongoing civil war in Yemen. Houthi rebels claimed several coalition airplanes (led by Saudi Arabia) were shot down using indigenous modification named 'Fater' – that uses components identical to the 3M9 used with the 2K12 Kub/Kvadrat (SA-6 'Gainful') system.

The U.S. military said that the MQ-9 drone was shot down over Yemen on 6 June 2019 by what it suspects was Houthi SA-6 surface-to-air missile.

On 14 February 2020, the Houthi rebels announced they had downed a Saudi Tornado in the northern al-Jawf province, in Yemen. Later on the same day, a Royal Saudi Air Force spokesperson said that '*at 23:45LT on Friday evening, an RSAF Tornado jet crashed while conducting a CAS mission in support of the Yemeni National Army operations in Al Jouf governorate.*'

Houthis have modified R-27T AAMs (air-to-air missiles) to be launched from pick-ups. The R-27 (AA-10 Alamo-B), is an IR-homing, missile with a maximum range of 63 km and a theoretical maximum allowed vertical separation of 10 km altitude. A modified R-27 was claimed to be responsible for the downing of a Saudi F-15 in 2018.

Artsakh/Nagorno Karabakh War

During the Armenian - Azerbaijani war over Artsakh/Nagorno Karabakh in the fall of 2020, several Armenian SA-6 units were hit by Azerbaijani drones. Based on the video clips from these engagements, these SA-6 units were not operational and there is a probability that they were used just as decoys to attract drones (Fig. 3-25, 3-26, 3-27 and 3-28) and to lure them into the engagement zone of the other missile systems such as OSA AKM (SA-8).

Figure 3-25: Armenian 2K12 Kub position near Shushi/Shusha, Artsakh/Nagorno Karabakh. This photo is from the peacetime and prepared combat positions are clearly visible. (Source: Twitter IntelLab)

Figure 3-26: Armenian 2P25 launcher at the position during the 2020 Karabakh war. Based on the missile position, it appears that the launcher was not in the combat readiness. It is possible that Armenians used these older launchers as a decoys to lure Azerbaijani drones.
(Source: still from the loitering munition attack clip, Azerbaijani MoD)

Figure 3-27: Captured Armenian 2P25 launcher at the position during the 2020 Nagorno Karabakh war. The impact of the loitering munition destroyed the launching platform and the missile. (Source: Azerbaijani MoD)

Figure 3-28: Captured Armenian 1S91 RStON ire control radar during the 2020 Artsakh/Nagorno Karabakh war. (Source: Azerbaijani MoD)

CHAPTER FOUR

Yugoslav Civil War

Outbreak

The first clashes of the Yugoslav civil war started in Slovenia by the end of June 1991. Slovenian territorial defense accompanied by the local police blocked and attacked the garrisons of the Yugoslav People's Army. Croatia was the next one. The same scenario: in the parts with the majority of Croatian population, territorial defense, pro-Nazi paramilitary groups and police blocked federal troops garrisons. The first clashes started in August and since 13 September, some isolated garrisons, with the Croatian command cadre in the ranks of the federal army started to surrender.

Some of the units were able to avoid blockades taking in timely manner positions in the field. Out of all blocked units and garrisons in the Zadar area (school center for the artillery and missile troops) only 271st light artillery air defense regiment and 60th medium self-propelled missile regiment (2K12 Kvadrat) were able to exit Šepurine garrison and join the forces with 9th army corps which was relocated in the areas with the majority Serbian population.

After the signed agreement between the federal forces and Croatian paramilitary forces, the rest of the federal units were able to evacuate local garrisons, military objects and join the rest of the forces. The majority of the equipment was evacuated except some which were intentionally sabotaged by the local employees and military personnel who stayed with the paramilitary forces.

The 60th SA-6 regiment, firstly relocated in the area of responsibility of the 9th corps, was ordered to move to the Montenegro territory, which was not accepted likely by the local Serbian population in the area of Benkovac and Knin which formed the territory of 'Srpska Krajina'. The regiment was transported by railway and by roads firstly to Titograd (nowadays Podgorica) than to Danilovgrad as a permanent base.

The second 2K12 regiment that was located on the Croatian territory, was 146th regiment in Zagreb. After the initial try by the Croatian separatists to block the regiment base and agreement of the peaceful withdraw, the regiment was transferred from the Pleso airport to Banja Luka in November 1991. Almost all equipment that was in need for repairs were relocated to the 'Kosmos' repair center. Regiment personnel was sent to Novi Sad. All equipment that was withdrawn from Zagreb was equivalent for five missile batteries, including all RStONs and one 'Bear' radar. Equipment stayed in 'Kosmos' even after federal troops withdraw from Bosnia and Herzegovina.

First Blood

During the clashes and negotiations for unblocking of the federal troops' garrisons and bases in Croatia, in Vukovar (eastern defense zone of the Croatian national guard) the first independent air force platoon was formed on 8 October. This first Croatian air force platoon was formed from the members of the civilian agricultural society and Osijek aero-club. Soon after the forming, the air platoon started with operations on the east. The workhorse was venerable An-2. During the battle of Vukovar, this aircraft was used to drop supplies to the surrounded Croatian troops. The same aircraft were also used to drop makeshift boiler bombs onto the Serbian positions. Boiler bombs were made form the gas cylinders filled with explosives, nails and other metals. An-2, even archaic, is very capable airplane for the quite approaches and bombing where there is no adequate air defense. The plane was always employed during the night, when anti-aircraft artillery without night visions and radars was not able to do anything. Frustration of the local commanders and protest to the federal army HQ made the commander of the air defense to order dislocation of 310th regiment from Kraljevo. Arrival of 2K12 within days change the situation: on 2 December 1991, RStON was able to locate and track An-2. One missile hit the plane which crashed near the Otok, a village near Vinkovci. All crew of four perished (Fig. 4-1).

It was interesting that long time after the hit, by unknown reason the radar showed a blip, so the crews launched few more missiles until the blip disappeared. Shooting down the only airplane forced the Croatian platoon to withdraw from the area which were protected by missile units.

After Slovenia and Croatia, the next clashes erupted in Bosnia and

Herzegovina in the beginning of 1992 with very similar Croatian scenarios. By then, federal units were withdrawn to the territories with the majority of Serbian population. On 17 March 240th regiment from Lukavica garrison (near Sarajevo), was relocated on mountain Romanija, near Sokolac. After the order for the federal troops to leave all territory of Bosnia and Herzegovina, the regiment was sent to Novi Sad.

Figure 4-1: Croatian An-2, a "boiler bomb bomber", the first airplane of the new formed Croatian Air Force, downed on 2 December 1992. (Source: authors)

On 11 February 1992, the last SA-6 regiment (311th) left the base near Skopje, which became Republic of Macedonia. The regiment withdraw peacefully. The biggest problem was the lack of people. Whoever knew to drive anything, was tasked to drive one of the vehicles. There were no hostilities by the Macedonian population but entering the province of Kosovo and Metohija could be challenging because the local Albanian population more or less showed hostilities toward the Serbian population and military. All regiment members were armed: assault rifles, hand grenades, submachine guns. Fortunately everything went well and, beside the dense fog during the night when the regiment entered Kosovo and Metohija, the Serbian population was happy to see the army coming and many people went to the streets to great the troops serving them with drinks and food. The regiment came to the permanent base in the early morning hours of 12 March at the military part of the Slatina airport, near Priština.

With this withdraw, federal troops finished basically dismantling the former Socialist Federal Republic of Yugoslavia territory. Yugoslav People's Army ceased to exist.

SA-6 in the Army of Republika Srpska[43]

Withdraw of the 149th regiment from Zagreb to Banja Luka brought considerable equipment to the Bosnian Serb territory. Beside the 149th regiment equipment, in Kosmos Technical center there were also equipment from the other regiments that was there for the maintenance and overhaul. With the equipment, some personnel also stayed. It was a mix of older S-75M system and newer 2K12 Kub/Kvadrat systems.

After the constitution of the new federal republic of Yugoslavia was proclaimed on 27 April 1992, the Serbian population in Republika Srpska found itself technically in the diaspora. The new military leadership in Belgrade planned to dislocate remaining federal troops onto Serbia and Montenegro territory. Some federal high ranking officers that remained on the Bosnia and Herzegovina territory, as well as the territory of Srpska Krajina, sensing that the civil war is inevitable, decided to organize and build up a new army from scratch: to form the Serbian army to protect the Serbian population. The new army will need air defense and from the equipment located in 'Kosmos' (five batteries with associate radars and one P-40 radar), it was decided to form Army of Republika Srpska air defense missile corps. By the order of the general stuff No. 30/18-17 as of 16 June 1992[44], the 155th missile regiment was formed. In the beginning, there was no plan for the establishment of the air force and air defense branch but

---

43   Republika Srpska is one of the two entities of Bosnia and Herzegovina, the other being the Federation of Bosnia and Herzegovina. Its largest city and administrative center is Banja Luka, lying on the Vrbas river. The entity encompasses most of the Serbs of Bosnia and Herzegovina-populated portions of Bosnia and Herzegovina situated in the north and east of the country. Formed in 1992 at the outset of the breakup of Yugoslavia, Republika Srpska, following the Dayton Accords, achieved international recognition as part of a federal Bosnia and Herzegovina.

44   At the beginning, the name of the entity was Serbian Republic of Bosnia and Herzegovina but that name was changed by the parliament decision on 12 August 1992 into Republika Srpska and the armed forces got the name Army of Republika Srpska.

the situation in the field dictated a necessity for this branch of the military. Initial steps were made to transfer the people with adequate specialities from the army units, even the preparation for the operation 'Corridor-92' was ongoing.[45]

The newly formed 155th regiment consisted of three SA-2C Volhov battalions and one SA-2A Dvina battalion. Besides these systems, air defense also had some number of short-range 9K35 Strela-10 and 9K31 Strela-1, and MANPADS such as 9K32M Strela-2M and 9K310 Igla-1 as well as a considerable number of artillery 20 mm, 30 mm and 40 mm. The most valuable system was 2K12 Kvadrat. Air defense had three battalions[46]. The number of different missile systems dictated reorganization so the 155th regiment was renamed into the 155th missile defense brigade with HQ in Zalužani, near Banja Luka.

In June 1992 the first independent self-propelled missile battery equipped with the 2K12 system was formed at the village Rijekavica, at the Manjača mountain. Technical center 'Kosmos' was able to refurbish and repair two 1S91M2 radars with few launchers. This was enough to form two batteries.

Figure 4-2: Patch of the 1st Kub missile battery, (Source: authors)

---

45   Operation 'Corridor-92' was an operation conducted during the Bosnian War by the Army of Republika Srpska (VRS) against the forces of the Croatian Defense Council (HVO) and the Croatian Army (HV) fought in northern Bosnia and Herzegovina between 24 July and 6 October 1992. The objective of the offensive was to re-establish a road link between the city of Banja Luka in the west of the country and the eastern parts of the territory controlled by the Bosnian Serbs

46   According to Danko Borojević, Dragi Ivić, Željko Ubović book "Vazduhoplovne snage bivsih republika SFRJ" (Air forces of the former Yugoslav Republics) Army of Republika Srpska had five Kub battalions-three located in the Republika Srpska territory and 2 located in Republika Srpska Krajina territory. After the fall of Republika Srpska Krajina, these two battalions were returned to Republika Srpska.

The first battery was equipped with one radar 1S91M2 and two launchers. The reason for this was the shortage of the trained crews and other trained troops. At the same time, the first recruits were accepted. The second battery was formed in the second half of 1992. By 1993, a number of officers from the Yugoslav army has been transferred from Yugoslavia. The third battery was formed at the Zalužani airbase in November 1993.

In the beginning, it was suggested to the VRS army HQ to form an SA-6 battalion for defense of the Banja Luka region but in the end, it was decided that it is not realistic because of the lack of qualified personnel. The intermediate decision was made to attach two batteries in the new formed 155th regiment. It was the first-time decision in any army that the territorial and troop mobile defense are merged into one unit. Missiles were supplied from Serbia and in total 72 were delivered.

Until April 1994, individual units were more or less staffed to the full number with the ongoing training of the new recruits.

The first combat duties were performed on the east, by 2nd battery, which was tasked to observe NATO C-130 transport airplanes that dropped food and munition supplies to the Bosnian troops in Tuzla. The unit had locked multiple time on the airplanes but didn't open fire on them (Fig. 4-5).

Figure 4-3: 2K12 of the 1st battery at the fire position near Banja Luka, 1994. (Source: Drago Vejnović)

By the end of 1993, all three batteries were employed in the limited number during the combat duties, acting with one 1S91M2 and 2 launchers. It was a decision based on the crew's availability and shortening the maneuvering time (Fig. 4-3 and 4-4).

By the end of 1993 NATO aircraft flight over the Serbian territory intensified and the HQ conclusion was that the Eastern parts of Republika Srpska is not adequately protected. Because of this, the decision was made in 1994 to form 172nd regiment in Sokolac. Interestingly, the regiment number was chosen based on the date when the regiment is formed – 17 February (Fig. 4-2).

Figure 4-4: RStON from the 1st battery at the combat position, vicinity of Banja Luka. (Source: Drago Vejnović)

NATO aggressive and provoking flights over the Serbian positions intensified and as a result, the first downing of the NATO combat aircraft happened. The first was UK Sea Harrier, XZ498, from the 801 squadron,

Royal Navy. On 16 April 1994, while flying a combat mission near Goražde, it was caught by a Strela-2M MANPAD operator which launched one missile.[47]

Figure 4-5: 2nd missile battery men. (Source: Danko Borojević)

After the end of the Croatian operation 'Flash', during the night of 2 May, 1995. the 1st self-propelled medium missile battery of the Republika Srpska Air Defense was transferred to the region of Gradiška and occupied a combat position in the village of Cerovljani, but Croatian airplanes then no longer flew over the territory of the Republika Srpska.[48]

In May 1995, NATO aviation conducted sporadic attacks on Serbian forces warehouses.

The first opportunity for action the 1st battery got on 2 June 1995, when she was located at the position between Petrovac and Ključ, in a place named Bravsko. On that combat position battery has been around for three days, waiting in an ambush and monitoring NATO aviation flights but without turning on radars, which could definitely unmask the position.

---

47   Danko Borojević, Dragi Ivić, Orlovi sa Vrbasa, istorija vojnog vazduhoplovstva na teritoriji Republike Srpske, D.O.O „Štampa", Ruma, 2014, str.151-152.
48   Danko Borojević, Dragi Ivić, Orlovi sa Vrbasa, istorija vojnog vazduhoplovstva na teritoriji Republike Srpske, D.O.O „Štampa", Ruma, 2014, str.161.

In the afternoon of 2 June, when a pair of F-16C fighters approached about 20 km from the battery combat position, target tracking radar was turned on. As soon as the lead F-16C is located, the fire control radar is turned on as well. At that moment the plane changed direction and took cover behind the Srnetica mountain. The battery saw a strong jamming signal. Under this circumstance, it was not possible for the operators to acquire a fire solution and the radars were turned off after 3-4 seconds.

Fifteen minutes later the same pair of planes approached again the battery zone of engagement. In the meantime, the crew changed the fire control radar frequency and when the planes approached at about 22 kilometers, they turned on target tracking radar again. After 3-4 rotation of the target tracking radar antenna, another plane from the pair was spotted at a 20 km distance. At that moment, a fire control radar is turned on.

The fire solution was acquired at 18 km and at that moment all conditions for the launch were acquired. The battery had two launchers ready with five 3M9 missiles. The battery commander decided to engage the target with two missiles and when the target got at 17 km distance, the first missile was launched. The second one followed after 3 seconds (regime II). The tracking of both missiles was stable and the first hit was observed at 15 km distance and 5.5 km altitude. After the first hit, the target split up and the second missile hit one of the parts. The plane parts fell mostly at two locations about 1.5 km apart. The pilot managed to eject and land about 6 km from one of the wrecks (Fig. 4-6 and 4-7).

The battery immediately turned off the radar and left the position and hide in the woods nearby. In total, the tracking and fire control radars worked for 26 seconds. During the night, the battery left the area where it was hidden and moved to a new location 100 kilometers from the combat position from where the missiles were launched.

Downed F-16C number AF 89-2032 belonged to the 555-fighter squadron, 31 fighter wing from Aviano. The pilot was Captain Scott O'Grady. After landing he spent six days in the territory of Republika Srpska before he was successfully rescued on 8 June.

The downing of F-16 by the older SA-6 system had an important reflection on the future flight procedures in the following operations.

Determining the vulnerability of fighters to this system, in later air operation against the FRY in 1999 strict rules of engagement have been introduced in US Air Force.

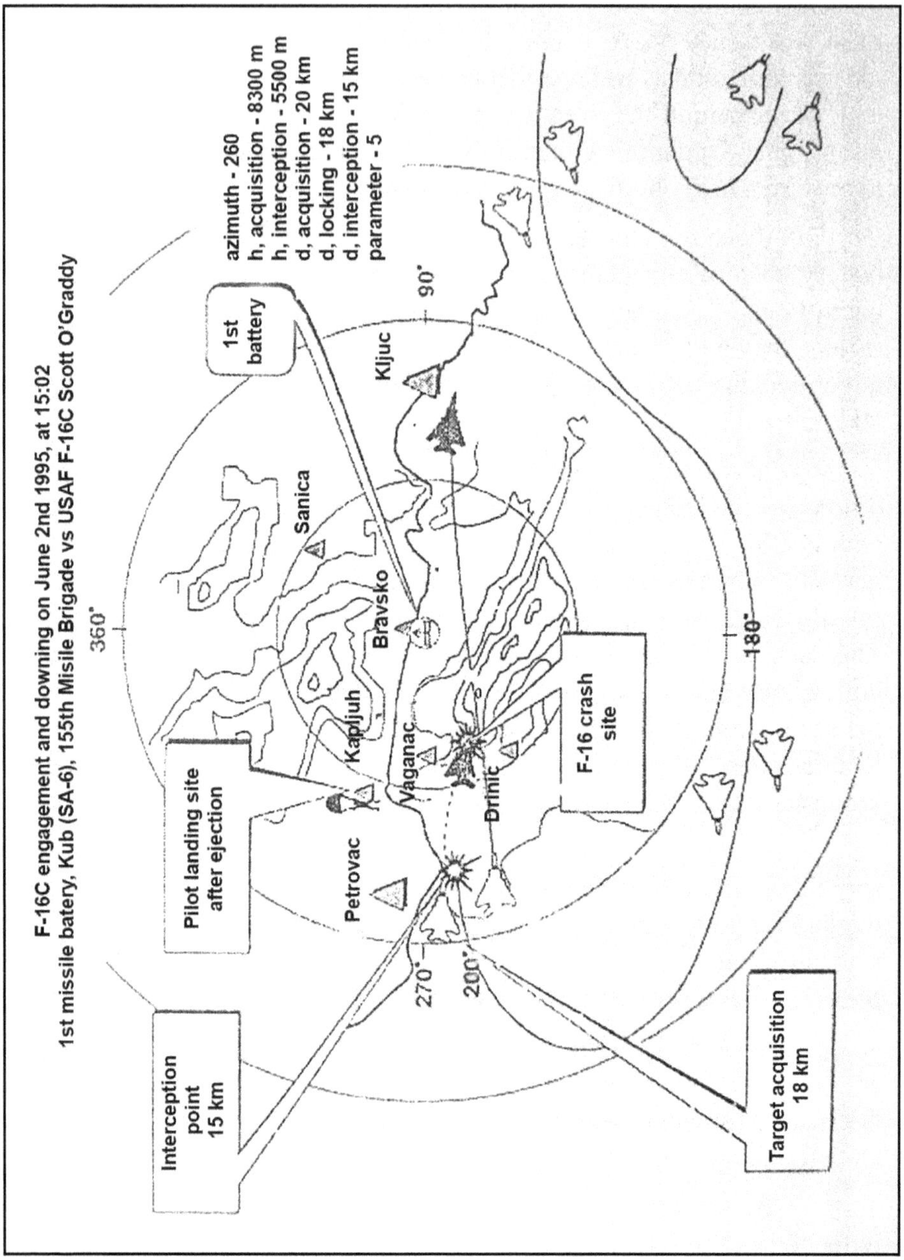

Figure 4-6: F-16 (pilot Captain Scott O'Grady) engagement by 1st missile battery. (Source: authors)

The airplanes did not enter the potential SA-6 engagement zones without EW support or before designated SEAD groups tried to neutralize air defense. Stringent minimum altitude limitations were introduced as well.

Figure 4-7: F-16C engine wreck, near Petrovac. (Source: Ratko Ćuković)

Basher Five-Two [49]

Captain Scott O'Grady

I broke through scattered cloud cover at 12,000 feet and stared into a magnificently clear sky. I had already locked on to Wilbur with my radar, and now fixed my airspeed so that I would stay two miles behind him. At our current speed, we could cover two miles in all of twenty seconds. (Fig 4-8, 4-9 and 4-10).

'Two is visual,' I radioed to Wilbur on our interflight frequency.

This meant that I had him in my sights.

'Clear to rejoin,' he replied. We were now over the Adri-

---
49   Scott O'Grady, Michael French - Basher Five-Two; The True Story of F-16 Fighter Pilot Captain Scott O'Grady-Doubleday Books for Young Readers (1997).

Figure 4-8: Captain Scott O'Grady. (Source: USAF)

atic Sea and would be in Bosnian airspace in about fifteen minutes. I closed the gap between us until we were in fingertip formation. We flew side by side, separated only by a few feet, and held our positions. This allowed Wilbur and me to make a visual inspection of each other's aircraft, to make sure that there were no fluid leaks and that all external systems were working. We also tested our chaff and flares, both part of the F-16's defense system. Chaff was a substance like tinfoil that was discharged from the plane to give enemy radar a false image to read. Flares were discharged to try to attract incoming heatseeking missiles away from our planes.

Everything looked perfect. Inspection over, we moved into a formation known as tactical line abreast. As the wingman, I flew a mile and a half from Wilbur and about 2,000 feet above him. Wilburs role was to lead our mission and to be the eyes and ears of our two-ship element. My responsibility was to maintain the basic flight formation and to support Wilbur in his decisions during the mission.

We were now at 27,000 feet and cruising at 500 miles an hour, an altitude and speed similar to those of a commercial jetliner. The only difference was, we were flying over unfriendly territory.

Our flight pattern carried us over the lush, green boundary separating Croatia and Bosnia, just south of a city named Bihac. We were running into a fair amount of clouds, and the air was choppy, but we decided to establish our combat air patrol, or 'cap.' We patrolled the skies by flying an oval pattern, similar to the shape of a racetrack, with each leg covering about twenty-five miles. Each oval took about eight minutes to complete, including making the two 180-degree counterclockwise turns. Flying the same pattern over and over might sound boring, but you never knew who would try to enter the no-fly zone. This was called our "vul" time, when we were vulnerable over hostile territory. A few minutes after we started our vul time, our radars showed a low-flying aircraft to the west, near the Udbina airfield. This was the stronghold of the Krajanian Serbs, and they were an aggressive bunch. Sixteen months earlier, despite NATO planes protecting the no-fly zone, the Krajanian Serbs had boldly launched an air attack against Muslim sites in Bosnia. To show that we meant business, NATO pilots had had to shoot down four Serbian jets.

The lone plane stayed clear of the no-fly zone, avoiding any hostile action by me.

Figure 4-9: F-16C (AF 89-2032) taxing at Aviano base. The same plane was shot down on 2 June 1995. (Source: USAF)

After about an hour of combat air patrol, we began to run low on fuel. The F-16 uses an enormous amount of fuel - a mixture of kerosene and gasoline, about 10,000 pounds for every hour and a half of flying. That's the same as a car getting two or three miles to the gallon. Following Wilbur's lead, I headed back over the Adriatic to meet our specially equipped Boeing 707

plane. This was our airborne gas station. While I 'parked' on the tanker's wing, Wilbur took a position directly under the fuselage of the 707. As we all flew at the same speed, Wilbur flipped a toggle switch to open his fuel door, which sat right behind his cockpit. At the same time, the operator of the 707 extended a boom and probe - like a gas hose - into Wilbur's open fuel tank. Then it was just like any other gas station. The pump was turned on, and you waited until your gauge showed Full.

After Wilburs turn it was mine, and I passed the seven-minute refueling time talking to the tanker crew on my intercom. I discovered one of the crew was a former 'Juvat,' a pilot with the Eightieth Fighter Squadron in Korea, with whom I had served a tour of duty. We Juvats, past and present, were a tight bunch. We even had a squadron coin that summed up our close bonds. The coin read:

'You will always be a Juvat no matter where you go.'

'Audentes fortuna juvat,' I called out to my fellow Juvat as I left the tanker. The Latin words were our squadron's motto: 'Fortune favors the bold.'

For our second vul time, Wilbur led me slightly north of our last location, in search of better weather. Finding a relatively clear patch of sky, we settled into our routine. Instead of running our ovals northwest and southeast as we had last time, we rotated to due west and east. I was 1,000 feet above Wilbur and continually moved my eyes between the sky and the dials and digital instruments in front of me. While we had no reason to worry about anything specific, we knew to stay far away from the Bosnian Serbs' SAM rings to the north and to the east. SAMs - surface-to-air missiles - were a definite threat to an F-16, even with our high-tech defense systems.

What Wilbur and I had no way of knowing was that a Bosnian Serb unit had secretly trucked a SAM battery into an area underneath where we were patrolling. And their missiles were already lined up, ready to fire at us.

The first sign of trouble came when Wilbur's threat warning system showed a blip on his screen. He had been "spiked,"

spotted by radar on the ground. By itself, this was no major concern. In Bosnia, radar was extremely common as a general tracking device, much like traffic control centers at major airports. A blip on a screen wasn't necessarily connected with missiles. But the F-16's electronics could pick out different types of radar. Wilbur had been spiked by 'acquisition,' or threat, radar—the kind that SAM operators liked to use. With threat radar, the enemy can learn enough about a plane's location, speed, and flight pattern to launch a missile in seconds.

'Basher Five-One, mud six, bearing zero-nine-zero,' Wilbur radioed to me on our open frequency. He wanted me to know there was possibly threat radar to the east.

"Basher Five-Two naked," I shot back. That told him my threat warning system hadn't picked up anything.

On the same open radio frequency, I listened for Magic, NATO's nearby airborne command center. Equipped with special intel electronics, the airborne center served to help pilots as an early warning system. In touch with spy satellites and U-2 spy planes, Magic could tell Wilbur and me if there was active radar from the SAM rings to the north and to the east as well as in any other location. If the radar was coming from the north and the east, we didn't have to worry because we were out of their missiles' range. The blip on Wilbur's threat warning system would have been a false alarm.

It took Magic only seconds to get back to us. 'Basher Five One,' a calm voice called over our radios, 'your mud six report is uncorrelated.'

Magic was saying that they couldn't really confirm where the radar was coming from. Cautiously, Wilbur and I continued to fly our ovals.

At exactly 3:03 P.M., Aviano time, my threat warning system showed a bright blip. I stared at my console in disbelief. At the same time, an alarm shrilled over my headset. I had been spiked by threat radar.

Forget any threat from the north. This was coming from due east, just like the one Wilbur had picked up. Could it really

be a second false alarm? My stomach did a flip.

'Basher Five-Two, mud six, bearing zero-nine-zero,' I said into my radio.

'Basher Five-One naked,' Wilbur reported back.

Our roles had been reversed. It was now my turn to be hunted. I knew I had to prepare myself for the worst. Through my canopy I scanned the skies for any evidence of a missile. The actual rocket that fires a SAM leaves a trail of white smoke. That smoke is a pilot's only chance to make a visual identification. Once the rocket turns off, the smoke stops. Then the missile sails on toward its target, silent and deadly, at a speed almost twice as fast as my F-16.

Seeing nothing in the sky, my eyes swam back to the video display on my threat warning system. The bright blip had not gone away, which meant I was still being spiked. A moment later, a second alarm blared over my headset. My glance jumped back to my screen. A new warning was there, brighter than the one before.

This was all happening in seconds. Split seconds. But it was long enough for me to understand I had just been locked up by a target tracking radar. This was the type that guided a missile to its target.

While I didn't know it, Magic had received information from a spy satellite that there were missiles right below Wilbur and me, but because of a garbled radio communication, we never got the message.

It hardly mattered. My instrument panel had already delivered the bad news.

I was in somebody's deadly sights. As I thought out the meaning of those words, I realized a missile might already have been launched. I was angry that we had all been outsmarted by the enemy, but I tried to stay calm. This was what our years of training had prepared us for, and I was ready.

A programmed voice from the plane's computer system rang out over my headset. 'Counter, counter.'

A second later, a brilliant red flash lit up the sky between Wilbur and me. A missile had passed between us, just missing us both. My heart sped up. I knew that SAMs were usually launched in packages of two. The chances were likely that another missile was already in the air, coming straight at me. As the adrenaline pumped through my veins, my thumb traveled down to the button that would release my chaff and flares. At the same time, I thought about pushing my aircraft into a series of steep climbs and dives to avoid the missile.

I had time to do neither. What happened in the next tick of a second, I'm not sure. Wilbur would later tell me that he had screamed over the radio, 'Missiles in the air!' I never heard him. What I did hear was a thunderous roar that almost shattered my eardrums. Then came a blow like nothing I had ever felt. It was like getting rear-ended by an 18-wheeler with a rocket tied to its front grill.

The missile had found its mark.

A burst of flames and intense heat spread through my cockpit. I began to pitch and roll wildly. It felt as if a giant hand had reached down, grabbed me with brute force, and shaken me in a frenzy. What was left of my plane was like a straw in the wind, totally out of control.

For all its space-age electronics, its supersonic speed, its defensive powers, the F-16 is not perfect. In the blink of an eye, it can be turned from the prince of the skies into a burning scrap heap of wire and twisted metal. The missile had blindsided me, coming up through cloud cover below. It had struck the plane's underbelly, hitting one of the fuel tanks and cutting my F-16 in two. It took me another moment to understand. The nose and cockpit had broken away—and I was now in a free fall to Earth.

As I spun out of control, I worried about blacking out from the sudden and unexpected G forces. I watched my console break and twist apart before me. My mind was outracing my ability to react.

Flames from the exploding gas tank had found a crack between my oxygen mask and visor. They had also reached the back of my neck.

Part of me was waiting for the cockpit to explode. Somehow, the heat and the pain and the insanity of the moment focused my thoughts.

Dear God, I prayed, please don't let me die now—don't let me die from this.

I gazed down, through the flames, and saw a fat yellow handle attached to my seat. The handle pushed up between my legs, bigger than life, staring at me like the miracle I took it to be. The beautiful words stamped across the top were impossible to miss, even in the fire and smoke: PULL TO EJECT.

I had no idea how much time had passed since the missile had struck. In reality it had been only seconds. It felt like an eternity. I knew I wasn't waiting much longer. For another microsecond, I worried that my damaged canopy wouldn't open, or if it did, that the seat wouldn't eject. But I really didn't have time to worry.

My left hand dropped down to the handle, and I pulled with all my might...

Figure 4-10: F-16C AF 89-2032 tail section and TIME magazine cover page featuring Scott O'Grady. (Source: Times)

In defense of Republika Srpska

After the fall of Republika Srpska Krajina (RSK), two SA-6 batteries which were located in the Krajina territory were pulled back to the territory of the Republika Srpska. During the Croatian offensive on Krajina, in the lack of Croatian air force actions, these batteries didn't have any engagement. The equipment of both batteries was sent to the 'Kosmos' center for technical maintenance.

The moment which NATO waited to strike Republika Srpska air defense came on 30 August 1995 when they launched the operation 'Deliberate Force'. The difference from the previous operations was that 'Deliberate Force' was planned as all alliance coordinate attacks to neutralize Serbian air defense in eastern Bosnia.

The action named 'Dead Eye South East' started around 03:00 with coordinate attacks executed by 17 airplanes against 14 targets: air defense batteries, radar positions, command centers and communication hubs. The brunt of the first attacks fell on the radars, communication and command centers. Fighter airplanes were supported with a strong EW asset – E6A Prowlers and EC-130H.

Overwhelming air power didn't reflect the intended goals: many targets were missed partially because of the weather conditions. NATO pilots had to take low-level flights in search of the well-camouflaged targets which exposed them to light AD – MANPADs and AAA. Mountain terrain and dense forests presented a challenging environment for air attacks. Stationary objects, which were abandoned anyway, were hit without any tactical or strategic goal except propaganda videos for the mass media and briefings.

On 10 August, operation 'Deliberate Force' was extended to western Bosnia. This brought NATO airplanes back to the area of Bihać and Banja Luka.

The SA-6 batteries that were tasked to protect the communication and radar object on mountain Kozara constantly presented a danger for the NATO airplanes. The attempt of the missile batteries to frontally confront NATO aviation during the first night of the operation, around 01:30 in the area of Čavarina was unsuccessful: bombs completely destroyed one of the battery radars and on 10 September at 21:30 in the vicinity Cerovljani,

one anti-radiation missile hit the antenna post of the 1st missile battery. The battery was targeted with two anti-radiation missiles and the second one missed the radar completely and went in the direction of the village but fortunately didn't cause any damage. There were no human casualties but the battery mascots – a dog, was near the radar and it was killed. The anti-radiation missiles were employed against the second missile battery in the next few days, but they all missed. NATO power was overwhelming, both in electronic warfare and fighters, and it was decided that the batteries cease any engagement. Only a week after the two batteries were taken out of action, US F-15Es were able to find their targets and hit them but a while before that all stationary objects were abandoned.

What was important is that all destroyed and damaged equipment were sent to the maintenance and repair center - destroyed radar was replaced with the new one and the damaged one was repaired and sent back to the unit.

In the press conference held at the beginning of October 1995, a commander of the 31 combat wing and 7490 composite (provisional) wing, colonel Charles 'Chuck' F. Wald stated that *'air defense of Republika Srpska presents the high threat level for NATO air attacks during the operation Deliberate Force: Serbs have much less missile systems than Iraqis but were more effective and skillful than Iraqis during the Desert Storm.'*

The air attacks were able to disrupt the integrated air defense but were far away from destroying it. Colonel Wald, who personally participated in some of these attacks stated that *'the Serbian air defense forces held the high capability with the very skilled crews and personnel which presented a clear and present danger in some areas.'* During the operation, a considerable number of cruise missiles were also used in an attempt to disrupt the Serbian command and control.

In NATO analyses after the operation, it was declared that the whole operation was successful forcing the Serbian side to accept the requirements and join the negotiations which eventually lead to the Dayton agreement which effectively stopped the civil war[50]. For the Serbian side, the greatest success was that even under the overwhelming pressure and airpower, the main goal of NATO to destroy the air defense systems failed

---

50   Deliberate Force A Case Study in Effective Air Campaigning Final Report of the Air University Balkans Air Campaign Study Edited by Col Robert C. Owen, USAF, Air University Press Maxwell Air Force Base, Alabama January 2000

simply because of the skillful employment of the available assets meaning that the vast majority of the equipment and means were saved.

SA-6 in Srpska Krajina

On 18 August 1992, the Republic of Srpska Krajina accepted a number of amendments to the Krajina constitution which lead to the legal basis for the establishment of the Army of Republika Srpska Krajina (Srpska Vojska Krajine – SVK). SVK consisted of two branches – the army and air force. From the beginning until they fell under the Croatian military action the armed forces were called "an army" but in fact it was a regional organized militia. There was a fundamental difference between VSK and the proper armed forces of Republika Srpska, Croatian Army or Yugoslav Army. The biggest difference was that the units organized by the territories had the area of responsibility only to their respected areas and didn't participate in the operations in the other areas. Organizationally, it closely resembled the structure of the territorial defense during the former Yugoslavia. The biggest problem for the SVK was the command cadre as well as an optimal number of troops. When the territorial defense was abolished in December 1992, the regional territorial defense units were organized in 6 army corps, again based on the geographic area. This kind of organization and the scattering of the Serbian territories from the beginning pointed that it will be hard to organize an effective defense in the case of eventual Croatian attacks. For this reason, the effective defense of Srpska Krajina relied on help of Republika Srpska and Yugoslavia. When Republika Srpska got engaged in the war with Bosnian Muslim formations and Yugoslavia fell under the sanctions, the position of Srpska Krajina as territorial integrity became highly questionable. The destiny of the Serbian territories in independent Croatia was doomed basically because of the international situation and it was a matter of time when Croatian military and paramilitary forces, with the intensive help of the western democracies in training, weaponry and munition, as well as financially, will be ready to finally expel the Serbian population fulfilling the Croatian Nazi dream from 1941 of the ethnically clean state.

Besides the sideshow role, the air defense of Krajina still played some role during 1994 and 1995. Serbian Krajina militia and army played a protective role to the local Serbian population preventing the repeating of the 1941-1945 Nazi Croatian genocide. In the end, Krajina was territorially lost but the majority of Serbian population were able to escape protected by the troops ahead of the Croatian army advance.

From 22 January 1993, Croatian forces started limited offensives probing the Serbian defense. Croatian action "Maslenica" was stopped with Krajina troops which had to take weapons stored and "protected" by UN forces. With the help of Republika Srpska, at Udbine base the air defense detachment was formed while the SA-6 was transferred from the 'Kosmos' repair center. In the beginning, two launchers and one radar manned with the crews from Republika Srpska were sent, followed by more launchers and radars. In total, two batteries were transferred, and the crews were replaced with VSK crews. One battery was tasked for Udbine air base defense while the second SA-6 battery was relocated in the area between Vrgin-most and Knin. Krajina 44th missile air defense brigade had one S-75 Dvina battalion and two new SA-6 batteries from Republika Srpska were also included. Brigade was under the command of Lieutenant Colonel Ranko Dašić. Based on the territorial organization, 1st missile battery became 'Lička' and the 2nd battery became 'Dalmatinska'. These two batteries were completed by January/February 1994.

The first blood of SVK air defense was drawn on 14 September 1993 when Croatian MiG-21 piloted by Colonel Miroslav Peris was downed. MiG-21, named 'The Avenger of Vukovar' was on task to bomb the missile battery position. The plane flew very low, between 80 – 100 m to avoid the radar. During this low-level flight, it was observed by AAA battery which opened fire. The plane was hit by few rounds and the pilot in an attempt to save himself and plane ascended to 350 m where it was hit by SA-6 missile. The MiG crashed in the vicinity of Stipan village, in the municipality of Vrginmost. The pilot did not eject (Fig. 4-11).

At the beginning of 1994, both batteries were stationed in the warehouse Golubić. Because of the lack of trained crew, both batteries had one radar and three launchers with support equipment. The battery had only 36 men. During the war, the 1st battery was typically assigned to the Udbine airbase and 2nd battery on the mountain Kordun area. From 14 June 1st battery was located at combat position Tepavci while 2nd battery was in Padjani.

On 2 August 1994, at 01:26 (and some sources mentioned night on 31 July/1 August) the 1st battery engaged and destroyed Ukrainian An-26 transport airplane (number UR-26207). The plane transported munition to Bosnian 5th corps. The whole crew of 5 perished and one member of the Bosnian army as well. The airplane crashed in the vicinity of Saborsko.

Figure 4-11: Croatian MiG-21 piloted by Colonel Miroslav Peris was downed on 14 September 1993. (Source: authors).

After the downing of An-26, 1st battery was ordered to get position around Udbine airbase and 2nd battery took position around Dreznik Grad. Both batteries were engaged during the Bihać operation in the fall of 1994. The typical composition was of one radar and two launchers so it can be considered as a half-strength. Taking into consideration that the trained crew were not available for the other launchers, both units still fulfilled their tasks and practically spent all the time in readiness No. 1 – ready for combat.

The first NATO action against Krajina SA-6 was on 1 November 1994. The 1st battery was positioned in the Vasići village. The battery came 10 days earlier and spent all the time in one position. In the day before the attack, the fire control radar worked 40-60 minutes. NATO took all measures to precisely located the battery. Just before the attack, technicians from Kosmos worked on the radar while the crew was nearby. The attack started with 2 HARM[51] missiles which both missed. The attack executed with laser -guided bombs and gravity Mk-82 and Mk-83 followed. The radar and one launcher were heavily damaged, and the second launcher caught fire which initiated a missiles explosion. Power supply PES-100 and UPPC were also destroyed.

---

51 More information about AGM-88 HARM can be found in Appendix B

After this attack, the 1st battery was taken out of service for some time. Taking the lesson about the attack on the 1st battery, the 2nd battery was more often relocated to the alternative combat positions.

The new commander of the 44th brigade, Lieutenant Colonel Miloš Djošan was appointed in January 1995. Upon his appointment, the brigade was reorganized and the remaining SA-6 equipment was used to form 3 batteries with reduced staff. To reinforce Krajina air defense, from Republika Srpska one Strela – 10M arrived as a support to the 2nd battery but was withdrawn back very soon.

In March the 1st battery got the repaired equipment from Kosmos which brought the strength to one RStON and two launchers. Using two launchers per battery gave the opportunity for the forming of 3rd battery.

After the fall of Western Slavonia, Krajina SA-6 batteries were again engaged in bunting for the helicopters which were involved in Bosnian Muslim forces supplies. The 1st battery was located in Slunj area, 2nd battery at Veljun and new formed 3rd battery at the Tepavci position.

After the midnight of 28 May 1995, the Ukrainian & Bosnian crew in Mi – 8MTV-1 (factory number 95822, Bosnian army registration T9-HAB)[52] was in preparation for the flight to Cazinska Krajina from the Zagreb airport. The helicopter took off at 01:32. During the flyover the position of Krajina forces, it was detected, and some sporadic fire opened but without any effect. The helicopter landed at Ćoralići airport at 02:07. After unloading the supplies and loading the passengers the helicopter took off again at 02:40. The flyover was reported to the command and the SA-6 battery was on alert. As soon as the helicopter took off, it was detected and tracked by 2nd battery. The helicopter flew at 280 m altitude trying to avoid radar that Bosnian Muslim forces knew was in the wider area.

The radar at Veljun position, about 20 km away was able to track the helicopter the whole flight, constantly feeding launcher. At 02:45 a missile was launched and hit the helicopter. The whole crew perished – Bosnian pilot Mirsad Dupajić and Ukrainians Maksimenko and Dudayev. Besides the crew, Bosnian foreign minister Irfan Ljubijankić, who was the passenger, also perished.

In the helicopter wreck, the GPS guidance system was found as well as a map with the precise location of Serbian air defense by days. Only

[52] There is also information that was Mi-8MTV-1, factory number 95921, former ATK Vityaz RA-27-085)

two last days were missing. Immediately after the engagement, the SA-6 battery left the combat position and relocated to the new one.

According to the Bosnian sources, there were about 90 flights performed from June 1994 until August 1995 in an attempt to resupply 5th corps. This information could not be independently verified.

Shooting down Mi-8MTV-1 was the last Krajina SA-6 air defense engagement.

On the first day of Croatian operation 'Storm' the 1st battery was exposed to jamming while the 2nd and 3rd battery didn't experience any action. Knowing the rough positions of the SA-6 batteries, Croatian airplanes avoided any approach to the potential zone of destruction. Krajina batteries used also radar emission imitators. The order to withdraw missile batteries from Krajina to Republika Srpska was issued on 5 August, after some of the militia defense lines collapsed. All three batteries arrived at Banja Luka where they were offered to join the Republika Srpska army, but the crews refused and were transported by buses to Serbia. The equipment of these three batteries was used to reinforce the Republika Srpska batteries. During the retreat, Krajina forces abandoned one 2P25M2E launcher and one 2T7M missile transfer and reloader truck with three training missiles.

From Republika Srpska to Bosnia and Herzegovina forces

For the SA-6 crews, NATO intervention in the second half of 1995, prior to the truce agreement, provided a valuable opportunity to further improve the tactics and procedures in the air enemy superiority environment. Of particular importance was the fast taking the firing positions, shortened radar emission and even faster moving to the alternative positions. The major component was the military technical center 'Kosmos' which provided the full maintenance and repairs for the air defense equipment. Supplies of the reserve parts were enough. Missile brigade HQ had on its disposal spares guidance stations. After the fall of Krajina, the arsenal was completed with spare missiles and parts. The problem was in people – it was never enough trained crews and operators.

As soon as the combat operation stopped, all SA-6 batteries were withdrawn to the garrisons. Air Defense of Republika Srpska at the end of the war had four SA-6 batteries. Peacetime conditions dictated reorganization so basic units got the new designations. For example, the 155th missile brigade (Fig. 4-12) was renamed into the 855th brigade and the 172nd missile regiment into the 872nd missile regiment. One battery stayed in the 855th brigade while the rest three stayed in the 872nd regiment.

*Figure 4-12: Men of 155th missile brigade with the Republika Srpska air defense and air force commander, General Živomir Ninković, 1994.
(Source: authors)*

During the NATO aggression on Yugoslavia, in 1999, many troops were sent to Yugoslav SA-6 units. After the war, officers returned to their units. The consequences of the NATO aggression on Yugoslavia also reflected on Republika Srpska. In particular, the maintenance of the equipment and education and training of the new staff.

After the international pressure toward the Republika Srpska leadership, it was decided to disband the armed forces of the republic and incorporate them into the federal armed forces. The consequences of this forced reconciliation between three fighting sides lead that much qualified staff left the military.

The new federal armed forces of Bosnia and Herzegovina formed an air defense brigade. This "integration" was anything but smooth: it was evident confusion and dilettantism of the newly formed united military. For example, somebody from the federal Bosnian authorities decided that the new air defense shall scrap off the missile reloading equipment as non-perspective. That decision leads that at one point it was impossible to do simple operations such as reloading the missiles on the launchers.

After this first steps of the federal armed forces, a considerable number of the Republika Srpska office cadre joined the commission which was in charge of the air defense organization, some of the initial missteps were corrected. Today air defense of Bosnia and Herzegovina SA-6 components consists of three batteries that are located in Sarajevo, Tuzla and Banja Luka.

CHAPTER FIVE

2K12 Kvadrat/SA-6 in FR Yugoslavia army

The breakup of Yugoslavia in 1992 caused that many federal army units were forced to relocate to the Serbia and Montenegro territory. Two missile regiments were relocated to Serbia and one regiment was relocated to Montenegro. The newly formed Federal Republic of Yugoslavia army faced numerous organizational problems. The role of the air defense was assigned to the Air Defense Corps which consisted of air forces with fighter/interceptor's component, the surface to air missile component and air surveillance and airspace control component. From the army component, five SA-6/Kvadrat/Kub-M missile regiments were transferred into the Air Defense Corps.

For example, the 60th missile regiment equipped with Kub-M after the arrival into the permanent location in Danilovgrad was reinforced with two battalions of light air defense weapons and renamed into the medium mobile air defense brigade.

Not all Kub-M equipment was operational after the arrival into the new locations but by the end of 1992, all five regiments were declared operational. Each regiment consisted of four Kub-M batteries, a fire control battery, technical missile battery, missile equipment maintenance company and support units. Because of the ongoing civil war on the borders, these regiments were constantly rotated providing security in the designated areas.

The newly formed Corps had a problem with the qualified cadre. This was a particular problem in the regiments that came from the other republics. It is estimated that the whole Corps had about 60% of the staff. The new reorganization from the regimental composition to the brigade composition didn't show the proper advantage and it was decided to go back to the previous organization. For example, the 60th brigade in Danilovgrad was renamed back to the 60th regiment. This type of regimental organization for all Kub-M units stayed until after NATO aggression in 1999.

After the situation worsened during 1994 and 1995, Kub-M batteries were relocated from the home bases to protect the strategic objects and areas on the western parts. For example, 230th regiment batteries were relocated near Bogatić in Mačva for the lower river Drina protection; 240th regiment from Novi Sad was relocated on the western border with Croatia; 310th regiment from Kraljevo was relocated on Tara mountain and 60th regiment from Danilovgrad to the Boka Kotorska bay.

Dayton peace agreement signed by all parties by the end of 1995 effectively finished the civil war in Yugoslavia. Kub-M units withdrew to their home basis and the peacetime daily routine kicked in. After almost 4 years, the education and training for the non-commissioned cadre which was in particular deficit in Kub-M batteries finally can be restarted. This relatively short period between the end of the civil war and the aggression of NATO on Yugoslavia provided the opportunity to improve the overall situation in all Kub-M units. From the military academy, the newly trained junior officers' cadre also started their military service in the assigned units.

1999 - Prelude to War[53]

The Balkan peninsula throughout history has been known as a 'powder keg' that needs a very small spark to explode. Those sparks occurred often and the explosions occasionally ignited wars far beyond its borders.

The last decade of the last century was a time when Yugoslavia as a federal country of six republics and two provinces disintegrated in the nationalistic civil war sponsored by the 'democratic' west, which created new states in the Balkans. At that time, Serbia and Montenegro kept what was left of Yugoslavia. Brutal civil war followed.

How to summarize the whole western approach in one sentence? Maybe we can quote an analysis written by David Golpert, then vice-president of RAND and ex-director of national intelligence:

> *'How to defeat Serbia?'... for years, decades perhaps, Serbia would have to be subjected to isolation and misery, that it would have to be quarantined for as long as it takes to eradicate the virus that Serbia carries within it. Because the Serbs should be treated as lepers. The sanctions against Serbia do not have to be hermetically tight provided that they are permanent.'*

The Serbian-Kosovar-Albanian conflict had its roots in the centu-

---

[53] M. Mihajlović, D. Aničić: Shooting Down the Stealth Fighter: Eyewitness Accounts From Those Who Were There, Pen and Sword Air World, 2021

ries before the 1999 conflict. The territory of Kosovo and Metohija has been considered the birthplace of the Serbian state during medieval times. Albanian tribes came to Serbian territory as shepherds and populated mountainous regions. During the decline and disintegration of the medieval Serbian kingdom, Albanians converted to Islam and integrated themselves into the Ottoman Empire. Since then the two peoples have had problems with each other. Kosovo was liberated from Ottoman rule in the first Balkan war but at that time the Serbian population was mostly expelled from the territory as the Albanian tribes thrived. The Serbian government has never been accepted and occasional riots, sometimes paid for by foreign powers such as Austro-Hungary and Italy, arose. During the Second World War the majority of the Albanian population sided with fascist Italy and even formed SS division Skanderbeg. What was left of the Serbian population in many Kosovo areas was expelled or killed in a series of pogroms. After the war, the anti-Serbian communist regime banned the return of the Serbian refugees to their homes. Some Serbian politicians objected.

The 1950s and 1960s were a period marked by policies in Kosovo under Aleksandar Ranković, a Serbian communist who later fell out with and was dismissed by Yugoslav president and communist dictator Tito. During this time nationalism for Kosovar Albanians became a conduit to alleviate the conditions of the time. In 1968 Yugoslav Serb officials warned about rising Albanian nationalism and by November unrest and demonstrations by thousands of Albanians followed calling for Kosovo to attain republic status, an independent Albanian language and an Albanian university. The ultimate goal of Kosovar Albanians is to unify with Albania forming Greater Albania, which would include some Macedonian and Greek territories.

Tito and his henchman Edvard Kardelj rewrote the Yugoslav constitution in 1974 and tried to address Albanian complaints by awarding the province of Kosovo autonomy and powers such as a veto in the federal decision making process similar to that of the republics. Kosovo functioned as a de facto republic because Kosovar Albanians attained the ability to pursue near-independent foreign relations, trade and cultural links with Albania, an independent Albanian language university and Albanology institute, an Academy of Sciences and a Writers association with the ability to fly the Albanian flag.

Military precursors to the separatist 'Kosovo Liberation Army'

(KLA) began in the late 1980s with armed resistance to Serb police trying to take Albanian separatists into custody. Before the KLA, its members had been part of organizations such as the 'National Kosovo Movement' and the 'Popular Movement for Kosovo Liberation'. The founders of the later KLA were involved in the 1981 protests in Kosovo. Considerable numbers of ethnic Albanian dissidents were arrested or emigrated to European countries, such as Switzerland and Germany, where they continued subversive activities. Repression of Albanian nationalism and Albanian nationalists by authorities in Belgrade strengthened the independence movement and focused international attention on the plight of Kosovar Albanians.

From 1991 to 1992, Albanian radical nationalist Adem Jashari and about 100 other ethnic Albanians wishing to fight for the independence of Kosovo underwent military training in the municipality of Labinot-Mal in Albania. Afterwards, Jashari and other ethnic Albanians committed several acts of sabotage aimed at the Serbian administrative apparatus in Kosovo. Attempting to capture or kill him, Serbian police surrounded Jashari and his older brother, Hamëz, at their home in Prekaz village on 30 December 1991. In the ensuing siege, large numbers of Kosovo Albanians flocked to Prekaz, forcing the police to withdraw from the village. While in Albania, Jashari was arrested in 1993 by the government of Sali Berisha and sent to jail in Tirana before being released alongside other Kosovo Albanian militants at the demand of the Albanian Army. Jashari launched several terrorist attacks over the next few years, targeting the Yugoslav Army (VJ) and Serbian police in Kosovo. In the spring of 1993, Homeland Calls meetings were held in Aarau, Switzerland, organized by Xhavit Halili, Azem Syla, Jashar Salihu and others. KLA strategist Xhavit Halili said that in 1993 the KLA 'considered and then rejected the IRA, PLO and ETA models.

Some journalists claim that a May 1993 attack in Glogovac that left five Serbian policemen dead and two wounded was the first attack carried out by the KLA. In the early 1990s there were attacks on police forces and secret-service officials.

A Serbian policeman was killed in 1995, allegedly by the KLA. Since 1995, the KLA sought to destabilize the region, hoping the USA and NATO would intervene. Serbian patrols were ambushed, and policemen killed. It was only the next year that the organization of KLA officially took responsibility for the attacks. In 1996-97 The KLA, originally composed out of a few hundred Kosovar Bosnian War veterans, attacked several police stations and wounded many police officers.

In 1996 the British weekly magazine The European carried an article by a French expert stating: 'German civil and military intelligence services have been involved in training and equipping the rebels with the aim of cementing German influence in the Balkan area... The birth of the KLA in 1996 coincided with the appointment of Hansjoerg Geiger as the new head of the BND [German secret Service] ... The BND men were in charge of selecting recruits for the KLA command structure from the 500,000 Kosovars in Albania.'

A former senior adviser to the German parliament Matthias Küntzel tried to prove later on that German secret diplomacy had been instrumental in helping the KLA since its creation.

KLA representatives met with American, British, and Swiss intelligence agencies in 1996, and possibly 'several years earlier', and according to The Sunday Times, American intelligence agents admitted they helped to train the Kosovo Liberation Army before NATO's bombing of Yugoslavia. Intelligence agents denied, however, that they were involved in arming the KLA.

In February 1996 the KLA undertook a series of attacks against police stations and Yugoslav government employees, saying that the Yugoslav authorities had killed Albanian civilians as part of an ethnic cleansing campaign. Serbian authorities denounced the KLA as a terrorist organization and increased the number of security forces in the region. This had the counter-productive effect of boosting the credibility of the embryonic KLA among the Kosovo Albanian population. On 26 April 1996, four attacks on Serbian security personnel were carried out almost simultaneously in several parts of Kosovo.

In January 1997, Serbian security forces assassinated KLA commander Zahir Pajaziti and two other leaders in a highway attack between Priština and Mitrovica and arrested more than 100 Albanian militants. Jashari was convicted of terrorism in absentia by a Yugoslav court on 11 July 1997. Human Rights Watch subsequently described the trial, in which fourteen other Kosovo Albanians were also convicted, as 'failing to conform to international standards'.

The Albanian interior conflict and collapse of security of 1997 enabled the KLA to acquire large amounts of weaponry looted from Albanian armories. A 1997 intelligence report stated that the KLA received drug trafficking proceeds, which they used to purchase arms. They also received funds from Albanian diaspora organizations.

Some non-Albanians such as the Serbs and Romani fled Kosovo fearing revenge attacks, others were pressured by the KLA and armed gangs to leave. According to the report of the US Committee for Refugees the KLA attacks 'aimed at trying to cleanse Kosovo of its ethnic Serb population'. The Yugoslav Red Cross estimated 30,000 refugees and internally displaced persons from Kosovo, most of who were Serb. The UNHCR estimated at least 55,000 refugees had fled to Montenegro and Central Serbia, most of whom were Kosovo Serbs: 'Over 90 mixed villages in Kosovo have now been emptied of Serb inhabitants and other Serbs continue leaving, either to be displaced in other parts of Kosovo or fleeing into central Serbia.'

Pursuing Adem Jashari for the murder of a Serbian policeman, Serbian forces again attempted to assault the Jashari compound in Prekaz on 22 January 1998. With Jashari not present, thousands of Kosovo Albanians descended on Prekaz and again succeeded in pushing the government forces out of the village and its surroundings.

The next month, a small unit of the KLA was ambushed by Serbian policemen. Four Serbs were killed and two were injured in the ensuing clashes. At dawn on 5 March 1998, the KLA launched an attack against a police patrol in Prekaz, which was answered by a police operation on the Jashari compound which left fifty-eight Albanians dead, including Jashari. Four days after this, a NATO meeting was convoked, during which Madeleine Albright pushed for an anti-Serbian response. NATO now threatened Serbia with a military response. The Kosovo War ensued, with subsequent NATO intervention. A NATO-facilitated ceasefire was signed on 15 October, but both sides broke it two months later and fighting resumed.

The infamous spark which lit the powder keg happened with the killing of forty-five Kosovar Albanians in the village of Racak. The massacre – the veracity of which was disputed by the Serbs – was reported in the western media in January 1999. After OSCE mission head William Walker filed the report, NATO decided that the conflict could only be settled by introducing a military peacekeeping force. After the Rambouillet Accords broke down on 23 March with Yugoslav rejection of an external peacekeeping force, NATO prepared to install the 'peace-keepers by force'. That was the culmination of something that started much earlier and now it was time for the coup de grâce.

SA-6 Units Situation in 1998

The post-civil war training of all SA-6/Kub-M units was performed in the garrison Šipčanik which was part of the Golubovci military air base. Besides the crews from Yugoslavia, crews from Republika Srpska also participated. Every missile unit training shall consider also live missile launches. For that, an area of the Montenegro coast was designed. However, the increasing tension in February of 1998 between Albanian separatists and the Serbian government and Albanian UCK terrorists' attacks against law enforcement and Serbian civilian population forced the army to intervene. NATO and western powers didn't want to allow the legal government to deal with the terrorists and openly supported Albanian terrorism which was absolutely against all international regulations and norms.

This caused that air defense units started to take their combat positions in the case of aggression and be prepared for the eventual NATO action. All units were combat ready by September. Fortunately, on 13 October the situation temporary deescalated after the agreement between Richard Halbrook and Slobodan Milosević. With this agreement, law enforcement units should withdraw to the home bases and Albanians shall stop all armed activities. An international verification mission was formed to overlook the situation in the field. The agreement was that NATO UAV assets be deployed in the area of 25 km of administrative border between the Republic of Serbia and the province of Kosovo and Metohija. The no-flight zone for all military aircrafts was established as well. In Yugoslav air defense command in Zemun and NATO command in Vicenza, Italy the liaison teams were established. These limitations effectively put the end of any training activities of the 311th regiment at Slatina base which will have some effects on the unit readiness in the days before the outbreak of war.

The whole situation before the outbreak of the war was pretty tense. In his own words, one of the authors of this book, Zoran Vukosavljević, a sergeant in the 60th regiment describes:

We got ready for the march and taking over the combat position on the Luštica peninsula. The whole unit was divided into two groups. The first group, with the wheeled vehicles and with the RStON radar on the trailer, went to the Radovići garrison and from there to the field position and started preparation on the combat position. The second group, where I was assigned, was tasked to prepare and load the launchers on the trailers and escort them to Radovići where they were taken by the other group and positioned at the combat position. As we didn't have enough trailers, the whole transport took multiple backs and forth drives. Every time I escorted those trailers to Radovići, I came back for the new round. It took us 3-4 days to transfer all equipment to the Luštica peninsula area. Technical missile battery was also involved in the transport of their 3M9ME and 3M9M3 missiles.

I particularly remembered the event of the beginning of October 1998 when I arrived in the Radovići garrison with the last tour and met senior sergeant I.G. who told me that the attack will start in 96 hours! After the missiles were loaded on the remaining launcher, I walked to the combat position. Senior Sargent I.G stopped me around 50 m from the camp and around 100 m from RStON and launchers. He asked me can I see where the camp and positions are. I have to prize that both the camp and RStON was masked very well with the camouflage nets and local vegetation. It took me a bit of time to find where they are. The masking was so well done that I couldn't determine the distances.

So, the beginning of October was marked with our relocation to the combat positions and the rest of the time we were occupied in the camp organization and usually in the early morning or later after the sunset routine inspection of the equipment and testing the radio communication between the RStON radar and launchers. We tried to avoid unnecessary movements on the combat position because we knew that NATO recce flights or UAV flights from Bosnia can pinpoint our location. The Navy was very helpful in providing supplies and helping us to organize the life at the position. We had enough food and water and everything else we needed. They also brought a few Strela-2M MANPADs to protect us in the case of low-level attack. We also established a full coverage of the airspace in cooperation with the navy radars.

I was also tasked by captain P.V. to prepare daily brief-

ings about the situation which I extracted from the daily press which we got usually in the evening. Officers from Republika Srpska also visited us. Their experience with NATO aviation over Bosnia was of great help. They told us that we have to use our imagination and be creative and not to stick blindly to the official regulations.

The situation de-escalated on 13 October when our president Milosevic and US envoy Holbrook verbally agreed on certain measures that our side need to take, and the agreement was signed on 15 October.

As the situation got better, we made a schedule for the officers and NCO for the home leaves. Every time I went home to Podgorica, I used the opportunity to also get to the Law School at the University to take some classes and lectures as well as to prepare the semester assignment "Introduction to Law".

We stayed at the combat position until the beginning of November when we got an order to prepare the equipment and return to Radovići garrison, where we got one portion of the building for our staff.

The time at the combat position and before our return to the garrison I always keep in my mind as a good time. The comradery was excellent. I remember that once with Lieutenant Prečko we tried to find a shortcut to the beach through the hedges and bushes and we succeeded but with a lot of scratches. After that our trips to the beaches were always by the paved road that we "discovered" lately. On our trips, we were amazed by the old stone houses and cottages as well as the landscape. The shoreline was steep but beautiful on that way. We spoke about how it would be good if somebody invests in tourism in this area. For sure that investment will not be a miss.

Our time in the Radovići garrison was satisfactory. Accommodations and food were ok. I had an opportunity to see one coastal defense battery with anti-ship missiles Rubezh – E. The whole system is installed on the large trailer and includes radar and launcher with two P-21 missiles. The missile has a range of 80 km and according to one of the officers who served on that system one missile is enough to sink a warship the size of a frig-

ate but with a volley of missiles even larger ships like cruiser or carrier can get significant damage or even sink. He told me that the same type of missile is installed on our warships such as frigates and missile boats. See, how somebody can learn many different things, I told to myself. All in all, I was impressed.

Our time off we spent in the Radovići town where there is always a place to have juice or few beers in the local pubs or taverns. The locals were adapted to the presence of soldiers and we didn't have any problems with them.

At the end of November, we got an order to go back to our base in Danilovgrad. We packed our equipment and stuff and went back by the same way we got to our combat position a month or so ago. This time the trip was much easier. It seemed that life is getting back to normal.

Indeed, it really started to get back to normal.

After the infamous incident in Račak on 15 January 1999, the hostilities between the police and Albanian terrorists started again. This triggered the additional pressure from NATO on Yugoslavia accompanied with the new threats. The situation calmed again because in Kosovo was almost 1000 members of the Kosovo verification mission which main task was to observe the situation and ceasefire, but a majority of them actually performed intelligence gathering. NATO didn't attack in January because they were afraid that the lives of their field assets may be endangered.

By then, it was clear to everybody that the NATO intervention is imminent and that they will wait for the weather to improve, meaning early spring or summer as the most likely time to start the bombing campaign.

Based on these estimates, all preparation for the war were speeded up. While the military commanders were occupied with the preparation of defense, on the political side the negotiation in Rambouillet, France was initiated to make the last attempt for a peaceful solution. Representatives of the Serbian government and Albanian separatists including the armed (terrorist) fraction with NATO and western power mediation tried to make a deal that may work for all sides, but in-depth, the decision to go to war has been made and this meeting was just an excuse to blame Serbian side on the political way.

While the negotiations in Rambouillet were on, the 311st regiment in Prišitina tried to do as much as possible to bring the unit readiness at the highest level. It was for sure that this unit will be the first to get attacked if the war breaks out.

The Rambouillet negotiations failed because the US, NATO and EU requested that the alliance troops be placed on the Yugoslav territory and take monitoring mission meaning a "soft occupation" which not a single sovereign country can allow. Besides this military proposal for the technically occupation of the part of the territory, the political proposal was also discriminatory dictating that the local Albanian population is the only one that will decide about the future of the province.

The Serbian side simply couldn't agree with this kind of ultimatums so, as it was already said, the dice for war is already cast.

Based on this negotiation failure, all SA-6 units were ordered to move out of the home basis and take defense combat position. The time for war arrived.

Yugoslav Air Defense Order of Battle[54]

Serbian air defense in operation 'Allied Force', as the air campaign was called by NATO, represented the typical pattern of Soviet air defenses from the 1960-70 period. It was representative of the effects of stagnation on modern surface-to-air missile system proliferation through much of the world that had been dependent on Soviet supplies.

Serbia's strategic air defense was handled by a declining number of vintage Almaz SA-2/S-75M Dvina and a small number of partly modernized Almaz SA-3/S-125 Neva systems. Before the Yugoslav civil war, the air defense command had six battalions of SA-2/S-75s, totaling about forty single-rail launchers, of which only three battalions were still operational in 1999. There were also twelve combat battalions of SA-3/S-125s with 60 x 4-rail launchers – of which about fifty were still operational in 1999. SA-3 systems were grouped in one missile brigade (250th Missile Brigade) and one independent missile regiment (450th Missile Regiment).

250th brigade consisted of eight battalions (1st Batajnica; 2nd Pančevo; 3rd Jakovo; 4th Zuce; 5th Jakovo; 6th Smederevo; 7th Mladeno-

---

54   Mike Mihajlović, Djordje Aničić: Shooting Down the Stealth Fighter: Eyewitness Accounts From Those Who Were There, Pen and Sword Air World, 2021

vac and 8th Obrenovac). Besides combat battalions, the 250th brigade also had two missile technical battalions whose main purpose was missile warehousing, maintenance, preparation and supplies to the combat battalions (1st Missile Technical Battalion in Sremčica and 2nd Missile Technical Battalion in Zuce). The missile defense technical school and training center also had training equipment including one missile guidance station, one engagement and fire control radar and four launchers. There was a total of eleven missile guiding stations available to the 250th Brigade whose task was defense of the capital city area. 450th Regiment with four battalions and one technical battalion covered the south-west parts of Serbia and the industrial city of Kraljevo. In total, there were fifteen missile guiding stations available for all SA-3 systems (Fig 5-1).

Figure 5-1: S-125 Neva at the combat position. (Source: authors)

Air defense of the field army was handled by five independent regiments of SA-6/2K12 Kub (Soviet export version 'Kvadrat') mobile radar-directed SAMs, with one of the regiments (311th Independent Regiment) based with the Serbian forces in or near the province of Kosovo and Metohija area and two regiments (230th from Niš and 310th from Kragujevac) based not too far from the province. The 60th Regiment was based in Danilovgrad (Montenegro) and 240th Regiment had a base in Novi Sad.

Each regiment had four batteries. The weakest point on the Serbian SA-6 system is the 1S91 (Straight Flush) radar vehicle which is needed to provide guidance for every four missile-launch vehicles. This cumbersome arrangement restricted the flexibility of the Kub batteries (Fig. 5-2).

Figure 5-2: 2K12 (SA-6) at the position: 2P25 launchers and 1S91 (Straight Flush) radar. (Source: authors)

Air defense at divisional level ('Trupna PVO' as per Serbian terminology) included SA-9/Strela-1 and SA-13/Strela-10 IR-guided, low altitude, vehicle-mounted SAMs (Fig. 5-3). The more common of these was the older SA-9/9K31 Strela-1, with some 113 launcher vehicles delivered to Yugoslavia in the 1970s. The associated missile was manufactured in Yugoslavia under license before the war. The SA-9 system consisted of four missile launchers mounted on a wheeled BRDM-2 light armored vehicle and had an effective ceiling of 3,500 meters. It employed an older uncooled lead-sulphide seeker with no IR counter-countermeasure capabilities. Yugoslavia received a total of seventeen of the more modern SA-13/9K35M Strela-10 in the 1980s. This system descended from the Strela-1 but was mounted on a tracked MT-LB chassis. The SA-13/Strela-10 had IR counter-countermeasures with later versions of the missile having a two-channel seeker. Besides these standard systems, Serbian air-force units attempted to create improvised air defense missiles for their bases using IR guided air-to-air missiles. The normal aircraft rail-launchers for AA-8 Aphid/R-60 and AA-11 Archer/R-73 were lashed to ground mountings codenamed 'Praćka' (Slingshot) (Fig. 5-4).

Small unit air defense was handled by anti-aircraft guns and a significant number of old SA-7/Strela-2M and new SA-16,18/9K310 Igla man-portable SAMs. The SA-7/Strela-2M was produced in Yugoslavia under the name Strela-2M2J 'Sava' and was available in large numbers. Serbia managed to purchase about seventy-five of the new SA-16/9K310

Figure 5-3: Strela-10/SA-13 IR-guided, low altitude, vehicle-mounted missile system. (Source: Serbian DoD)

Figure 5-4: M53/59 Praga with R-73 air-to-air missile. (Source: authors)

Igla-1 man-portable IR-guided SAMs from Kazakhstan and other sources in the mid-1990s. In total there were about 850 man-portable IR-guided SAMs in the Serbian armed forces in 1999. NATO took the threat posed by IR-guided SAMs the most seriously, as these had been the primary source of casualties in Operation Desert Storm. There was some confidence that the radar-directed missiles could be dealt with using traditional means of suppression of enemy air defenses (SEAD) and electronic countermeasures (ECM). Unlike radar-guided SAMs, IR-guided SAMs present a serious suppression problem since the launchers rely entirely on passive sensors and are generally smaller, more mobile and easier to conceal (Fig. 5-5).

Figure 5-5: Strela-2M (SA-7). (Source: Serbian DoD)

The older-generation IR-guided SAMs, such as the Strela-2M (SA-7) and Strela-1 (SA-9), use seekers that are more susceptible to conventional ECM, such as flares and 'hot brick' infrared countermeasures (IRCM). The newer IR-guided systems, such as the man-portable Igla (SA-16/-18) and vehicle-mounted Strela-10/SA-13, have more robust counter-countermeasures. Rather than risk aircrews to these systems, NATO planners restricted most air operations to above 10,000 ft, where these small SAMs had a very low kill probability. Furthermore, the presence of these SAMs raised concerns about operating attack helicopters such as the AH-64 Apache deep behind Serbian lines and was a significant factor in US reluctance to deploy the Apaches in combat.

The altitude limits succeeded in minimizing casualties to IR-guided SAMs. As per NATO reports, a single aircraft was hit by a shoulder-fired SAM, but it failed to fuse and bounced off the aircraft. Several other aircraft were damaged, possibly by this type of weapon. The mere presence of these weapons, however, inhibited air operations to a significant extent. Weather conditions forced NATO to abandon air missions when cloud cover precluded operations below the altitude limit, and none of the air forces other than the US had munitions such as the Joint Direct Attack Munition (JDAM) that could be used in all weathers. Secondly, it contributed to collateral damage against civilian targets. Although NATO aircraft did have electro-optical sensors for surveying targets before the strike when used from medium altitude the resolution of the image in the cockpit was often mediocre. Civilian tractors and buses could be mistaken for military vehicles (for further details see section: Successful deceptions measures).

The Yugoslav side paid close attention to the experience of both coalition and Iraqi sides during operation 'Desert Storm'. In the command and information department of the air defense forces numerous analyses were performed about the capabilities and tactics of allied strike forces. For example, one of the analyses was about F-117A capabilities. The first conclusion was that the performance of the airplane such as altitudes and velocities were within the missile system envelopes for both SA-3 and SA-6. The issue was from how far it could be detected on the surveillance radar and were the capabilities of the existing engagement and fire control radars enough to perform target acquisition, tracking and engagement. What was not known was the radar cross-section. The Yugoslav side got help from an unexpected source: the US Air Force. In one of its publications there was an article about the achieved level of stealth accompanied with appropriate graphics. The Yugoslav side conducted numerous calculations comparing the available information about the airplane and the capabilities of the radars. The conclusion was that the available radars in the air defense system were able to track and provide fire control solutions and guidance to engage the stealth aircraft. One of the conditions was that all combat procedures had to be performed very precisely and accurately.

During the meeting, which was held on 10 September 1998 in the Air Defense Command center, the analysis was presented to the Air Force and Defense commander. Shortly after, the year 4 students of the air defense academy started training how to calculate the range and altitude of stealth aircraft for all surveillance radars in air defense. With very limited equipment, the Yugoslav side had done everything possible to get ready for the imminent war.

USAF and NATO Order of Battle[55]

In the US Forces Order of Battle, notable is the high proportion of F-16CJ defense suppression aircraft, around 40% of the total fast jet strike component. Even accounting for the provision of escorts to aircraft flown by other NATO nations and US heavy bombers, this is a very high proportion of the strike force committed to protection against a collection of mostly obsolescent Soviet-era SA systems (Fig. 5-6 and 5-7).

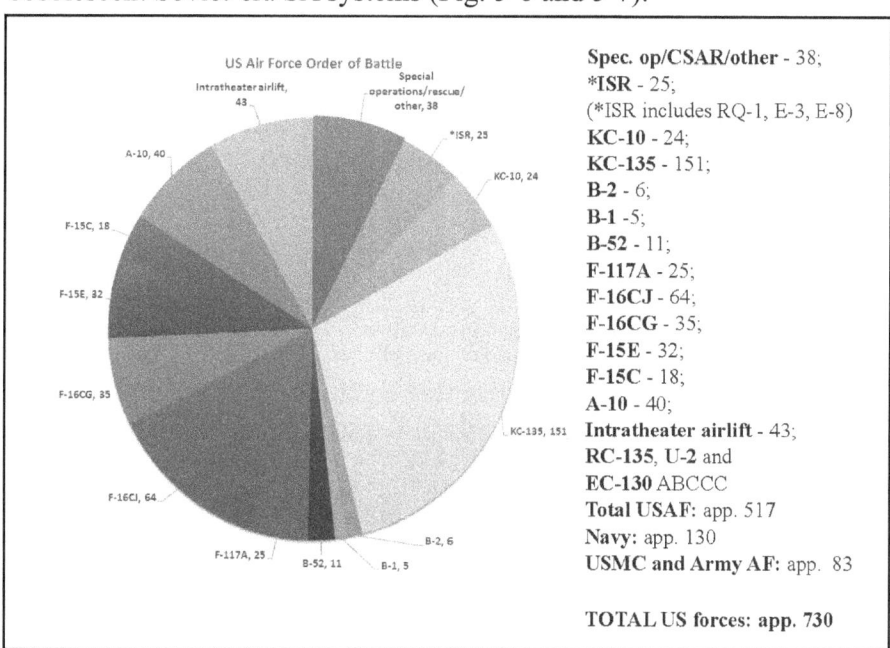

Figure 5-6: USAF order of battle as a most numerous air component. (it does not include US Navy aircraft). (Source: AWOS Fact Sheet)

Also engaged was the aircraft carrier USS Theodore Roosevelt's amphibious group and support vessels. In total, more than 1,000 aircraft

---
55 M. Mihajlović, Dj. Aničić: Shooting Down the Stealth Fighter: Eyewitness Accounts From Those Who Were There, Pen and Sword Air World, 2021

against the few.

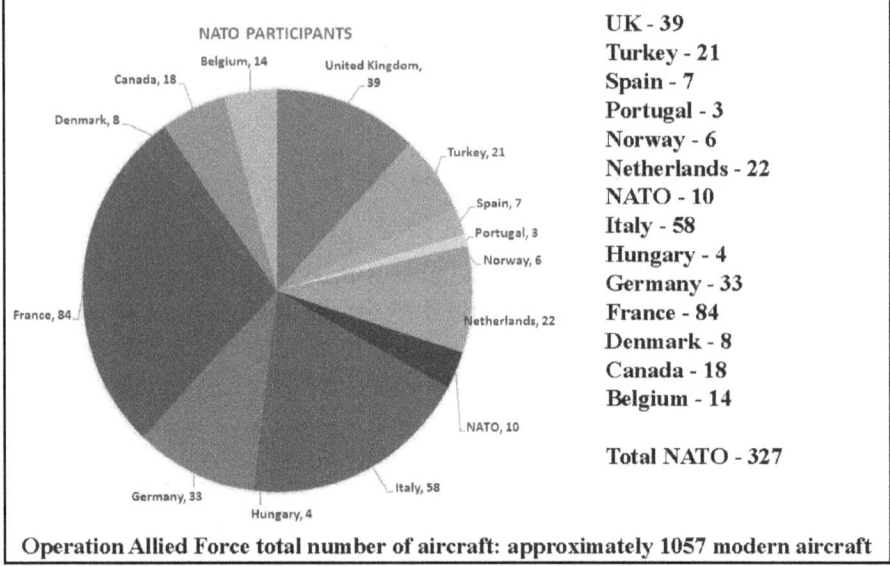

Figure 5-7: *NATO countries order of battle.*
(Source: www.ausairpower.net, modified by authors)

Attack

The armed forces of Yugoslavia were able to defend the country against the combined attack of two neighboring countries, but to fight against the most powerful military organization in the world the chances of success were almost zero.

The first indication of imminent attack was when during the night of 23 March all international air traffic, which is very dense over Yugoslavia, was re-routed over surrounding countries. The sky was cleared. Long range surveillance radar couldn't pick up a single airplane over Yugoslav air space. The NATO air attacks started on 24 March 1999.

What NATO tried was to deliver a knock-out punch on the very first night, pretty much like the attack on Iraq. In modern war there is no chivalry – the attacker uses everything at his disposal to achieve the goal: cripple or destroy the enemy without casualties to his own side. Salvos of cruise missiles launched from NATO airplanes (B-52s), US and UK submarines and warships in the Mediterranean and the Adriatic Sea, and laser guided bombs, hit radar positions, missile batteries, command centers, military airports, warehouses etc. Tomahawk missiles were timed to hit command and control centers (C2). Air-launched missiles from the 2nd Louisiana Bomb Wing hit similar targets. A pair of B-2s from Whitman Missouri 509th Bomb Wing base made a 32-hour round trip to strike air defense, arms factories, airfields and weapon storage areas. Bombers were escorted by F-15C fighters, EA-6B electronic warfare aircraft, KC-135 aerial tankers and NATO E-3 Sentry airborne command and control airplanes (Fig. 5-8 and 5-9).

Figure 5-8: F-117A taking off from Aviano base on 24 March 1999 - the night of the first attack. (Source: USAF)

Yugoslav's had enough information through intelligence reports of NATO build-up around the borders, intensifying terrorist attacks in Kosovo by Kosovar separatists, re-routing of air traffic over surrounding countries. In the days before the attack, the air force's most modern MiG-29s were relocated in pairs in the different airports. The few that were flightworthy were simply no match for those of NATO. Pilots were basically sacrificed in the opening hours of the war. Air defense units were just starting deployment but were by no means ready for combat. What plagued Yugoslav air defense and with them, the whole military was political negligence, no investment in the new weapons systems, lack of training, lack of funding, unhappy junior officers, incompetent high-ranking officers who advance

through the ranks only because of their connections. With some exceptions, most of the generals in key positions were not up to the task of fighting the whole of the NATO pact, but they couldn't say 'no' to the president because that would mean automatic dismissal and loss of privileges.

Figure 5-9: Lieutenant Colonel Waltering in the middle (8th squadron CO) after the first F-117A bombing mission over Serbia. (Source: USAF)

The air defense of the Federal Republic of Yugoslavia was presented to the population as "formidable". That was also picked up by the western press and can be seen in some documentaries. It was anything but formidable! As seen in the section 'order of battle' Yugoslav air defenses were obsolete. Equipment was old and prone to breakages. There were no funds to buy the new systems or even spare parts. Routine maintenance was simply to try to make something workable, often re-using parts from the other systems which were broken.

To have a combat-motivated and effective unit, investment in people and technique is necessary. Yugoslav air defense didn't have that at all. People didn't even get regular paychecks. Even so, they did their best to do their jobs.

NATO was aware of the capabilities of Yugoslav air defense. It was a fraction of the strength of the Iraqi's air defense which were defeated and almost destroyed in the first few weeks of fighting. All peacetime locations of combat positions, radars, munition warehouses, and command centers were well known, and they were first to be attacked. The question for air defense command was how to survive the first blow. Since the clearing of Yugoslav air space, command had almost twenty-four hours to relocate units to alternative positions. The units waited for marching orders.

The SA-6 regiments were in their assigned areas:

60th regiment (Danilovgrad) with regimental command in the vicinity of the town

- 1st missile battery at Ćemovsko Polje
- 2nd missile battery at Golubovci airport, toward the Tuzi village
- 3rd missile battery at Luštica peninsula – Boka Kotorska bay
- 4th missile battery in the vicinity of Podgorica

230th regiment from Niš with regimental command at Kalač hill

- 1st missile battery in the vicinity of Lisinac village
- 2nd missile battery at Kremenac village area
- 3rd missile battery at Čamurije village area
- 4th missile battery in the vicinity of Znojnica village

240th regiment from Novi Sad with regimental command in Planta farm

- 1st missile battery at Kisač area
- 2nd missile battery at Futog area
- 3rd missile battery at Kisač area
- 4th missile battery in the vicinity of the city of Novi Sad

310th regiment from Kragujevac with the regimental command in the Tromić village

- 1st missile battery at Sjenica township
- 2nd missile battery at Divostin
- 3rd missile battery at Ponikve airbase near Užice
- 4th missile battery in the Mašići village area

311th regiment from Priština with the regimental command at Be-

laćevac

- 1st missile battery in the vicinity of Obilić
- 2nd missile battery at Belaćevac
- 3rd missile battery at Gračanica
- 4th missile battery in the Gornje Dobrevo

On the evening of 24 March, the first missiles and bombs fell on the targets in the Federal Republic of Yugoslavia. The first targets to be hit were garrisons, warehouses and peacetime position of the missile air defense units. NATO planners knew very well the peacetime location for every single SA-6 unit and the positions of all warehouses and radars. Regimental commands in the days and hours before the attack made a good decision to relocate all units to the field combat positions or to spread them around. Even knowing that the attack is imminent, some smaller units were still in the garrisons but not in the most likely objects that will be attacked in the first wave. This decision by the higher command resulted that there was not a single fatality among all SA-6 units nor any of the combat ready equipment was seriously hit or taken out of service. Some of the equipments which were non-functional and was stored was slightly damaged and was later repaired and sent to the combat units.

On the contrary, significant material damage was inflicted on the stationary objects such as warehouses and buildings, which was in general known that it would happen.

It is important that not a single missile was destroyed or damaged during this initial attack because the missile technical batteries, who were in charge of storing, maintenance and delivery to the combat units, were moved to the alternative positions right on time. The other missile systems, S-125 Neva from the Air Force and Air Defense branch were not that lucky: the command of the 250th missile brigade didn't order on time to evacuate and relocate their missiles so in the first attack about 80 of these missiles were destroyed. That was a blow for the S-125 Neva missile units which fortunately didn't happen with the 2K12 Kub units.

The order for all SA-6 units was to stay passive and not to do any radar emissions at the first wave of the attackers because the command wanted to keep the combat positions secret. This decision was based on the Iraqi experience during Operation Desert Storm when all Iraqi SA-6 units for the prolonged period of time kept their radars on and launched barrages of missiles and this provided the coalition forces with the opportunity to precisely locate the majority of Iraqi batteries and attack them in the second wave.

How that first night of the war looked like through the eyes of the eyewitness, sergeant Zoran Vukosavljević (Fig. 5-10):

> *After we got information about the imminent war, we took our full combat gear and went into the bomb shelter, which was located not far from our building, inside the Danilovgrad garrison. Besides me, there were also two other sergeants, one corporal on contract and 4-5 troopers. My place was just by the shelter's edge with my back on the communication trench wall. Suddenly, with just a glance that lasted maybe one millisecond I saw a fire tail flying behind us. In just a moment later, a tremendous explosion erupted 40-50 meters from us. Immediately we jumped into the farthest corner of the shelter with our faces down and covering our heads. In the next few seconds, another three powerful explosions rocked the ground, but they were farther away than the first one. I had a feeling that the air pressure from the explosions is going to lift us from the shelter and toss us all around. I yield "Gas, gas, gas!" and we all put our gas masks on our faces and lay down still. Some of the missiles fragments struck the small ammunition depot. The air was full of explosion thundering and whistling bullets. We had the feeling that the attack is still ongoing even in reality it lasted barely a minute.*
>
> *After some time we raised our heads just a bit from the shelter and we saw flames pouring out of the artillery brigade warehouses as well as from our warehouses and storages.*
>
> *At that moment, senior sergeant Stanke, a section commander of PRV-16 radar, ordered us to crawl toward the small hill at the garrison edge. We crawled about 50 meters to the first trees. From there we looked at what happened to the garrison. The fire was raging in all the buildings that were hit. Not too long after that, the fire control battery commander, a captain and a battery sergeant came to us. They told us that we were attacked by 4 BGM 109 Tomahawk cruise missiles and that it seems that one member of the artillery brigade lost his life when the first cruise missile hit the warehouse. He was in front of the building.*

What can I say about myself: I was in a state of shock. I couldn't believe that the NATO aggression really started. I watched the flames from our storages and warehouses with disbelief. It seemed that I didn't think of anything... A full mind blockade.

The captain told us that we must move out of the garrison area, and we have to get ready and form a column as soon as possible. It didn't take too long for us to do so. One major, who was the duty officer in the HQ joined us.

Our column arrived at Podgorica outskirts around 22:00. There were plenty of trees there, so it provided a decent hiding place for our equipment, rest for the men and to get some information about what is going on around us. It was also an opportunity that we make a phone calls from the houses nearby and at least tell our families that we are ok. We knew that we can't stay in this position for any prolonged time. The forest was ok for hiding but there were houses around and if NATO is able to locate us and attack, there was a possibility that surrounding houses may be hit causing civilian casualties.

During the night, the captain told us that the 1st missile battery at the Golubovci airport was attacked as well and that there is one seriously injured soldier and RStON was lightly damaged but operational. In the 1st battery, there were two of my buddies, sergeant I class Dzek, an operator on RStON and sergeant Baki, data transmitter UPPC section commander who was also my buddy from the military school. Today is Dzek's 26 birthday and I'm sure that he will remember this day for the rest of his days.

That wounded soldier would turn the only casualty from the 60th regiment for the whole duration of the war.

It would be good to explain how our soldier was wounded. The 1st battery was on combat duty at Šipčanik which is in the area of the Golubovci dual-purpose (military and civilian) airport. That position was very well known, and most likely NATO intelligences obtained the latest photos prior to the attack with the precise location of the equipment. Around 20:00, the battery commander got a phone call from the regimental command with

the very simple order: 'Open fire on anything you see in the air!'. The high voltage is turned on in the RStON and suddenly the whole screen was full of blips. The air was full of the approaching airplanes. The commander quickly selected the target and was about to transfer it to the fire control radar when suddenly the explosion cut off the power supply to the RStON. Anti-radiation AGM-88 HARM exploded between the RStON position and the power supply PES-100 and severed the power cable. The soldier who was an operator on the power supply unit was in the shelter, but he went out to see what is going on and was hit by the HARM shrapnel in the stomach. Even the wound was hard, he was able to recover. The rest of the batteries as well as the other regiment units were not attacked during the first night.

The impact of the Tomahawks on our home base and warehouses was such that one of the PRV-9 altitude finder radar was lightly damaged together with another truck but they were quickly repaired. One of the self-propelled AAA 30/2 mm Praga

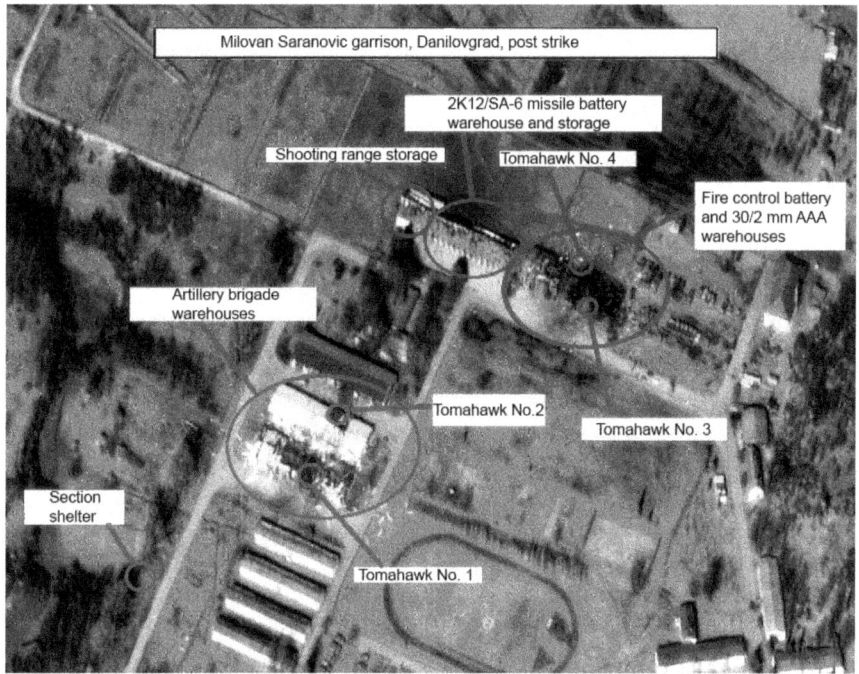

Figure 5-10: Danilovgrad army base after the first attack. (Source: NATO)

was also lightly damaged but functional.

It was evident from the very beginning that a self-propelled missile battery with its own mobile engagement radar 1S91, with tracking 1S11M radar and precision tracking and illumination (fire control and guidance) 1S31M radar, will be immediately exposed to the swarms of anti-radiation missiles. This is an Achilles heel of the SA-6 system. During the whole duration of the war, only three times the system successfully engaged the enemy using the prescribed methods: the missile battery independently detected the target, determined the fire solution and launched and guided the missiles before it was hit by the anti-radiation missile. In some instances, some batteries were hit after the launches.

It was also determined that the centralized command system with K-1M will be hard to apply in practice because the telecode radio signal was immediately prone to extensive jamming. It is possible to have wired communications that are basically immune to the EW actions, but that kind of connection requires significant logistics which limits the mobility of the batteries. The challenge was that batteries will be located closer to each other, wired transfer is slower than the radio transfer, laying the communication lines and providing the security require significant manpower. To connect batteries, tens of kilometers of cables are necessary. One of the disadvantages was also the limited use of the altitude finder radars PRV-16 or PRV-9. Without these radars, the target altitude can be only estimated based on the information from 1RL128D 'Bear'.

One of the options to mitigate the issues with the altitude finder was to set up the "zero" altitude on a certain level which can be used as a base. In practice, NATO airplanes rarely flew beneath 5000 m because the potential danger from the IR short-range missiles and AAA. If the fire control radar set up 5,000 m as zero then based on the search radar information, it can do a fast target search from 5,000 m to most typical 6-7,000 m then start from the sea level as a zero one. Few seconds for missile battery often mean the difference between life and death or between fulfilled mission and failure. This method worked well in the S-125 Neva system.

Taking into consideration that automatic system K-1M didn't function most of the time, in use was the older "planchette" system where at the regimental command post the fire control center 9S416M (UKUV) and based on the information from 1RL128D 'Bear', P-15 or P-12 radars the individual batteries 1S91 RStON were directed to the NATO aviation approaching paths.

It was mentioned earlier that 2K12 Kub has also integrated a 9Sh33 optical tracker which uses a TV camera for visual angle tracking of targets with an optical device. In Yugoslav use, it is designated as a TOV – Television Optical Visor. The disadvantage of TOV is that it can be applied only during daylight and in the initial phase of the war NATO aviation didn't fly during the day. The only exemption was the territory of province Kosovo and Metohija where NATO aviation started earlier with the daytime missions. Typical TOV is shown in Fig. 5-11.

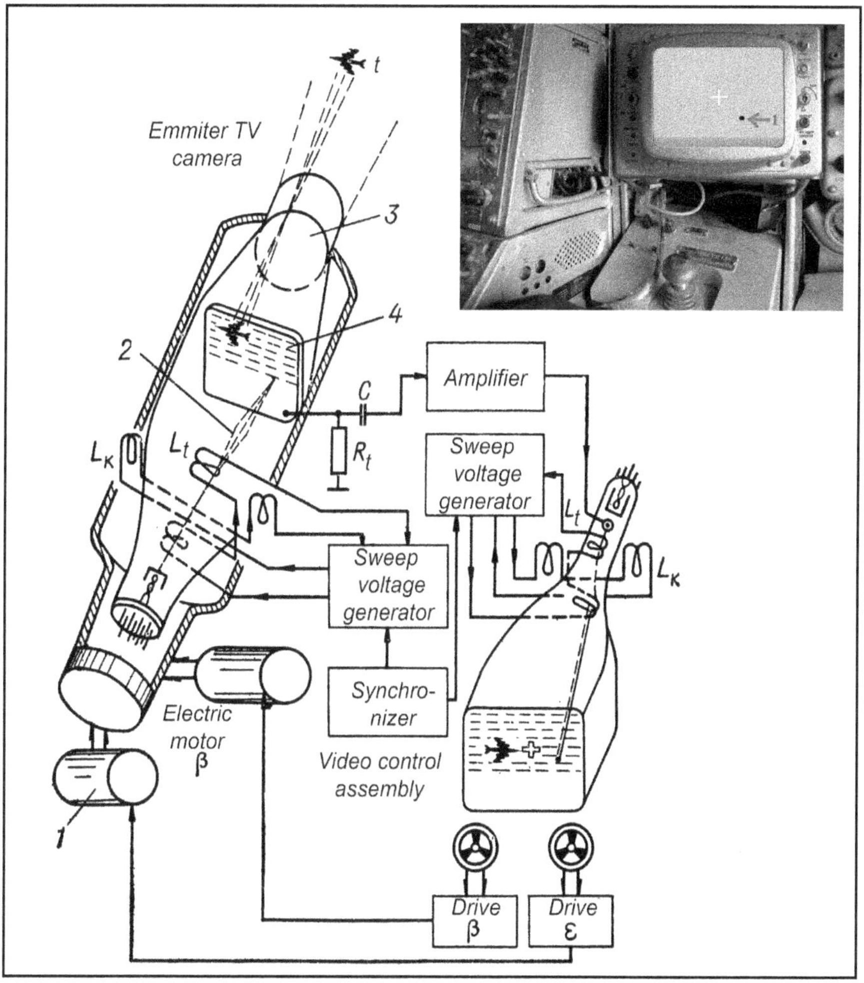

Figure 5-11: Typical television optical visor (TOV) - optical tracker diagram. (Source: authors)

When the enemy airplanes enter in the 30 km zone radius and with the flight direction toward the individual battery, the battery commander order the target tracking and acquisition radar 1S11 to turn on the electromagnetic waves' emission. After 3-6 seconds, the target is detected, and the coordinates determined, and the operator turns the 1S31 fire control radar in the target direction. After this, the target is handed over to the fire control operator which turns on the mono pulse emitter. Within few seconds the target is locked. At that moment, the target is also visible on the TOV. The operator turns "on" the target illumination transmitter switch to activate the 1S61 datalink so that the missile self-guidance head can also lock the target.

At the same moment when the missile guidance system acquires the target, the missile readiness lights in RstON are illuminated confirming that the missiles are ready for launch. Information to the individual launcher is transmitted through the battery synchro communication and orientation system (SSVuO). While the first missile is launched, the operator at the fire control radar immediately turns off the fire control radar emission and switch the system into the "equivalent" mode and transfer the control to the TOV control stick. The target is visible on the screen and, with the manipulation of the control stick, the target is kept in the crosshair.

In the radar cabin, the operator must keep the target all the time in the crosshair. Moving the control stick, the fire control radar antenna is moving as the TOV is moving to provide the emitter to illuminate the target all the time.

In this regime, the crew can visually see if the missile is activated in the proximity of the target.

The advantage of this combat procedure is in shortening the mono pulse radar emitter working sequence only on the time of locking the target when the role is taken over by the TOV. One of the disadvantages is that the target illumination emitter must be "on" because the SA-6 missile is semi-active radar guided.

This method of engagement provided the opportunity to execute more firings but even with this method, it did not eliminate radar emission into space which is used by the enemies to launch HARMS. The cumulative time of the target surveillance and tracking radar and the fire control radar mono pulse tracking emitter sometimes were too long and provided the opportunity for the aircraft to launch the antiradiation missile either in automatic or manual modes.

The missile operators faced the challenge of how to engage the enemy while cutting the radar emissions even more. The use of TOV without turning "on" the radar station is one of the options but with certain limitations: the detection distance is limited by the camera, the amplifier block and video signal receiver. Atmospheric conditions such as rain or fog can greatly limit the use of TOV. With the ideal optical conditions, the visibility is 21-30 km for the smaller fighter airplane such as F-16 at the altitude of 7 km. Visually detecting the target at this distance is enough for the missile flight to the maximum engagement range of 24 km.

TOV provides the ability of the system in the equivalent mode (placed right beside the mono pulse emitter) to scan the air space without turning on the tracking radar. The combat rules in detail describe how this procedure works. At the moment when the target is detected on the TV screen, the mono pulse tracking emitter on the fire control radar is turned "on" so that the distance to the target can be determined. After the target is acquired, the target illuminator emitter is turned "on". At the same time, at the commander's station the control indicator lamp "Ready" is illuminated informing the commander that the missiles are ready for launch. The battery commander then performing the launch. The operator of the fire control radar turns "off" the mono pulse emitter emission and switch again to the TOV tracking. The fire control operator uses a control stick to keep the target in the crosshair on the screen and in parallel directing the fire control radar which emitter constantly illuminates the target and the missile and guides the missile to the target. The radar crew can see on the TV screen if the missile hit the target or missed it.

In this mode of operation, the time for engagement of the target tracking mono pulse emitter on the fire control radar is shortened and the emission of the target detection radar is fully eliminated. The emission of the fire control radar for the target illumination is necessary for the missile guidance, as mentioned before.

With this mode, the targets are usually detected in the shorter distances based on the facts that the operator must visually detect the target and that is by the rule shorter than the abilities of the acquisition (detection) and tracking radar.

The shorter detection range is one of the disadvantages of this method. The other disadvantage is that the directing of the individual launchers is not precise because the TV tracking doesn't have the same tracking precision as the radar. What can happen is that because of the vibrations and the manual manipulating, the missile may lose the lock on the target which require the launch of the second missile. This increases the operation time by at least 3-4 seconds.

The great advantage of using this guidance method is that the batteries that were engaged in Kosovo and Metohija were able to launch on multiple targets and at the same time avoiding to be hit with the anti-radiation missiles or bombs, saving the people and equipment.

Engaging the aerial targets with TOV without the turning "on" engagement and fire control radar on RStON is mostly used against the hovering helicopters or low flying airplanes but the batteries at Kosovo and Metohija had to use this method against the maneuverable targets at the medium altitudes which limited the probabilities of hit and destructions of the targets. Launching the missiles in this mode even without the hit disrupted and often break the attacking formations thus protecting the troops and the equipment on the ground. This kind of engagements were not prescribed in the rules and procedures of the combat engagements and it can be considered as a "proprietary tactical modification".

Some of the tactical uses include an "innovation" when one of the crew members stands on the RStON cabin and manually aim the TOV, guiding the operator in the cabin. When the operator in the cabin observe the target, the soldier operator jumps from the cabin and run to the shelter. The TOV is interlocked with the fire control and target tracking radar (Fig. 5-12).

This following may sound complicated and confusing, but the intention of the procedure and commands is to "confuse" the missile guidance block to think that it is locked onto the target only from the signal from the guidance block but not from the launcher. What is happening is that when the target is visually detected, the RStON mode "Regime II" is turned "on" and the command is transmitted to the selected individual launcher. The command "capture in the air" (LOAL - lock on after launch -) on the individual launcher analog command computer is transmitted to the selected missile and in the missile self-guidance block the command "capture ban" is activated. In the launcher launching command block, the command "capture ban", which in the normal circumstances would capture the target in the self-guiding block, is annulated. In practice, it means that the missile is ready only by the signal for the self-guidance block that informs the launcher that it has steady capture (target lock) and tracking. The launcher will issue the command "ready for launch" that will show on the RStON even the missile guidance block didn't capture (lock-on) the target. Upon the command "launch" is issued, the missile leaves the launcher with the guidance block ready to search, capture and lock the target.

Figure 5-12: RStON at the combat position. A crew member can stay by the radar and guide the operator. This method shortened the radar emission time. (Source: authors)

At this moment, and sometimes with 2-3 seconds delay, the operator on the fire control radar turns "on" the illumination transmitter while the target tracking radar is turned "off" because the tracking of the target is performed through the TOV with the operator using the command stick to keep the target in the crosshair.

After 4.5 seconds, the command to annulate the "capture ban" is issued in the missile guidance block and the missile continues the flight while the seeker is searching for the target by frequencies. When the target is acquired by the seeker, the guidance system guides to the interception point. In the case that the target is in the near engagement zone, meaning short and medium engagement distances, the "capture ban" on the guidance block is annulated after 3 seconds. This method is more appropriate for low-level flying targets. As the possibilities to engage the low flying targets are limited, following the rules, two missiles on the launcher are selected which gives a probability of 90% for the successful target destruction.

The same method with one of the crew members guiding the passive TOV operator is applicable with even shorter radar emissions 2-3 seconds after the missile is launched.

The greatest advantage of these methods was that the anti-radiation missiles launched at the source of electromagnetic radiation in the vast majority missed the batteries. These methods also provided better safety for the operators and send a "message" for the aggressors that even after hundreds of anti-radiation missiles and bombs, the SA-6 batteries are pretty much alive and active.

The negative side of this methods is the increased number of launched missiles because some of the missiles lost track after the launch or during the flight.

All in all, not sticking blindly to the procedures increase the battlefield survivability of the SA-6 batteries, far longer than in the most optimistic prediction.

The important component was also field camouflage and the use of decoys not only by the SA-6 batteries but the other short-range missile systems as well. Mobility and changing the position often was one of the measures. For 78 days of the war, the SA-6 batteries were relocated 378 times.

After the initial strikes, it was determined that the main engagements of the NATO airplanes are on Kosovo and Metohija and the wider area around the capital Belgrade. This dictated sometimes longer transfers from one combat position to another combat position which increased the risk that the units may be detected and attacked while on the march. It is worth saying that it has never happened that any of the combat units or technical and support units were ever detected and attacked during the transition from one position to another.

As the war progressed, the 60th regiment from Danilovgrad was ordered to deploy two batteries to Kosovo and Metohija and two batteries to the Belgrade area. The regiment command with 1RL128D 'Bear' and PRV-16 radars moved to Kosovo and the reserve command with P-15M and PRV-9 moved to Belgrade while the K-1M command and control unit moved to Novi Sad area. This move required marches of a couple of hundreds of kilometers. The same was for the 310th regiment – moving to Sjenica with one battery and to the Mačva region with two batteries. In the later phase of the war, one battery was relocated to the Southern Banat.

Two batteries from the 230th regiment based in Niš operated in Kosovo to be later relocated to Niš again. 240th regiment from Novi Sad spent the entire war in the northern part of the country while the 311th regiment from Priština spent the war in Kosovo.

At the begging of the war, all relocations were performed during the night but later it was often performed during the day, passing often through the villages and towns. In Kosovo that was risky because the local Kosovar Albanian population or at least some of their parts were hostile to the army and there was a constant danger that the moves will be reported to the UCK terrorist and from there to NATO.

The general rule was that after every engagement, the battery must leave the position immediately. Even if there was no engagement at all, 24 hours was the maximum time that the unit can be at one location. In practice, this was not always executed.

What is important to say is that the engagements of SA-6 batteries were often performed in a way that actually limited the true potential of the system. The mobility of the system is one of the reasons why the air defense HQ decided to move these units from one place to another more often and without thorough planning. One example is that after the Belgrade air defense network was damaged, mobile SA-6 units were taken from the base units and sent as a help to the S-125 Neva units tasked with the Belgrade area air defense but without the long-range surveillance radars. There was no real coordination between the units and this practice showed as unsuccessful and was abandoned. The ambush tactics in which some of the batteries were engaged were not performed according to the tactics principles and methods. The lack of the proper and correct information about aerial targets within the engagement zones was one of the weaknesses. In some instances it was required that batteries turn on their tracking radars too early, providing the NATO signal intelligence and electronic intelligence assets to locate the positions rendering the ambush positions useless. There were also individual mistakes because of the lack of proficiency levels necessary to operate these systems and perform the tactical moves.

It was evident that the 'divided' regiment use didn't have any success. The idea was that the missile regiment was used to defend two assigned objects but without the overlap and cover by the other part of the regiment.

As it was mentioned before, the idea to support the S-125 Neva systems without the long-range surveillance radars was fruitless because the battery radar has a limited range of 60-70 km and 7 km altitude which caused that the radars were used with prolonged but unsuccessful emissions and in a few circumstances the batteries were attacked and people killed and equipment destroyed. This will be addressed in the following section.

There was an attempt to reinforce the batteries with P-15 surveillance and acquisition radars, but this radar has limited abilities with the altitude (for fighter bombers around 6,000 m). The radar was very sensitive to the jamming and the practice was soon abandoned. In few instances, the radars were hit with the anti-radiation missiles causing casualties.

Besides the difficulties reflected in the technical inferiority to the modern warfare, lack of qualified officers and NCOs, lack of previous combat experience, lack of training in the modern electronic warfare saturated battlefield, absolute enemy superiority and domination in the airspace, 12 years since the last live missile launches were performed on the exercises, one of the additional measures that rendered the ability of the batteries to use the best that can be extracted from the old system was often ineffective tactics ordered by the superior command and pressure by the same to use the radars extensively and launch even when the conditions were absolutely against the individual batteries. All of this took a heavy toll on the equipment and people. The damaged equipment can be replaced, but the people can't.

The most successful SA-6 units (considering the number of launches) were the ones that had an area of operation determined in the pre-war plans and who spent the entire war in their regiments - the 240th regiment from Novi Sad and 311th regiment from Priština.

The biggest problem to all SA-6 units and the same problem was in Neva (SA-3) units as well, was the optimal duration for the radar emissions for both tracking and fire control radars. A certain time is necessary to detect, track and lock onto the target and to launch and guide missiles. The existing regulations and prescribed values in the official manuals were at the very beginning proven to be too long and the gradual shortening of the emissions was widely applied. Combat crews basically re-wrote the rules of engagements and modules of actions. Some units were more efficient, and some were not, and they didn't solve the problem for the entire duration of the war. SA-6 batteries had a mobility advantage over the Neva batteries. The SEAD actions against Neva batteries were more effective and the majority of them were taken out by the end of the war. One of the surviving units with Neva system was the legendary 3rd battalion, which was targeted with anti-radiation missiles 22 times but never hit and never lost a single piece of equipment. The same battalion downed F-117A and F-16CG as well as one big still unidentified target and damaged one more F-117A.

According to some of the parameters, the Kub battery shall turn on their radar when the target is below 30 km distance, in the case of the approaching target, so that the search of the target with the fire control radar last a maximum 5-6 seconds and the cumulative emission for both detection and target tracking radar shall not be longer than 18 seconds, including the target search time. This requirement put an additional burden on the combat crew in the case that the target is not found, and the battery needs to move.

In the second half of the war, almost all batteries switched to the new and more creative way of using TV mode which wasn't defined in the standard operation and engagement procedures, by using a TV camera system to search for the targets, and to launch the missiles without the turning the radar "on" and only a few seconds after the missile launch, the radar is turned on (target and missile illuminator) thus shortening the cumulative emission for 40%. The use of this method resulted also in extensive missile consumption, which was often recorded by the NATO pilots as launching in series. Units that used this method had a much better chance to survive the counterattacks either by anti-radiation missiles or by fighter bombers.

The fire control battery at the regimental command post, equipped with 1RL128D or P-15M also applied a non-continual model of the radar emissions. The radar worked for a few rotations then it is switched to the "equivalent" mode for a few rotations, then turned the high voltage again for the few rotations with the electromagnetic emission, and so on in irregular patterns. The idea was to do airspace surveillance without repeating intervals on a regular pattern. The scanning zone changed accordingly without sticking to the patterns as well. The altitude finder radar PRV-16 was turned on only by the order directly from the regimental command based on the situation at the combat position.

Besides the radar emission timing, one of the issues was reducing the heat signatures of the equipment. In order to do that, the power supply units (diesel generators), were moved away from the combat equipment whenever that was possible, concealed and cooled down. There was also attempts to extend the exhaust pipes. Camouflage also included wide use of camouflage nets, wood, tires, industrial conveyors, rubber belts etc. More will be discussed in the following chapter.

Communication between the individual batteries, fire control battery and the regimental HQ was one of the most vulnerable parts. It was already described how the radio communication between the units is prone to jamming. Because of that, wired communication was used but that created certain limitations such as the functioning in a "real time" wherein "planchet" (also described earlier) there was a problem in determining the parallaxes between the units that were scattered which caused that the differences in directions and azimuths were too big. The SA-6 units simple had obsolete communication systems which were easy to jam.

To counter the enemy electronic warfare abilities, SA-6 units used radar emission imitators combined with a radar reflector as one of the means of electronic masking. These imitators worked in conjunction with the battery radars. In the air defense corps, only 15 imitators were available. At the beginning of the war, additional eight imitators were distributed to the units. Around 500 passive radar reflectors were distributed between SA-6 and Neva units and additional quantities were fabricated during the war.

The use of the radar imitator showed very good results but toward the end of the war, NATO aviation learned their lesson and didn't pay too much attention to imitators. These electronic devices were used as much as possible to cover the fire control radar emission channel by turning on not only the battery imitator but also imitators from the nearby batteries.

The most efficient way was to use a combination of imitators, passive radar reflectors, decoys and fake combat positions. It was recorded that NATO aircraft bombed three decoy positions made by 60th, 310th and 311th regiments. During the war, more and more radar emission imitators of different size and power are introduced. SA-6 batteries used them on 1,000 – 2,500 m meters from the radar position. Passive radar reflectors were positioned up to 500 m from the position. The idea of passive radar reflector use is that they reflect the radar electromagnetic energy in space and this energy may attract the anti-radiation seeker to prematurely activate the missile warhead confusing the reflector as a real radar (Fig. 5-13, 5-14 and 5-15).

Figure 5-13: Fire control radar imitator - antiradiation missile decoy system, very effective way to lure the antiradation missile guidance system. (Source: mycitymilitary.com)

After the initial problems and temporary elimination of few batteries, the rest of the units consolidated and acted more cautiously and applying limitations for the radar emissions, faster and more often relocations and effective field camouflage. These measures contributed that for the 78 days of NATO bombing, besides the enormous enemy advantages, these units were always clear and present danger for the aggressors. From time to time, some of these units were out of service for a short period of time, but the majority continued to fight to the end of the war.

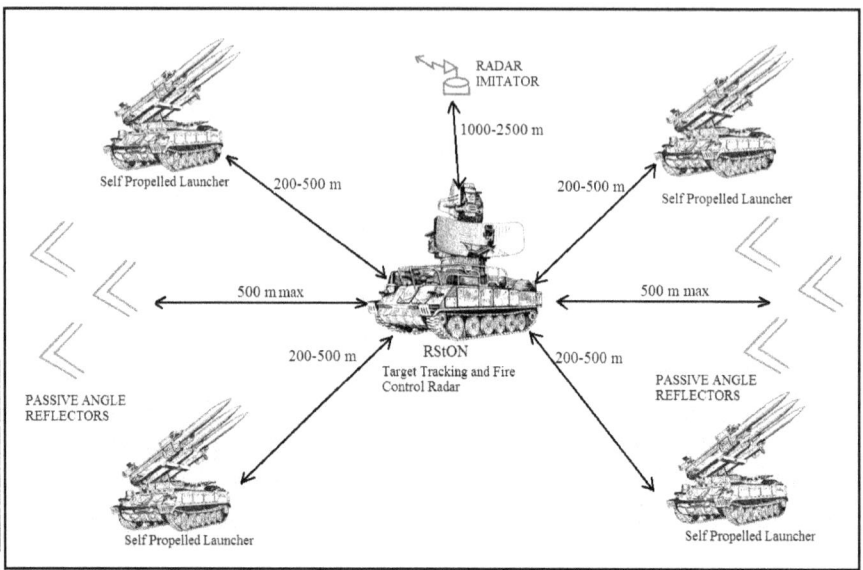

Figure 5-14: Application of passive radar angle reflectors and radar imitator at 2K12 battery position. (Source: authors)

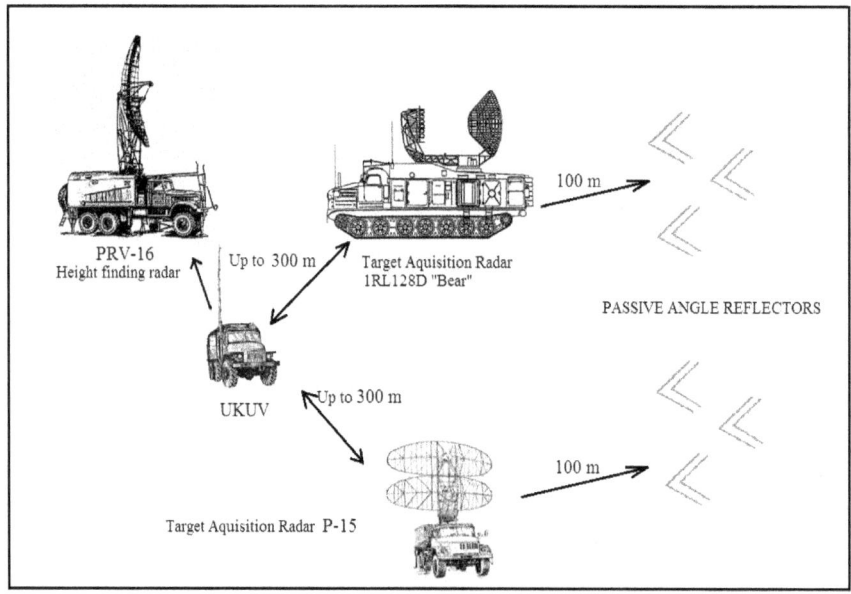

Figure 5-15: Application of passive radar angle reflectors at 2K12 regiment position. (Source: authors)

Eyewitness accounts and controversies of the air war 1999

2K12 Kub-M vs B-1B Lancer – lightning or SAM strike?

Captain Gerald Goodfellow
(as published in Osprey's B-1B Lancer Units in Combat)

The first B-1B mission occurred on 2 April against the Novi Sud petroleum production facility at Pancevo, northeast of Belgrade. Although ONA was originally limited to only 'tactical' targets at the start of the campaign, it became clear that hitting such sites alone would not persuade President Milosevic to fold. Instead, the target set was expanded to cover 'strategic' installations such as the Novi Sad facility, which was literally helping to oil the Serbian war machine. The combined load of 168 Mk 82 'slicks' dropped from the two bombers that were sortied had no trouble knocking out the key sections of the plant. These Mk 82 bombs are lined up on an ammunition handling truck, waiting to be loaded into the weapons bay of the 77th BS Lancer parked in the background. The access ladder in the crew compartment is down and the aircraft awaits the arrival of the four-man team who will fly the bomber over western Europe and the Adriatic Sea and then onto its targets in Serbia and Kosovo (B-1B Systems Program Office).

However, after the bomb run, the weapons bay doors on one of the B-1Bs failed to close. The Lancer was subsequently targeted by a Serbian SAM, although a combination of defensive maneuvers, chaff and electronic countermeasures defeated the missile. The weapon succeeded in forcing the bomber into the engagement zone of a second SAM, however, which the crew was also able to defeat. According to the pilot of the aircraft, Captain Gerald Goodfellow *at the first indication of a SAM launch your training kicks in. It feels very natural. You don't really think about it until later on, when the mission is completed. You take on*

an almost business-like attitude.

You have to beat that missile. When I'm up there, my biggest worry isn't about getting shot down, but about missing the target. As a whole, the crew is concentrating as one putting those bombs on target'. The open weapons bay doors and the maneuvering of the aircraft caused Goodfellow's Lancer to use more fuel than anticipated, leaving the bomber with insufficient fuel to return to Fairford. During the mission, the B-1B was also struck by lightning, which blew off a section of the aircraft's horizontal stabilizer, but the crew was still able to get the aircraft home.

Goodfellow remembered that 'we felt a huge relief at the completion of the mission. The SAMs came closer than we'd anticipated, and after thinking about it for a couple of days, we were glad to have survived'.

...

'Lancer 85-0075 of the 77th BS sits under a partially cloudy Gloucestershire sky whilst being readied for another mission. to Serbia. This aircraft left Fairford a mere 11 days after its arrival. The jet's early departure, in contrast with some of the other aircraft deployed, may have been due to mechanical problems (B-1B Program Office)'.

...

General John Jumper

'The pair of B-1Bs came down south over the Adriatic Sea information with their ALE-50 towed decoys deployed, and we watched the radars in Montenegro track the bombers as they turned the corner around Macedonia and headed up into Kosovo. We watched the radars, in real time, hand off the targets to the SA-6s, which came upon full-target track and fired their missiles. Those missiles took the ALE-50s off the back end of the B-1s just like they were designed to...' [56]

It is clear that not many details of this mission are relieved in these citations except prizing the professionalism of the American airmen and quality of the equipment.

However, years later, in an audio interview that, now general Good-

---

56 For more information about the ALE-50 towed decoy, see Appendix C

fellow gave to his nephew, some interesting details are revealed. General Goodfellow further explains the known details about that mission but also reveal something new.

The following are some extract:

After the bomb run at the first target and failing to close the bomb bay doors his aircraft is caught in the missile guiding radar. He observed a launching of the first missile and attempts to take evasive actions. At one moment, is aircraft broke the sound barrier and accelerate to 1.6 Mach at an altitude of 20,000 feet (about 6,000 m). With evasive maneuvers he tried to put the towed decoy AN/ALE-50 between the plane and the missile. At one moment the whole crew registered a loud explosion. The next they saw was the second missile that after about 10 seconds flew over them. Evasive maneuvers and activation of afterburners cause much bigger fuel consumption, so they had to be refueled before the return to the UK base. At the landing, the lightning struck the horizontal stabilizer. At the moment they made a touchdown, the bomb bay suddenly closed.

What is interesting in this extended interview is that they acknowledged an explosion in the proximity, but the proximity of what? Was that the proximity of the towed decoy, or the proximity of the airplane itself. If the crew knew about the explosion in the airplane that is flying supersonic, with a lot of noise such as airflow, instrumentation, jet engines etc. it means that the explosion was very close and the 3M9 missile proximity fuse is set up to activate at 30-35 m from the target.

The details about the second missile that "flew over the airplane" may have a different meaning than the crew think that happened: if the missile flew over the airplane, that could mean that it was guided to the airplane, otherwise, if it was guided to the towed decoy, it would flew over the decoy, which is towed a hundred or so meters behind.

It is highly likely, based on the technical performances of the missile and guidance method that the first missile was indeed guided into the airplane and the activation of the warhead by the proximity fuse happened behind the airplane, between the towed decoy and the airplane but closer to the airplane itself. The crew heard the explosion and some of the warhead fragments hit the horizontal stabilizer.

It is important to say that this kind of damage is minimal and couldn't jeopardize the airplane functionality. After the landing in Fairford

base, this airplane was withdrawn from the combat service for repairs and replaced with the other one and most probably didn't take any other combat missions against Yugoslavia. It is still operational as of the writing of this book.

According to the crew, the airplane was struck by lightning at about 200 feet (app 60 m) during the landing but was able to land safely. The routine inspection is performed right away. The information about the lightning strike was revealed by the crew. With respect to the American bomber crew, they are airmen, not the specialized technical people to know right away the cause of damage. This information they can hear only from some of the technicians from the maintenance support or most likely they rafted that conclusion by themselves. Since then this information holds on. More information about the lighting strikes on the airplane can be found in Appendix E. Boeing also confirms that the majority of the lighting strikes may occur between 5,000 to 15,000 feet (1,524 to 4,572 meters).

In the interview, Goodfellow said that it was his first experience with the lightning strike on the airplane so definitely he is the one who had no experience in this kind of situation.

It is interesting that not a single photo of the damaged stabilizer is publicly available. It is well known that even bird strikes or hail strikes are often publicly shown on fighters and other airplanes. Also, there is not recorded information about the lightning strike in the Fairford area for that exact day. Fairford is not known to have many lightning strikes anyway.

It is also possible that the lightning strike was intentionally placed for the sake of keeping the "high spirit" among the bomber crews. It wouldn't sound good if it was published that the modern fourth-generation bomber was damaged by a second-generation missile, launched by an inferior enemy, on its first combat mission. Besides this, the efficiency of AN/ALE-50 that started to be installed on the B-1B bombers just a week or so before could be questioned.

One more thing is interesting as well: it was announced that the airplane was returned to the US because of mechanical problems. The question is what kind of mechanical problems? The mechanical problem can be, for example, damaged stabilizers and controls that can't be repaired by the field maintenance units and require specific tools and expertise and even support by the manufacturer.

It is worth saying, and that is very well known to all pilots and aeronautical engineers and enthusiasts that the airplanes are protected from lightning strikes. Since the outer skin of most airplanes is primarily aluminum, which is a very good conductor of electricity; the secret to safe lightning hits is to allow the current to flow through the skin from the point of impact to some other point without interruption or diversion to the interior of the aircraft. This is a practical application of the "Faraday cage". It is a higher probability that the lightning will strike the vertical stabilizer or edges of the wings but, for the sake of objectivity, there is a possibility of the horizontal stabilizers strike as well. Punching the hole is not an impossible event but the probability is extremely low. Maybe it was the "lightning", but the one that came from the ground.

And to conclude this analysis with the mathematical probability theory, what is the real probability that the only B-1B airplane that was forced to abandon the bombing mission of Yugoslavia because of unspecified 'mechanical problems' was the only one that reported the surface-to-air missile attack.

And the last, but not the least, for comparison, it was rumors that, besides the downed F-117A over Serbian territory, one additional F-117A was damaged during the bombing mission but for 20 years US officials denied that until one of the pilots who flew that mission publicly acknowledged that the airplane was indeed damaged and effectively taken out of service for the duration of the war. There are also some other rumors circulating.[57] We will stop here and let the readers make their own conclusion.

Two other crewmen also talked about that night:

Captain Greg Payne was flying as a 'weapons systems officer,' or 'WSO' ('Whizzo') on the lead bomber. Lt. Col. Ben Leitzel, He was a Whizzo on the second aircraft:

To understand the difficulty of the first mission, you have to start a week before the air war over Kosovo.

Friday, March 26, 1999, was a normal workday at Ellsworth AFB, Payne said. 'We had no indication we were going

---

57 https://www.thedrive.com/the-war-zone/37894/yes-serbian-air-defenses-did-hit-another-f-117-during-operation-allied-force-in-1999#:~:text=An%20F%2D117%20deploys%20its,%2C%20on%20April%204%2C%201999.&text=%E2%80%9CTuna%E2%80%9D%20doesn't%20provide,occurred%20on%20April%2030%2C%201999.

anywhere.'

Over the weekend, the 28th Bomb Wing at Ellsworth was notified its bombers might be needed for Operation Allied Force. Planning began.

The official 'tasking' came the following Monday.

On Wednesday two aircrews - the eight men who would fly the first mission - flew to the Royal Air Force Base at Fairford, England, so they could get the required 12 hours rest before their missions.

Their B-1Bs arrived the next day, and crews loaded each of them with 84 500-pound bombs, which had been prepared at Ellsworth.

Weapons maintainers here also chalked messages on the bombs, such as: 'This is the last day of the rest of your life' and 'Greetings to Milosevic from the 28th Bomb Wing.'

By 3 p.m. Thursday, April 1, the two B-1B crews were being briefed for their first combat mission. Mission planners described the targets. Survival experts explained what to expect if they had to bail out. Air Force lawyers briefed them on avoiding civilian targets.

The aircrews also planned for 'crunch points.'

'That's when a lot of things are happening at once,' Leitzel said. For a B-1B crew those few minutes include approaching and departing a target.

The mission was to drop bombs on two areas in hilly terrain, while avoiding surface-to-air missile launchers known to be operating in the area.

The two B-1Bs took off shortly after sunset for the five-hour flight to the Adriatic Sea, which served as a staging area for the 'packages' of fighters and bombers that attacked together.

It took about 20 minutes for the two B-1Bs to fly from the coast to their first target, and it was a busy 20 minutes.

A B-1B bomber has a crew of four: two pilots up front and two Whizzos, who sit in ejection seats in back, in closet-size

spaces crammed with an array of computer screens, gauges, dials and keyboards.

There are two kinds of Whizzos: defensive systems officers, or DSOs, who sit in the left seat, and offensive systems officers or OSOs, in the right seat. OSOs are the equivalent of the old bombardier.

DSOs deploy such systems as flares, metal chaff and a towed decoy that fool anti-aircraft missiles.

Leitzel and Payne were flying from the DSO seats that night, but they could see radar images of the target tanks, and they helped the OSOs verify them.

Payne's aircraft dropped its bombs without a hitch. The crew could feel the explosive bolts pushing 42 bombs out of the aircraft. 'It feels like someone is shaking a table,' Payne said.

Leitzel's aircraft, however, had a problem. The B-1B has three sets of bomb doors. All three open, even to drop half a bomb load, because the weapons are released in a sequence from each bay.

The bomb doors on Leitzel's aircraft were stuck open, with less than two minutes to the next target.

'This was a crunch point,' Leitzel explained.

The crew recycled the system, but that didn't help. The crew made a quick decision to continue the mission with doors open.

The two B-1Bs hit their second target, each aircraft dropping another 42 bombs. The crews were preparing to turn for home when one of the pilots noticed a flash.

'We had a SAM launch,' Leitzel said. A surface-to-air missile. To a pilot, a SAM looks like a bottle rocket that gets bigger very, very fast, Payne said.

At the same instant the pilot saw the flash, Payne and Leitzel heard the wavering 'whoop, whoop, whoop' tones in their headsets that warn of a launch.

The pilots turned hard and the DSOs deployed defensive

systems. *'All of them,'* Payne said.

After a tense minute - maybe a minute and a half - the two crews knew the missile had failed.

The open bomb bay on Leitzel's aircraft and the hard maneuvering away from the SAM had burned lots of fuel, so Leitzel's crew called for an unscheduled mid-air refueling over the Adriatic.

Then they turned for England.

'You really feel the adrenaline draining out of your body,' said Leitzel, who two weeks ago placed fourth overall in the Mount Rushmore Marathon.

The rest of the bombing run should have been easy, but on the approach to RAF Fairford, a lightning bolt hit Leitzel's aircraft and blew off a chunk of the horizontal stabilizer the size of a fist.

So ended the first combat bomb drop by B-1B bombers.

2K12 Kub-M against A-10A Thunderbolt

Major Dave "Devo" Gross[58]

'The first of May began like any other day in Gioia...

Just as I was about to roll in, I heard, 'SAM launch, SAM launch' over the UHF radio. Looking east towards Pristina Airfield, I saw a volley of two SAMs followed immediately by two more. I was amazed at the amount of white, billowy smoke they produced and the rapid speed at which they flew in our direction. All four SAMs were guiding towards us. I began evasive maneuvers and called the SAM launch out on the very high frequency (VHF) radio that all four A-10s were using to work the target-area handoff. All four A-10s began a SAM defense ballet, the likes of which I have never seen and hope to never see again. The sky was full of chaff, and the world's greatest attack pilots were maneuvering their Hogs like their lives depended on it—and they did! A SAM, the second launched, malfunctioned and detonated

---

58 Col. Christopher E. Haave, USAF, Lt. Col. Phil M. Haun, USAF, A-10s over Kosovo, Maxvell Air Force Base, Alabama, december 2003.

in spectacular fashion about 2,000 feet above the ground. From 63 MISSION LEADERSHIP AT THE TACTICAL LEVEL, page 99: my now-inverted cockpit, I could feel the concussion of the warhead detonating in a blaze of orange fire. The other three SAMs continued on course in an attempt to thwart our attack against the troops massed in the forest below us. All but one of the SAMs failed to guide—and that one chose Scud as its soon-to-be victim. Wouldn't you know it would pick Scud, who was the least-seasoned pilot in our fourship - a formation that had over 3,500 hours of combined Hog experience.

Meegs did an excellent job of defeating the threat, maintaining situational awareness on his wingman, and calling out the final evasive maneuvers that prevented the SAM from impacting Scud's jet and ruining our day. All four SAMs were defeated, and the Serb troops in the forest below awaited the wrath of the Panthers. The Serbs failed to take a lesson from Desert Storm. In that campaign, the Iraqis quickly learned that if they shot at an A-10 they had better kill it because if it survives, it is going to shoot back with a vengeance. Corn and I were out of gas, so we departed the area with our hearts in our throats and left the counterattack to Meegs. He dropped four Mk-82 airburst bombs on the troop concentration in the trees and eliminated those forces from the rest of the campaign. (I can make that statement with a high degree of certainty. One year later I received an Air Medal for my participation in that sortie) ...

After getting fuel from the tanker, Corn and I proceeded back into the KEZ to look for more targets in the northern region of the country. We had received numerous intel reports about troops and targets in this region, but we had not achieved much success in finding them. We flew approximately 15 miles northwest of Pristina Airfield and began searching for targets. I found one area of interest that appeared to have mobile AAA and possibly some other military vehicles in a small valley. I was just starting to talk Corn's eyes onto the area to get his opinion when I saw two SAM launches from just north of Pristina Airfield. I thought, 'Here we go again.' I called out the SAM launch to Corn and directed his break turn to defeat the attack. As I dumped out as much chaff as I could muster and made the appropriate break

turn, I looked back to see that Corn had turned in the wrong direction. He was heading straight towards the SAMs, increasing their probability of intercept. Realizing that he did not see the SAMs, I directed him to 'take it down! Break right now and roll out west! Chaff! Chaff! Chaff!' As the second SAM guided in Corn's direction, I continued to monitor his progress and update his maneuvers while attempting to talk his eyes onto the threat. I was certain the SAM was going to hit him, and I was just about to call out a last-ditch maneuver when it began to drift aft to pass about 1,000 feet behind...

On the Serbian side, this event is described as follow:

On 1 May 1999, in the afternoon hours, a group of A-10 escorted by F-16CJ was observed approaching the Slatina airport. After they entered the engagement zone, the 1st battery launched 4 missiles around 17:22. The missiles were launched using the TOV. The first missile exploded in the air after only 600-700 m. The reason for that is unknown. The second and third missile didn't lock-on onto the target and harmlessly passed by them. The fourth missile which was launched from the other launcher locked on to the target and exploded in the vicinity of the target (Fig. 5-16).

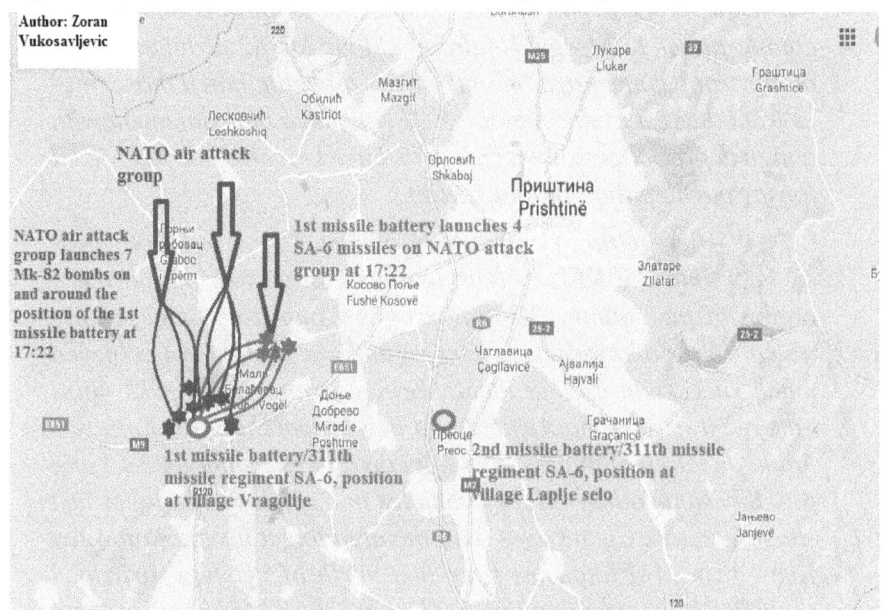

Figure 5-16: A-10A group first attack on the 1st battery, Kosovo. (Author: Zoran Vukosavljević)

After 10-15 minutes the airplanes conducted the counter-attack on the battery position, with 5 guided bombs and 2 guided missiles. The RStON sustained light shrapnel damage and there were no casualties among the people. American reports about this event are different, as we saw in the pilot own words.

In any case, the battery was exposed to combine attacks from multiple directions. Because of this, the 2nd battery tried to cover the 1st battery which was in great danger.

At 18:32, the 2nd battery launched two missiles using the TOV. The results are unknown but the loud explosion in the air was heard. In the US reports, there is no mentioning 'evading and defeating' the first missile but it was mentioned that the second missile 'followed' one of the A-10 which tried to 'shake' her off then suddenly the missile missed for about 300 m (Fig. 5-17, 5-18 and 5-19).

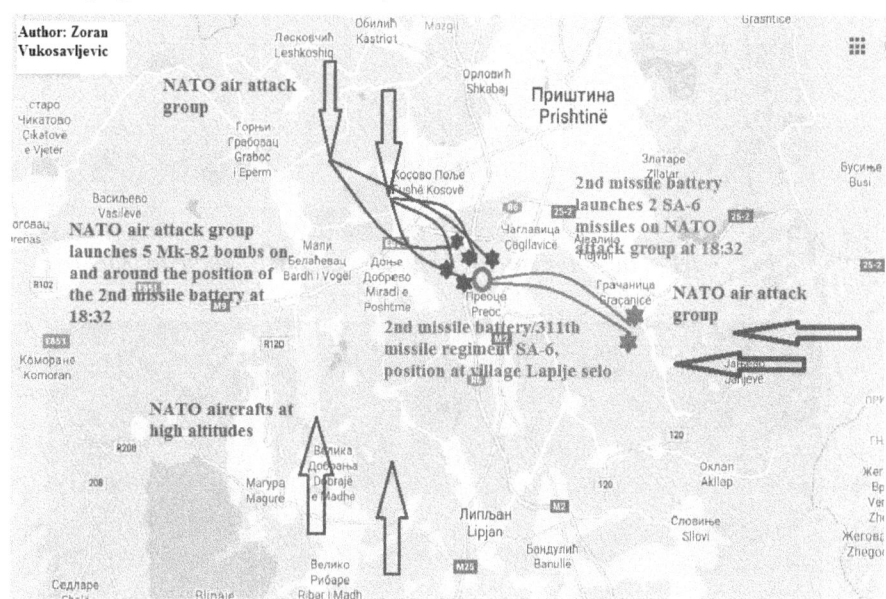

Figure 5-17: A-10A group second attack on the 2nd battery, Kosovo. (Author: Zoran Vukosavljević)

Not long after, the 2nd battery position was hit with 5 laser-guided bombs. The battery commander was lightly wounded but, unfortunately, one of the soldiers was killed.

This example shows the great devotion of the missile crews in at-

tempts to defend their position and fulfill their tasks.

In his own words, sergeant Vukosavljevic (one of the authors of this book) describes what he heard from one of the 2nd battery members during one of the A-10 attacks:

On 3 May 1999, in the area of Globočac village, province of Kosovo and Metohija, an air defense ambush group was formed. The group consisted of the 4th missile battery from the 311th regiment and a light self-propelled anti-aircraft artillery

Figure 5-18: The moment of 3M9M3 combat launch in Kosovo. (Source: authors).

Figure 5-19: 3M9M3 in fight toward the target. (Source: authors).

battery equipped with M-53/59 Praga with dual 30 mm canons. In the early evening hours, both batteries took their combat positions.

In the early evening hours of 3 May, around 16:30 hours, a group of A-10 was observed flying over the Albanian border. The group flew relatively low. Above them, F-16s from the SEAD group were also observed.

At that moment, 4th missile battery launched the first missile toward A-10 and after few seconds the other one blasted from the launcher. Both missiles exploded in the proximity of the A-10 group and for a few moments, the group disappeared.

After some time, the A-10 were back, attacking the position of the batteries with the cannon fire. A-10 action was random, spraying the area with GAU-8 30 mm rounds, but missing the equipment. Not a single round hit anything of our equipment and there were not any injuries among the people. As soon as the aircraft left, both batteries immediately left the position.

In his own words, sergeant first class Dragan Mitrović, then commander of the RStON radar station in the 2nd battery, from the 60th regiment:

It was a nice and sunny day on 17 May. We were located at the combat position in the vicinity of Smoluša village, near Lipljan. We were in readiness No. 1. It was slightly after 12:00 (Fig. 5-20)

In the battlespace environment with the enemy absolute air dominance, we applied a tactic with the use of TOV.

Sergeant Mirić was beside TOV. He came from the army of Republika Srpska. He was the one who visually guided the camera and while I was trying to get the target on the screen and have a lock-on. Our communication went through Lieutenant Dragan Janković, who stood at the plank in front of the RStON cabin and passed the information between me and Mirić and also helped Mirić to guide the camera toward the target.

Suddenly I saw a target on the screen, and we all jumped inside the cabin. It was an American A-10. Lieutenant Sreten Cvetković, a battery commander, also entered the cabin. The air-

plane flew from Albania and just flew over Šar-Planina mountain. I turned on the illumination transmitter and after getting the signal that the missile is ready and locked on the target, Lieutenant Cvetković launched the missile.

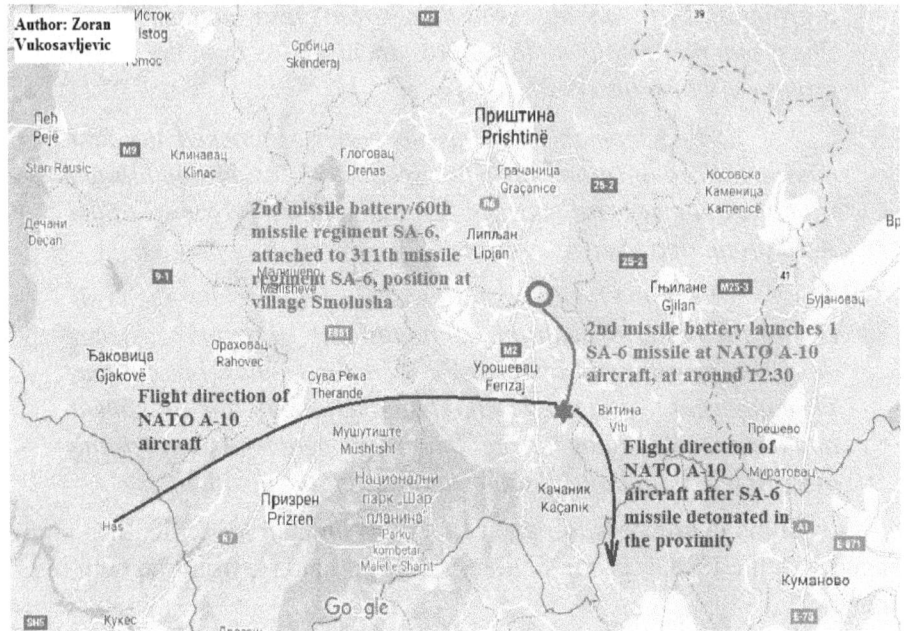

Figure 5-20: A-10A attack on the 2nd battery, Kosovo. (Author: Zoran Vukosavljević)

    The missile blasted off from the launcher and I saw very clearly that the guidance is functional based on my guiding the radar and the illuminator with the TOV control stick. The A-10 started a counter missile maneuver and went into the steep climb. The missile was steady behind his tail. Almost at the end of the effective engagement zone, the missile exploded. What I saw after, looked like the pilot catapulted. In this evasive action, the airplane flew in the direction of Macedonia when the missile exploded, and it was able to cross the border.

    I don't have any information about what happened with the airplane except some rumors from both sides of the border.

    We 'packed' our radar as fastest as we can and moved from our position in one of the hiding areas. We cover our equip-

ment with branches and camouflage nets. Not long after, maybe half an hour or a maximum one hour, a large group of NATO airplanes flew over or previous position hunting for us and waiting for us to activate our radar again. We stood very quiet for a couple of hours and after NATO airplanes left, we were able to relocate to another combat position.

2K12 Kub-M against the Drones

During the night of 3 May, in the northern part of the country, in the 240th regiment area of responsibility, there were activities by a considerable number of UAVs which flew at 2,000 – 3,000 m altitude. NATO aviation flew at about 6,000 m altitudes which is within the effective engagement zone of the SA-6 system.

The regiment command guided the battery radar toward the target and at 00:45 the 2nd battery launched one missile, but the hit was not observed (Fig. 5-21).

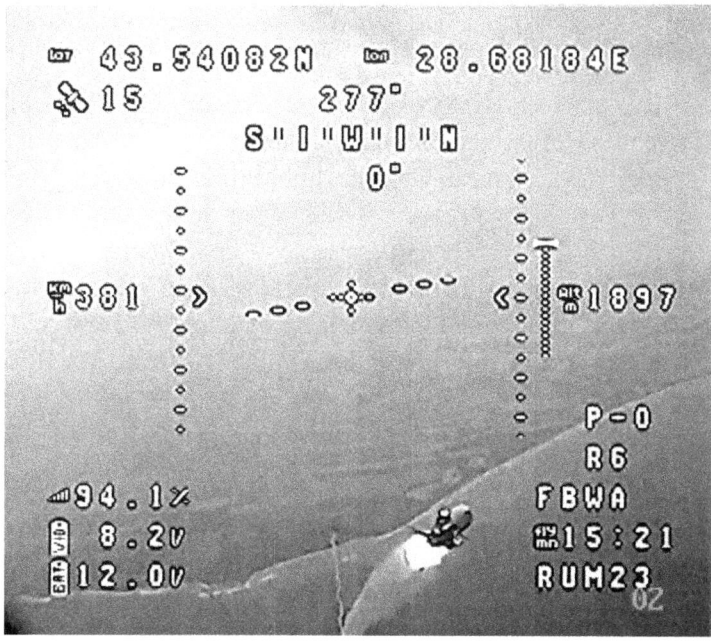

Figure 5-21: Photo made by target drone moment before impact - after the war exercise in Shabla, Bulgaria. (Source: authors).

At 00:58, again based on the guidance from the regimental command post, the 3rd battery launched one missile and this time the missile hit and destroyed the target (Fig. 5-22).

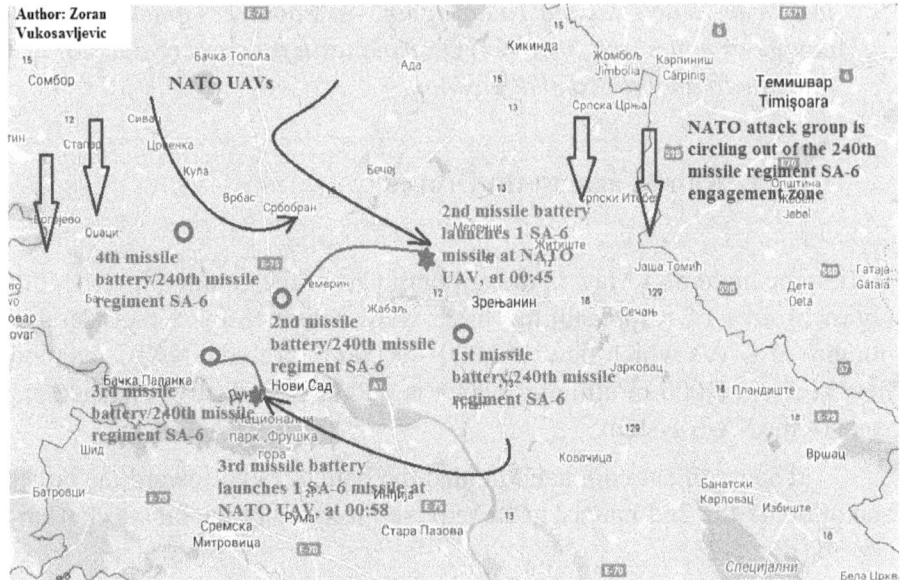

Figure 5-22: 240th regiment batteries against UAVs on 3 May 1999. (Source: Zoran Vukosavljevic).

It was not clear what type of UAV was hit that night but there are some references in the literature, like in the book 'NATO Air War for Kosovo: A Strategic and Operational Assessment' in the chapter 'Accomplishments of Air War, page 97', it is written than during the war over Yugoslavia, in total 8 US Hunter UAVs are lost: one was hit by radar-guided missile, 4 crashed because of the 'technical reasons' and 3 were shot with IR missiles. Based on this, we can assume that on the night of 3 May one Hunter was downed by the 3M9M3E missile.

Engaging the NATO airplane over Podgorica

In his own words, sergeant Zoran Vukosavljević describes this event (Fig. 5-23):

On 30 March 1999, I was on duty with my P-15 radar on the regiment command post located at one of the mountain

picks above Podgorica called Kakarička Gora. My shift ended just after midnight and I went out from the cabin to the fresh air. From my position, I could see the city from above, like it is sitting in the 'palm of my hand'. Two of my soldiers were with me. Around 00:30 we saw a missile launch from Podgorica direction, south-west from our position. We knew that our 4th battery was somewhere in that area. After few seconds, the second missile blasted off. We followed the flights of both missiles without blinking! The flight was stabile for both of them, not on the straight line, which is a clear indicator that they are guided. If there is no guidance established, the missile will fly on the ballistic trajectory. After 15-20 seconds (even that looked like an eternity for us) we saw and heard the activation of the first warhead then after few seconds the second one. We all tried to see if there are any traces in the air, like a falling fireball, scattered debris falling or any flames, but I couldn't see anything. It was very dark, and we were very far away.

Figure 5-23: 60th regiment P-15M radar at the combat position. (Source: authors).

I ran to the radar where my colleague, Lieutenant, was on duty and told him what I saw outside. He went to the command and communication car to hear what happened.

He returned after 10 minutes and told me that our 4th battery launched two missiles and hit the target. Few moments

after the engagement, they were hit with anti-radiation missile HARM but, fortunately, there were no casualties. The RStON was damaged and taken out of service but the damage can be repaired, which was done a month later and the battery was sent to Kosovo and Metohija.

After the war, I spoke with a sergeant first class who was commander of the radar and who participated in that engagement. He told me that the launch was a "school" one. The target was detected on the target detection radar, transferred to the fire control and guidance radar, the stable lock-on was established, two missiles launched and guided, and both exploded in the proximity of the target.

Now, the question is what happened with the target: was that an airplane who crashed in Albania or in the Adriatic sea, or was that airplane damaged but still managed to get out of the Yugoslav airspace and safely landed somewhere, or that was just a hit in the towed decoy is the question which is not yet answered.

There was also a rumor that it was Sea Harrier, the pilot ejected safely and was captured by Montenegro police but was immediately handed over to NATO representative in Albania because the Montenegro president wanted to please NATO and stop them to bomb any targets on the Montenegrin territory. Until today, it is still a rumor...

A few important hints: the missile trajectory is not on ballistic trajectory which means that the seeker has lock-on into the target. In other words, the missile had guidance.

The guidance is stabile meaning that the target is illuminated and tracked.

The explosion of the warhead – it appears that there were three visible distinguished flashes that associate with the warhead explosion. The first one is smaller, the second is bigger and brighter and the third one is again smaller. This is a typical event in the case of the proximity fuse activation, hit the target which causes larger and brighter light than the reflection of the fragments.

The second light trace is not associate with the antiradiation missile AGM-88 HARM rocket motor because HARM uses a smokeless component in the rocket motor so there is no visible combustion in the visible (optical) spectrum.

The most likely scenario is that it was a second airplane or a second pair which tactically make sense because one airplane or pair will attack the target while the second airplane or pair performs the cover and act as a SEAD either from F-18 or EA-6B. These aircraft were known to operate in the area: F-16CJ from Aviano and EA-6B from the aircraft carrier or from the airbase Singorela. There is also a possibility that it was F-16CJ engaged.

It is evident that the second light track suddenly took a steep dive with a sharp turn to the left for about 90 degrees or so. The size of that light

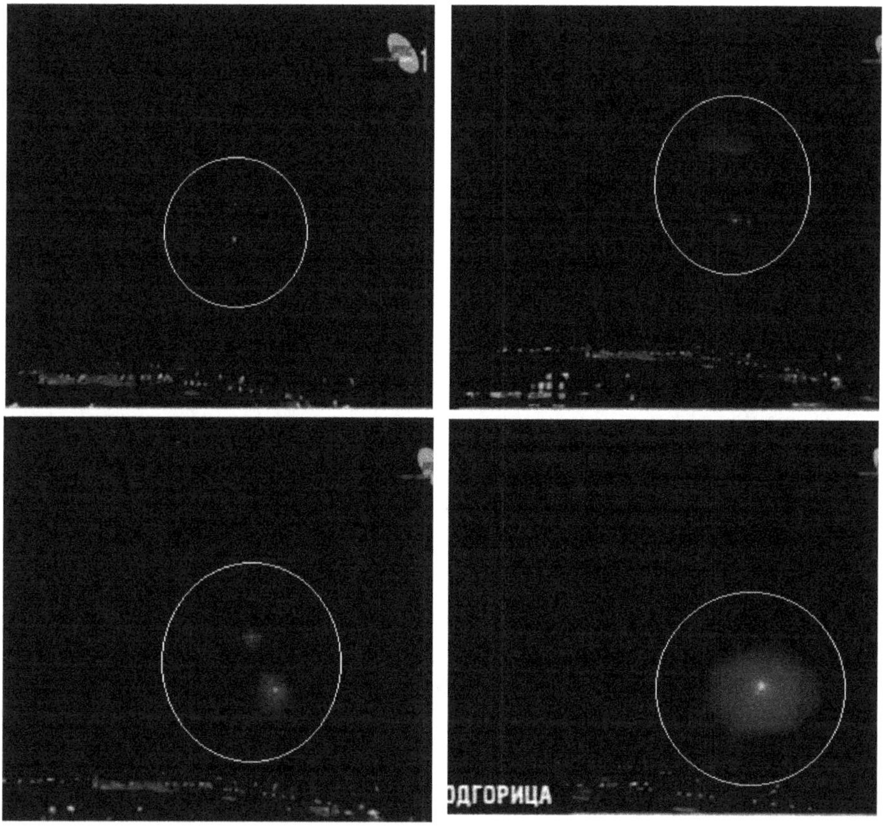

Figure 5-24: Stills from the news showing the engagement sequences (order left to right and top to bottom): the bottom right pictures shows highly illuminated object that associate with a damaged airplane in a steep dive. (Source: RTS news from 30 March 1999).

track is possible only when the airplane is at full-throttle or something is on the fire. The shape of the light track is almost round one. One of the possibilities is that the fuel tank caught fire and was jettisoned (Fig. 5-24).

If the first missile hit the target it is reasonable to estimate that the second missile also locked on into the target. If the airplane had a towed decoy such as AN/ALN-50 the second missile could easily lock on the decoy as well which the airplane can disconnect. A typical counter missile maneuver of the fighter bomber is to rapidly change the direction and go into the steep dive. In this case, if the decoy is disconnected, it would continue by inertia and follow by the missile.

The conclusion is that the first missile activated in the proximity of the target and caused significant but not total damage. The airplane was able to jettison the fuel tanks and escape but even with the light damage, it is recommended that the pilot land at the nearest "safe" airport. Even the carrier airplane will not risk landing at the sea when there are available airports within 15-20 minutes away.

The hardest night

The night of 31 May was one of the hardest ones for SA-6 units. Just before midnight on 31 May, a large group of NATO airplanes, anything between 50-80 airplanes entered into the Yugoslav airspace from Hungary heading toward Novi Sad. (Fig. 5-25)

In the vicinity of Srbobran, there were units of the 240th regiment. All units were in readiness No. 1. The corps ordered the regiment to engage incoming attackers. At 00:08 on 1 June, the forward group attacked the position of the 4th battery, which were located at Nadalj. The battery already launched 3 missiles when suddenly almost at the same moment when the third missile is launched, an anti-radiation missile struck the RStON. After that, a guided missile is launched which directly hit one of the launchers. Launcher commander, senior sergeant Dragan Bandić and reserve soldier Aleksandar Popović were unfortunately killed while the third crew member, private Ivan Petković was badly wounded. The strike group then bypass the position of the battery and went to the south Banat to patrol the line Zrenjanin-Vršac-Pančevo. Until 02:18.

In that area was 310th regiment.

Just before midnight, General Ljubiša Veličković, chief of staff of Air Force and Defense Corps came to visit the regiment. His first visit to the combat unit was the 2nd battery which was located in the vicinity of village Omoljica. With him was also Colonel Božidar Pejčić from the missile and artillery directorate. While on the battery position, they got a report that the enemy strike forces reached the area of responsibility of the 310th regiment and that previously the 240th regiment was attacked, one battery is taken out of action and there were casualties.

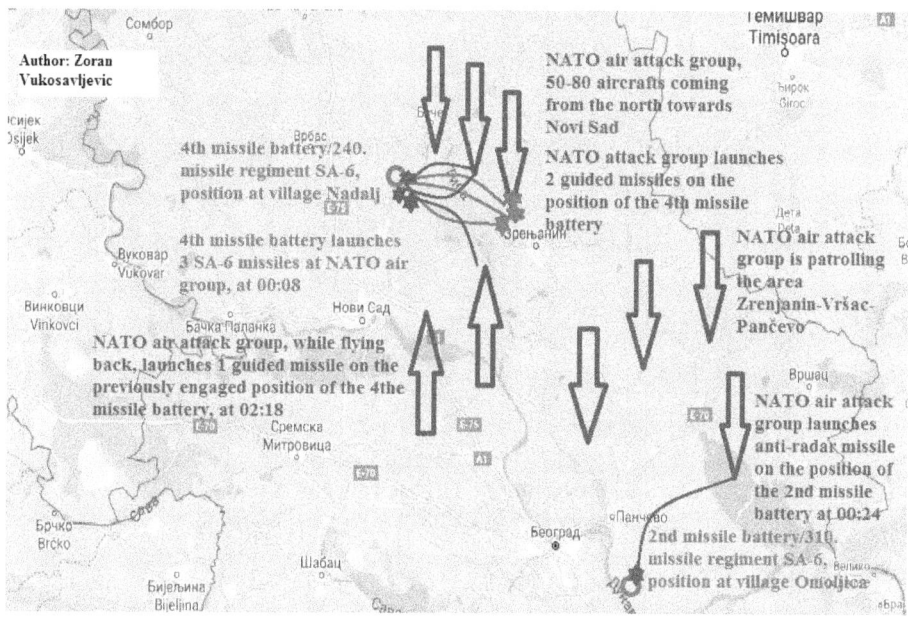

Figure 5-25: NATO attacks on 240th (near village Nadalj) and 310th regiment (near village Omoljica position). (Source: Zoran Vukosavljević).

After the arrival on the 2nd battery position, the general ordered the battery commander, Captain First Class Svetomir Trifunović, to turn on RStON and engage NATO airplanes. The captain ordered RStON to start the emission. Captain Trifunović entered into the radar and Colonel Pejčić also entered into the radar cabin and set beside him while General Veličković stayed outside observing the combat procedure through the open hatches.

At the seventh second after the radar was turned on, an anti-radiation missile struck the radar at 00:24. All three officers were killed instantly. The enemy strike force continued patrolling the area at about 8,000 m altitude until 02:00 when moved out of the zone.

During the return to their bases, this group again at 02:18 attacked the position of the 4th battery from the 240th regiment. This time already damaged RStON was hit with a laser-guided bomb. At that moment, the technical group was in the position trying to extract the bodies of the deceased and to move the other equipment. This time two officers Lieutenant Colonel Stanko Džomić and reserve Captain Jovo Pujić were wounded and, fortunately, there were no fatalities (Fig. 5-26).

Figure 5-26: RStON from one of the regiments, under NATO attack. (Source: still from NATO mission briefing)

How hard was this night the reader can see from the words of the participants of these events:

Sergeant Dano Jukić

Slightly after 23:00 on 31 May, while we were at Nadalj, we were ordered to get the battery ready for the eventual engagement that night. We were guided from the regimental HQ. Just after midnight, our RStON had a lock-on onto the enemy airplane and the battery started combat procedure for the launch. After few seconds, the first missile was launched, I went in front of my vehicle (UPPC) to see with my own eyes this battle between David and Goliath. After the third missile was blasted off from the launcher the antiradiation missile struck the radar and not long after, a bomb hit the launcher which launched the three missiles. Immediately I ordered the boys from my section to take a cover far from the vehicle until the situation is cleared. A few minutes later I called the RStON from my vehicle and asked them if they are OK. They told me they are OK and are about to leave the radar. Then I made the decision to go with my boys to the launcher that just got hit and see what the situation is there. When we arrived there, we open the hatches. There are no words that can describe what we saw there. That is something that I will remember for the rest of my life. Both commander and operator were killed instantly, and private Ivan Pavlović was badly wounded. With my soldiers, we took Ivan out. We carried him to our vehicle and gave him first aid, as much as we could, and transport him to the field hospital. At that moment at our position, a civilian Golf arrived. It was a random guy who saw that the missiles hit our position and he came to see if he can help. He told us that he was a member of the Army of Republika Srpska during the war in Bosnia and Herzegovina. We put Ivan in his car, and he drove him to the hospital in Novi Sad.

We stayed at our position. Shortly after, some guys from the regiment HQ and from the technical unit arrived. They were joined also by our regiment commander, Lieutenant Colonel Slobodan Petričković. The guard was dispatched by the undamaged launcher to observe the airspace.

Slightly after 02:00 few of us stood beside the damaged radar and talking how we can move it from the position. Medics arrived and they were around the destroyed launcher trying to extract the bodies of our fallen comrades.

At that moment, we saw a guard that was beside the undamaged launcher running toward us yelling that the enemy projectile is flying toward us. We looked at the sky and saw a projectile!!! Then the panic kicked in and we all ran as fastest as we can in all directions. Few of us, including the regiment commander, ran away from the incoming missile, while the other group, including Lieutenant Colonel Stanko Džomić, ran toward the projectile.

It happened so fast. The missile hit the radar and the shockwave kicked me to the ground. The other guys were also dropped onto the ground. We were just 10-15 meters from the

radar when the missile struck it. The shrapnel and parts from the radar flew over our heads. If we were a bit farther from the radar most likely we all would be hit. Proximity actually saved us. One of my colleagues was hit with an RStON piece right into his helmet. If he didn't wear the helmet, he could be killed. At this moment Lieutenant Colonel Džomić and Captain Pujić, who were in the other group running toward the missile were injured: Lieutenant Colonel Džomić sustained injuries and burns on the back lower extremities as well as Captain Pujić. (Fig. 5-27).

Figure 5-27: Destroyed 4th battery RStON near Nadalj village. (Source: Dano Jukić)

After this attack, for a short period of time, we left the position and took cover. Later we came back and extract the bodies of our killed comrades. In respect for their sacrifice later we erected a monument at the place where they were killed.

Senior Sergeant Vojislav Marinkov:

On that 31 May the destiny played it hard with some of us... Obeying the strict military rules valid in the peacetime partially are to blame for what happened that night.

To all of those who served the military and who knows the rigid regulations about the fuel consumption lists that need to be filled from the beginning to the end of each month, that "end

of the cycles" night at Srbobran was additionally complicated because I had to fill the tanks for additional loaders and bring the reserve troops and return the previous troops to the base camp. All I need is just additional administration besides other issues that I need to finish. I had to cross the Tisa river to get from one place to another. After the shifts were switched, just before midnight I went back to Banat side. When we got to the Novi Sad – Zrenjanin road slightly after midnight on our left-hand side, from the direction of Nadalj, we saw flashes from the launched missiles. Soon after that, at the Žabalj bridge where our crews were busy making the smoke screens people observed few pointed light traces for which later next day, I found out were AGM-88 HARM that NATO airplane launched on our missile battery. After I got to our base camp, I heard from the guard that they saw some combat going on in the area of Nadalj/Turia and that they saw an unknown large lighting object which had a curved trajectory and fell between Elemir synthetic rubber plant and the city of Zrenjanin, not far from the gas refinery in the cornfield.

That night I decided to sleep in the base because in the morning I had to be on the road to Pančevo to replace two autoloader handlers. During the night we received an information about the events in Nadalj. Our engineers were busy making the new combat position but, unfortunately, the battery wasn't able to take them anymore. At dawn, I was informed that there was also combat in the area of village Omoljica and there are casualties there. Also, the area of Village Ivanovo was also under enemy attack but nobody was hurt there.

In the morning two warrant officers from the Corps HQ came to us and told us that not far from us one of our SA-6 missiles fell and that we have to go find it and neutralize the warhead. As some guys from my crew were from the surrounding villages, we were able to quickly locate the missile. At the exit of Taraš village, a group of locals gave me the parts of one HARM missile.

That 1st of June was full of surprises. We found 5-6 HARMS scattered around. NATO launched HARMs both on arrival and during the flight back home.

In general, field camouflage worked very well during the entire war but there were situations where NATO was able to detect the real battery position and then attack.

Captain Mihajlo (Mike) Mihajlović

Immediately after I got information about the attacks I went to the field to investigate if there unexploded bombs or missiles. Locals gave us some general directions and I ordered MPs to prevent any civilians to get to that area and especially to not touch anything.

On our way there we met some guys from KUB batteries. Seemed to me that a lot of people are going around. We spoke with the other guys and they showed us some debris. It was immediately clear to me that the fragments are from AGM-88. We couldn't find warheads but tail stabilizers were almost intact. The guys took them as souvenirs.

Not long before that, I was able to get some HARM engagement manuals. Interesting material, restricted use, describing how F-16C/D employs the missile. I sent these materials directly to our intelligence guys. Didn't get any feedback from them. I wondered how much are they able to extract from the printouts. Based on the overall state, probably not too much. Hardly anybody in the 'chain' speaks English. Ideally, it got in the hands of some technical intelligence people who prepared briefings for the AD field units. That would be 'mission goal achieved'.

When the speed of handling information is more important than approval from some HQ parasites. Previously I bypassed the chain of command with some material related to the employment of US MLRS and sent it directly to the Priština Corps intelligence guys. I had to use an intercity bus driver to hand over printed material to my buddy in Belgrade who handed them to the Priština Corps boys that sent a driver to pick them up. By the evening, they were already down there. Effective way, almost private initiative, avoiding the complex and sometimes useless chain of command and it worked well. For that I got my 'wrist slammed' but who cares - boys there were able to extract what they need and NATO MLRS didn't cause any damage.

 *2K12 Kub/SA-6 in NATO aggression*

On 14 April one battery from the 310th regiment was hit not far from Debrc village. After NATO located the battery position, one airplane launched AGM-130 on the PES-100 power supply generator van. Unfortunately, private Zoran Virijević was killed instantly. After the aggregate was destroyed, NATO airplanes launched AGM-130 missiles on the battery radar. This attack was most likely carried on by US F-15E.

Counter missile maneuver by RStON

Sergeant Zoran Vukosavljević (Fig. 5-28)

Figure 5-28: Sergeant Zoran Vukosavljević in front of missile transport truck 2T7M. (Source: Zoran Vukosavljević)

Somewhere between 26 April and 29 April, NATO fiercely bombed the Golubovci airport and surrounding military objects. Especially hard were the attacks on the nights of 26 and 27 April.

One of these nights I slept with other NCO, officers and soldiers from my unit in a building about one hundred meters from the radar position.

We were wakened up by an extremely strong noise that was similar to the thunder. We were just 20-30 kilometers away from the Golubovci airport and could hear everything very well. I went out of the building with one Junior Lieutenant and a private and walked to our P-15 radar. From there we could see the

bombing of the airport. Suddenly, west of us, we saw a "lightning flash" rising from the ground and heading toward the enemy airplanes. A few seconds later, the second one followed. We knew that our buddies from the 1st missile battery fired on the enemy.

We didn't know what the outcome of the launches was but what we saw was that the NATO airplanes stopped momentarily with the attack.

Just a few weeks before the end of the war, I was ordered to join the 1st missile battery which was at that time located in the wider area of Belgrade. My duty was to be missile launcher section commander. In the off-duty time, I asked few guys about that engagement over Golubovci. Senior Sergeant Dača, who is an expert for 1S91 RStON radar told me that they were able to lock on onto the target. The shift commander, Lieutenant Riki, tried to launch the missiles but the command link from RStON couldn't get to the launcher. He then ordered the first launcher, which commander is, by the way my, classmate and friend sergeant Gliša, to manually launch the missile from the launcher. Gliša pushed the button and the missile blasted off from the launcher. After that Lieutenant Riki, ordered the commander of the second launcher to manually launch the second missile. Dača told me that he tracked the target and in one moment he noticed that the target launched the HARM anti-radiation missile toward them. He immediately informed Lieutenant about this and suggested anti-radiation missile evasive maneuver with antennas and turning off the radar emission. HARM missed the radar for a couple of hundreds of meters. Fortunately, nobody was hurt, nor any equipment damaged.

I thought to myself, how lucky was my classmate Gliša to manually and personally launch the missile from the launcher. Taking into consideration that I don't know if that error was corrected maybe it will be a good opportunity for me to launch one missile from my launcher, which would be a great pleasure for me!

Fire control battery

Sergeant Zoran Vukosavljević:

In the first half of April, the first long-range surveillance radar 1RL128D the 'Bear' and the altitude finder PRV-16 radars were sent to assist the 311th regiment in Kosovo. Since that moment my radar P-15 became the main radar of the 60th regiment.

On 15 April, in the middle of the day suddenly the attack started. We were in readiness No. 3 and P-15 radar from the light artillery regiment in the Masline garrison was working. We shared the shifts with that radar – one time it was our turn, and the next time it was theirs. They didn't see anything on their screens, and we were caught virtually with our pants down. Immediately we got an order to get into readiness No. 1. Both Lieutenant Laza and I were in the cabin. The radar was jammed with the active jamming noise and we couldn't discriminate any target in that noise. Automatic noise sweeper which was part of the DGBSO – digital noise remover) was able to lower the intensity of the noise for a bit but that didn't help us a lot.

We worked for about 45 minutes when we got an order to switch to readiness No. 3. The danger is over. We went out from the cabin then somebody told us that we were ordered to turn off the radar not because the danger is over but because the P-15 radar from the light artillery regiment was targeted with a Maverick guided missile but the missiles missed the cabin for about 5-6 meters. The radar was just "brushed" a bit. The damage was minimal, and it can be put in the service right away.

We found out that they were at the same position where we were before and from that position, we had some radar emissions. The position was very well prepared by the engineering units and that was probably the reason that they survived.

The bitter experience was that there was no real coordination between the two regiments and a mistake was that nobody from our regiment told the other regiment that we were already at that position and had an emission and probably that was recorded by NATO ELINT.

A few days later, a sergeant from that light artillery unit and radar commander came to visit us and we decided to communicate with each other and not to take previously used positions. It was a good decision because these errors were never *repeated again.*

The engagement tactics with P-15 was that we typically had three full circles (around 30 seconds) of radar emission than three cycles on the equivalent without any emission (30 seconds again) and so on. We planned the radar emissions: when the targets get into the "zone 50" (meaning that they are in 50 km zone) we run two cycles (about 20 seconds) than one cycle on equivalent (about 10 seconds). This means that we lowered the cycles of "on" and "off" of electromagnetic emission in space. We also avoided any patterns that can be easy recorded as well as the azimuth templates when turning the high voltage on and off. We also changed the working templates of the surveillance zones by height and regime (Fig. 5-29).

Figure 5-29: P-15 radar in working position.
(Source: 'Stalin Line' museum, Belarus)

This was an important moment – we stick to these agreed schemes of the radar operations to the end of the war. All in all, we were actively engaged for about 55 days, with 12 hours per day on "antenna" or "equivalent" (two shifts of six hours). Our radar was never hit and together with a crew, it survived the war.

Aftermath

"With regard to President Clinton's third objective — deflating Serb military capabilities — Milosevic's forces, particularly the land forces that are the bedrock of his military strength, remain intact. NATO's operational and tactical defeat."

Dr. E.Tilford [59]

The Yugoslav Air Defense System survived the NATO air campaign to force the removal of Serbian forces from Kosovo, which ran from 24 March to 9 June 1999 and at its height involved over 1,000 aircraft. Survival of the IADS was achieved by employing three different methods to negate NATO's air power. The NATO decision not to use ground forces certainly made Serb defensive measures much easier. By deliberately not employing all their defense assets at once, known as the strategy of withholding military force, the Yugoslavs could move their mobile surface-to-air missiles about to ensure they could not be targeted.

A defending ground force needs to be forced to expose itself, thus allowing it to be attacked by air power. A major lesson NATO learned was that an opposing force must be driven out from cover. One option is to stage an attack that is designed to compel a defending force to react. To enable air power to hunt down and destroy targets requires robust Intelligence, Surveillance and Reconnaissance (ISR) systems and Precision Guided Munitions (PGM). Terrain masking and deception measures by small forces in complex terrains, such as hilly and/or woodland terrain, as occurred in Kosovo and in the various conflicts in South East Asia, often negate the use of ISR systems, presenting difficulties in locating and positively identifying targets.

The aim of Operation Allied Force was 'to stop Serbian forces attacking' ethnic Albanians and eject them from Kosovo through the application of air power alone. This was to reduce casualties on the NATO side, but it made life for the Serbian forces in Kosovo easier as there were no ground troops to worry about, except KLA separatists and a few NATO special forces either fighting with the KLA or independently. By withhold-

---

59   Operation Allied Force and the Role of Air Power.
https://press.armywarcollege.edu/parameters/vol29/iss4/10/

ing military force the Serbs avoided having their air defense and field units being destroyed in the first days of the air campaign. They had absorbed the lessons of Operation Desert Storm and preserved their assets for the long haul. This was a successful strategy: Serb forces were still firing surface-to-air missiles on the last day of Operation Allied Force. Employing passive systems such as electro-optical tracking equipment further enhanced the survivability of IADS components, by not creating an emission signature that NATO defense suppression aircraft could lock on to.

Bad weather and the 'rigid' insistence on avoiding collateral damage and casualties to the attack force dogged NATO planners. It led to an over-reliance on Precision Guided Munitions (PGMs). In the first three weeks of Allied Force there were only seven days of favorable weather for air operations and ten days on which fifty per cent of the strikes had to be canceled for fear of collateral damage.

Ninety per cent of the ordnance dropped was PGMs which had their own problems. GPS-aided munitions, the only affordable all-weather munitions, can be inaccurate due to the cumulative effect of numerous errors, as well as small inaccuracies in the targeting aircraft, maps and the munition itself. This is called the 'sensor-to-shooter error budget' in US parlance. Further, the amount of cloud over Kosovo caused many laser-guided bombs (LGBs) to 'lose lock' and 'go rogue' often landing kilometers away from their intended target or hitting civilian targets.

The reliance on GPS guided bombs caused a shortage that became so acute in late April that the GPS guided Joint Direct Attack Munitions (JDAM) were available for only the B-2A Spirit bomber. By late April the ratio of PGMs to unguided munitions used had dropped to 69 per cent. Many of the targets struck by PGMs in Kosovo were not judged to be worth the cost of US$12,000 per Paveway II bomb kit (the price tag at the time), and could have been hit safely by unguided ordnance. The fire control avionics fitted to most NATO aircraft enabled very accurate bombing using 'dumb' bombs, albeit with a necessary reduction in bombing altitude.

Serbian ground forces were hard to locate due to their small unit size and movement, generally being company-sized units of 80 to 150 personnel and around six armored vehicles, operating autonomously or semi-autonomously of each other. Using the woods and mountains, and by not being a large target or moving in a set direction, prevented the building up of an intelligence picture and thus made these forces difficult to locate from the air.

The air campaign over Kosovo severely affected the readiness rates of the USAF's Air Combat Command during that period. Units in the United States were the most badly affected, as they were stripped of their personnel and spare parts to support ACC (Air Combat Command) and AMC (Air Mobility Command) units involved in Operation Allied Force. The Commander of the USAF's Air Combat Command, General Richard Hawley, outlined this in a speech to reporters on 29 April 1999. Further, aircraft would have to be replaced earlier than previously planned, PGM inventories would need to be restocked, and the war-stock of AGM-86C Conventional Air-Launched Cruise Missiles dropped to 100 rounds or fewer. Of the more than 25,000 bombs and missiles expended, nearly 8,500 were PGMs, with the replacement cost estimated at $US1.3 billion.

Thus the USAF suffered from virtual attrition of its air force without having scored a large number of kills in theatre. Even if the US's best estimates of Serbian casualties are used, the Serbians left Kosovo with a large part of their armored forces intact.

Successful Deception Measures

Sun Tzu wrote that all warfare is based on deception. Serbian deception measures were very successful. Decoys were a real problem for strike aircraft, as loitering over an area at low altitude made them targets for MANPADS, infrared guided point defense SAMs such as the SA-9 Gaskin and SA-13 Gopher, and SPAAGs such as the BOV-3/30 series and the Praga M53/59. Hundreds of decoys were hit that were thought to be real targets. Some decoys were hit multiple times. Pilots would not loiter over them trying to discriminate between them and real targets. Air forces have not always invested sufficiently in sensors to counter deception and camouflage techniques, and the Serbs exploited this quite successfully; this was noted in the post-Allied Force after-action study (Fig 5-30, 5-31, 5-32, 5-33 and 5-34).

NATO flew approximately 30,000 sorties during the war, and just under 2,000 of these saw ordnance expended. These sorties were claimed at the time to have destroyed 93 tanks and 153 armored personnel carriers (APCs) out of the approximately 350 tanks and 440 APCs believed to have been in Kosovo. NATO also claimed to have hit 339 military vehicles and

389 artillery pieces and mortars. These figures were wide of the mark, as General Clark, the Operation Allied Force commander, agreed, conceding that not all targets hit were destroyed, and that only twenty-six vehicles could be confirmed as kills.

In a New York Times article, there was an interesting view immediately after the war[60]:

> *Towards the end of the Balkans air war, rarely a day passed when NATO did not triumphantly declare that allied warplanes had destroyed several more Yugoslav tanks or artillery pieces with precision-guided bombs or missiles.*
>
> *Now it turns out that a significant fraction of those weapons that looked fearsome from 15,000 feet up may have been nothing more than artfully designed decoys meant to fool allied pilots. Indeed, the Serb military, outgunned by a technologically superior foe, proved to be a master of camouflage, concealment and deception. Yugoslav commanders built 'tanks' of wood and plastic sheeting, sometimes draping them with camouflage netting. To trick thermal sensors, they put metal tape or plates on some decoys and even set trays of water inside them that heated up in the sun, just like a real tank would.*
>
> *Some suspected artillery revetments turned out to be disguised pits, empty but for a long tube protruding towards the sky. And to the dismay of the NATO air commanders, several Yugoslav MIG-21 fighter jets emerged from hidden caves once the war was over.*
>
> *Of course, the air campaign's overall results were still devastating and no doubt instrumental in forcing the Yugoslav President Slobodan Milosević to cry uncle and withdraw his forces from Kosovo.*
>
> *But the phony targets have become a sore point with NATO's military commander, General Wesley K. Clark, who now says the alliance destroyed only 110 of the roughly 300 tanks that Yugoslavia poured into Kosovo, not the 150 tanks NATO initially thought it blasted into scrap.*

---

60   Eric Schmidt, 'The World; Bombs Are Smart, People Are Smarter', New York Times, 4 July 1999.

'For the most part, our pilots recognized those decoys,' General Clark bristled last week. *'There is a concerted disinformation campaign underway by the Government of Yugoslavia to protect the reputation of its armed forces and to diminish the reputation of NATO's air power campaign.'*

Yet one of the emerging lessons from the air war is that low-technology countermeasures can still fool high-technology weaponry and sensors enough of the time to make a difference. *'The history of warfare suggests there are always countermeasures, and human ingenuity will find its way,'* said Eliot A. Cohen, a professor at Johns Hopkins who directed the Air Force's definitive study of the 1991 Persian Gulf war.

'One of the big surprises was the extent to which the Yugoslav military was able to use ground decoys to cause us to strike targets that weren't real,' said one senior Defense Department official.

Serbian techniques included constructing false bridges, fake artillery pieces made of long telephone poles painted black with old truck wheels, anti-aircraft missile launchers constructed of old milk cartons, wooden mock-ups of MIG-29 aircraft, self-propelled artillery vehicles

Figure 5-30: 1S91 RStON plywood model. (Source: authors)

207

constructed on old vehicle shells and chassis from the scrapyards, radar reflectors and special camouflage nets (developed by one of the authors) around the real military equipment, extensive use of field camouflage, to name but a few. Some of the ingenious deceptions included cow manure in combination with metal plates to attract NATO thermal guided missiles. Manure naturally radiates heat similar to the heat radiation signature of a tank engine. Real tank engines were often covered with mattresses soaked

Figure 5-31: S-125 missile launcher decoy. (Source: authors)

Figure 5-32: Decoy field painting. (Source: authors)

with water to lower the thermal radiation. One of the authors designed thermal sleeves for artillery and tank cannons to prevent thermal emission detection after firing. To quote a NATO officer who performed field assess-

Figure 5-33: T-55 decoy equipped with a wooden log as a cannon. Decoy is covered with straw and manure. The manure during the biochemical reaction emits a similar thermal signature to the tank engine. (Source: authors)

Figure 5-34: AAA 3x20 M55 cannon with the mannequin crew decoy. (Source: authors)

ments after the war: 'Our guys in Kosovo have found hundreds of imitation tanks, trucks, artillery pieces, missiles and missile launchers, roads and even bridges that NATO aircraft and cruise missiles had "destroyed". From up close they look like junk, but from three miles up, they'd look like the real thing.'

In particular, radar imitators played a crucial role in the survival of the missile battalions, and in cooperation with fire control radar emission successfully defended the missile battalion when under attack. In today's air defense, radar imitators are a standard issue for every missile battalion. Russian battalions may use six or more imitators per unit (Fig. 5-13).

Fixed Air Defenses Damaged but Mobile Air Defenses Survived

NATO air planners were certainly concerned that not as many Serbian SAM batteries were destroyed as they would have liked, with the then commander of the USAF in Europe acknowledging the success of Serbian SAM battery shoot-and-scoot operational tactics.

Mobile systems suffered few casualties, but the fixed defenses were badly damaged. Two of Serbia's three static S-75 Dvina/SA-2 Guideline SAM battalions and seventy per cent of their static S-125 Neva/SA-3 Goa SAM sites were hit and most taken out of action. Some of the systems were damaged but repaired after.

Serbia certainly left Kosovo and suffered a tremendous amount of damage to its infrastructure in Serbia, but Serbian combat power remained substantially intact. Even if the Milosevic regime did not achieve its political objectives Serbia retained its ground combat strength in the face of overwhelming air power, and the Kosovo Liberation Army was 'disarmed' as part of the political settlement.

NATO expended a total of 743 AGM-88 HARM anti-radiation missile rounds, launched by EA-6B Prowlers, F-16CJ Weasels and Tornado ECRs. The most notable aspect of this chart is that more than 50% of HARMs were fired at mobile SA-6 batteries, which suffered the lowest attrition of any Serbian radar guided SAM type. At least twenty-two HARM missiles were launched against the 3rd battalion (S-125/SA-3) without any hit (Fig. 5-35 and 5-36).

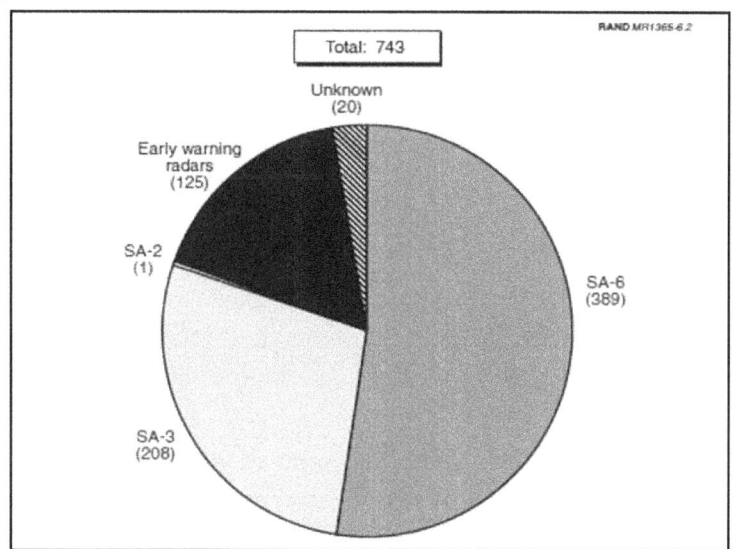

*Figure 5-35: AGM-88 HARM missiles launched against Yugoslav air defense..
(Source: AWOS Fact Sheets via www.ausairpower.net)*

*Figure 5-36: AGM-88 HARM missiles hit at 1S91 radar. Damage immobilized
the unit but later it was repaired and returned into service.
(Source: authors)*

As per NATO statistics, a total of 815 SAMs were fired at NATO aircraft, of which 665 were radar guided SA-3 and SA-6 rounds. Out of them, F-16CG and F-117A were downed and several other aircraft sustained significant or moderate damage through hit or near miss. Many SAM shots were unguided due to the radar shutting down to avoid HARM shots. (Source: AWOS Fact Sheet via www.ausairpower.net).

NATO and Serbian sources about the quantity of missiles launched are very different: the Serbian side launched a total of 163 SA-3 and SA-6 missiles (according to the material lists of expended ammunition). The Serbs also launched 168 missiles from portable shoulder launchers (MAN-PAD).

At the end of hostilities, the situation in the SA-6 missile units was not the easy one. Garrisons and bases including the infrastructure were destroyed or damaged.

From the 20 batteries at the beginning of the war, at the end 13 were fully operational and combat ready which represent 65%. This number is extraordinary taking into consideration what forces were applied against them. The fact is that there were only 47 launches, but the question is what could happen to the army units, especially in Kosovo and Metohija territory without this umbrella. The estimates made by the air defense command before the war was that all missile units, including the air force and air surveillance services can resist maximum 21 days. In the end, that estimate was exceeded three times.

Taking this into consideration and the mistakes made by the higher and lower commands, the SA-6 units deserve the passing marks, even with the higher standards because after the 78 days of bombing they kept 2/3 of the entire system force operational.

The official day for the end of the war is 24 June. During the aggression, 15 1S91 RStON units were hit and damaged. The majority of these units were repaired and returned to the service during the war. On the day when the war ended, SA-6 units had on their disposal 13 1S91 RStON radars and two are repaired in a weeks after so it gave the total number of 15 functional and combat-ready batteries (Fig. 5-37).

Heavy damage or full destruction sustained 4-5 units (depends on which source is used). These units are considered irrevocable loses because there was no feasible possibility for any repairs. One unit was written off because of the damage sustained during the traffic accident. According to the sources from the book: "NATO's Air War for Kosovo: A Strategic and Operational Assessment" chapter 6, page 110 during the whole campaign,

NATO launched 389 anti-radiation missiles and a considerable number of guided and unguided bombs against SA-6 units succeeding to take out of service just a few 1S91 RStON radar units which neutralize fire-power of just a few batteries.

Figure 5-37: Kub changing position during the war, Kosovo 1999. (Source: authors)

The other list of equipment that is hit includes 4 out of 5 engaged radars 1RL128D which were all repaired and returned to service. Two PRV-16B height finder radars were also damaged and one PRV-9. One of the command and control units is also damaged and written of. In total four launchers were destroyed and three damaged and repaired later. Two P-15 radars are destroyed and one damaged but repaired.

NATO engaged a considerable number of most modern fighter bombers and other assets in an attempt to find and destroy SA-6 units and had absolute advantage and control in the airspace but was never able to inflict any heavy casualties to the military units on the ground. During NATO briefings and conferences, streams of video clips showing hits on military equipment were presented to the public but after the war it was confirmed that a vast majority of these clips were just a hit into the well-placed decoys. This was already mentioned in the previous sections.

Statistic of the SA-6 engagements is as follow :

In total, SA-6 units launched at 47 targets with 70 missiles. 17 launches were with the use of the K-1M system, 16 with TOV, 10 was

combined and three in autonomous mode.

Missile consumption:
- one missile launched on 27 targets
- two missiles launched on 18 targets
- three and more missiles launched on 2 targets

The unit engagement is as follow:
- 60th regiment – 5 targets with 7 missiles
- 230th regiment – 11 targets with 15 missiles
- 240th regiment – 13 targets with 17 missiles
- 310th regiment – 6 targets with 9 missiles
- 311th – 12 targets with 22 missiles

The first SA-6 missile was launched by 1/230 on 26 March at 02:35. The last was performed by 2/230 on 2 June at 22:00.

It was previously mentioned that 19 members of the SA-6 units lost their lives in the NATO aggression. 32 were wounded. The losses by units are as follow:
- 60th regiment – 1 wounded
- 230th regiment – 4 killed, 6 wounded
- 240th regiment – 5 killed, 5 wounded, 1 injured
- 310th regiment – 4 killed, 7 wounded
- 311th regiment – 6 killed, 11 wounded

All of these killed, and wounded were just ordinary people, loyal to their oath and their country to the end.

According to the official data published by the air defense corps and based on the parametric analyses and eyewitnesses' reports, in total 13 airplanes, 2 helicopters and 2 UAVs were hit. It is important to say that for now there were no material evidence in the form of airplane wrecks, debris or other parts found on the Yugoslavian territory.

After the "Kumanovo agreement", the 311th regiment, which was based in Kosovo, was disbanded and the troops and equipment assigned to the other regiments.

How the return to the peacetime location looked like in the own

words of one of the 60th regiment members:

Sergeant Zoran Vukosavljević

By the end of June, we got an order to be ready for the march. We're going back to our garrison in Danilovgrad. This means that our 60th regiment is going to continue as a unit even we heard some rumors that we will stay in Serbia. A considerable number of SA-6 batteries were repaired and returned to service. We will continue our duties with 4 Kub missile regiments.

As the 311th regiment is disbanded, its batteries were sent to other regiments. Our marching order was to gather at the Dubinje airport, near Sjenica and from there the whole regiment will march as one unit to Danilvgrad. I was on my P-15 radar and we drove to the beautiful landscape of Šumadija. Here and there we could see signs of war – a destroyed bridge, factory ruins or damaged houses.

After some hours we finally reached Sjenica. After so many hours in the cabin on the uncomfortable seat, my back was stiff. I went out to stretch my legs when I saw my roommate and friend, sergeant Baki. We haven't seen each other since the beginning of the war and with our day leaves to get back to our apartment in Podgorica we passed each other. He was later transferred to Kosovo and Metohija, We spent the time talking and listening to the basketball match.

We got accommodation in the army barracks in Sjenica, if that can be called accommodation: not a single piece of window glass stayed unbroken. There were numerous craters from NATO bombs, and we were told not to go to the grass fields because nobody knows if there are any unexploded munition there. That night was bitterly cold even it was July. We had to sleep in our jackets. I will never forget that night because in the morning for two hours I felt a pain in my bones and kidneys. I was so cold that it seemed that I have a fever.

Later that day we got an order to form a marching column and hit the road. Everything was there – all our batteries, the 'Bear' radar, height finder PRV-16, launchers...

In northern Montenegro, people went out to the road to

see us. They waved to us and we waved to them. They looked happy that we are back. At that time the political situation between the Serbian and Montenegrin governments wasn't good. At least people here, in the north, liked us.

In the morning hours, we got to our garrison in Danilovgrad. In front of the main gate there's a new pub and coffee bar. Our guys from the logistics units were there, waiting for us. They stayed in the garrison for the entire war. We hug each other... it was an exciting time. For good luck we drank a few beers and brandies.

After that we entered the garrison... this was the first time that I had an opportunity to have a close look... two large craters were in the paved ground. Our hangar roof was full of holes. That is not a big deal because it was just a corrugated roof and relatively easy to replace. Seemed to me that the structural columns were not damaged. One crater was just in front of our launchers parking garage. Taking into consideration that was built with bricks, the damage wasn't too bad... missing roof tiles here and there, but that was it.

We went to the 326th artillery brigade hangar, the one that was hit on the very first night with Tomahawk and one of our comrades killed there. We took a step measures from that hangar to our shelter and it was around 40 steps. Our accommodation space was not hit and except for broken glass, everything looked ok. The glass windows can be replaced though... We concluded that taking into consideration all of those Tomahawks and bombs, our garrison wasn't damaged so bad. I just wondered where the government will find money to repair all that was damaged.

The peace is finally kicking in and we are at home...

After the war, Yugoslav air defense was weaker than the surrounding countries. Our equipment was an old one and worn in war. There was no money for any new equipment. The situation was bleak. That situation didn't change for years to come.

Renaming Yugoslavia to Serbia and Montenegro in February 2003 didn't change anything. That was an entrance into the 'divorce' of the two remaining republics of the once known great Yugoslavia. Next year 60th regiment was withdrawn to Serbia and disbanded. Equipment was transferred to other regiments. In 2006 Montenegro held a referendum where they decided to take independence. That was the end.

When Serbia finally got their 'freedom' that was lost in 1918 when the new country was formed after WWI, Serbia actually got her independence back. All military units became parts of the Army of Serbia. It was the time when reorganization and tiny modernization kicked in. Today

Figure 5-38: Serbian 2P25 launcher after the war. (Source: authors).

there are three 2K12/SA-6 regiments – 230th, 240th and 310th. All missile units of the Serbian army are under the command of the 250th air defense brigade. Serbia started with its own capacities modernization that includes the digitalization of the 1RL128D and 1S91 radars and a new thermal vision system instead of the TV system (Fig. 5-38 and 5-39). More about Serbian modernization can be found in the following Chapter.

Figure 5-39: Kub battery of Serbian army at the exhibition.
(Source: authors)

CHAPTER SIX

2K12 Kub/Kvadrat modernization

2K12/SA-6 after 50+ years in service in many countries is, by modern standards, obsolete nowadays, however, replacement of the air defense system is a very expensive task. Modernization and upgrades are some of the cost-effective measures but modernization has certain limitations. Because of the costs, many countries decided to keep their old AD systems and try to improve their present capabilities. It is also less expensive to utilize already trained operators who are currently trained to operate these systems than to teach them the operation of new types of equipment.

We already saw in the previous chapters about the improvements of the 2K12/SA-6 system in the Soviet service. As the 2K12 systems are still in use in many countries worldwide including the former Warsaw Pact countries which are now members of NATO, some NATO member countries decided to modernize the generic systems for their forces as well as to offer the improved systems to the foreign customers. Besides NATO countries, some other countries also prepared indigenous modernizations.

Ukrainian modernization

Kwadrat 2D system is a modernized and digitalized Russian 2K12 Kub SAM, developed by the Ukrainian 'Ukrobrononservice' company. The said system is quite popular in Poland as well. Modernization resulted in a significant increase in the detection range and increased reliability. Secondly, the target detection time has been significantly reduced.

2K12-2D Kwadrat 2D system (Fig. 6-1) was presented during the Kielce salon in a form of a modified 2P25M launcher, along with the 1S91M1 radar station. In both cases the changes covered mainly replacement of the elements that have been developed 50 years ago, with the use of modern, digitalized components. This is a similar modernization, like the one implemented in the case of the Polish Newa-SC systems, modernized by the Zielonka-based WZE (Military Electronic Works JSC) facility.

As a result of the Ukrainian modernization and 'digitalization', Kub's operational reliability was improved, operations and maintenance are easier, costs and workload required to operate the system were reduced. Additionally, the system was fitted with a simulation component which makes it possible to reduce the cost of training. The option of detecting the targets with the use of optronic devices, including thermal vision, was also implemented.

Figure 6-1: 2K12-2D Kwadrat-2D. (Source: Ukrobrononservice)

According to the data provided by the manufacturer, the 2K12-2D Kwadrat-2D system is capable of detecting 4th generation fighters at distances of up to 38 kilometers (in comparison with the prior range of 30 kilometers). Secondly, the launcher is capable of detecting low-flying cruise missiles, at distances exceeding 20 kilometers. Automated data transmission also shortened the reaction time two to four times – starting from the moment of detecting and identifying the target, to the event of launch. This offers an increased probability of neutralizing the threat – the level has gone up from 60-80 to 85%.

The above is not a solution that will make it possible for the obsolete missile system to compete against its state-of-the-art counterparts. However, the modernization package gives the less wealthy users a chance to increase the capabilities of the system.

Lithuanian modernization

Lithuanian company 'LiTak-Tak' performed modernization and upgrades that as a major program includes (Fig. 6-2):

Figure 6-2: Lithuanian 2K12-ML 'Kvadrat-ML'. (Source: LiTakTak)

- Improved survivability and control capabilities.
- New data processing algorithms.
- Increased engagement and kill envelopes.
- New GPS-based positioning and navigation system.
- Significantly reduced maintenance and power consumption.
- Crew protection from HARM.

Upgrades are up to the level of 2K12-ML "Kvadrat-ML" and performed to meet the following objectives:

- Restore service life of the SAM to 15 years by replacement of 99% of old component base with the new one.
- Increase combat capabilities through application of high performance computers, ability to conduct effective combat operations and destroy all classes of air targets in the complex

jamming environment.
- Increase reliability up to 1,500 hours of MTBF.
- Reduce power consumption.
- Reduce the crew.
- Simplify SAM operation procedures.

Composition:
- Self-propelled reconnaissance and guidance radar 1S91-ML;
- Self-propelled launcher 2P25-ML – 4 units;
- Transporting-loading vehicle 2T7M – 2 sets;
- Spare parts, tools and accessories kit.

Supporting systems:
- Remote command and control post (RCCP);
- Technical battery;
- External power supply;
- Radars P-18ML / MARS-L / PRV-16ML

Iraqi missile modernization

One of the interesting local modernization was performed in Iraq. After the invasion and occupation in 2003, US forces found original Iraqi modification. This Iraqi version includes hybridization of the 3M9 missile with a seeker section from the Molniya/Vympel R–60/AA–8 Aphid heat-seeking air–to–air missile (Fig. 6-3).

What is interesting in this hybridization is that the resulting heat-seeking 3M9 missile would retain similar susceptibility to flares or infrared jammers but the whole engagement sequence would be devoid of the CW illumination for the terminal phase of the missile's flight. As a result, the target would only have the command uplink signals and terminal phase from 1S91 tracking signals detected by the radar warning receiver to warn about the approaching missile. While the defensive countermeasures equipment relies on the continuous wave (CW) signal to jam the detected missile seeker, the heat seeking head would not be detected which could be potentially very effective and basically catch the target off-guard.

What is interesting in this development is that the technical people (engineers and designers) were able to rebuild missile, and mix its capability with another one to create an entirely new capability, which makes it more dangerous, mainly when no one is expecting this type of variant from the original one. For now, it is not known how advanced this modified missile was or if it was ever used during Operation Iraqi Freedom nor how effective it was but based on the sheer capabilities of the 3M9 missile and heat seeker from the R-60 missile it is realistic to conclude that the pilots in the airplane equipped with a standard missile jamming equipment shall always take in consideration that there is a modified heat seeking variants around.

Figure 6-3: Iraqi modification - combination of 3M9 missile with a heat seeker from R-60 air-to-air missile.

Romanian modernization

In Romania, 2K12/SA-6 is categorized as the medium range system. The idea of Romanian modernization is to equip the system with the different types of missiles.

Three different types of missiles are loaded on the 2P25 launcher.

Romanians installed ESSM, Spyder–MR and 3M9. This version includes the mounting beams modifications to affix the desired missile launching beams.

Czech Republic modernization

The Czech company Retia and the French company MBDA offers modernized SA–6 system with upgraded 1S91 Straight Flush radar, in which almost the whole system - the 1S11 and 1S31 surveillance and fire control radar electronics, target illuminator - have been upgraded and now have a new communication system and new operators' workstations (Fig. 6-4, 6-5, 6-6 and 6-7).

Figure 6-4: Czech modification - Main visual upgrade is Aspide 2000 missile containers installed on the 2P25 launcher. (Source: Retia)

1S91 vehicle upgrade starts with the repair of chassis and superstructure. The original equipment is subsequently replaced by new subsystems and cable trees. New units are installed into modified original frames. This huge replacement allows optimization on system level, performance and reliability improvement. Commander's and fire control radar operator's consoles are designed to reduce the complexity of the operation and the operator's load. Operators do decision and setting tasks, while routine tasks are performed by software. All units include built-in test equipment (BITE) for easier maintenance and repair. All BITE reports are collected and presented on the commander's console.

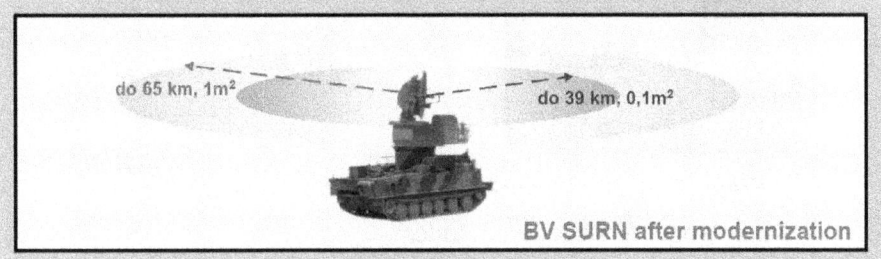

Figure 6-5: 1S91 SURN modernization (Source: Retia)

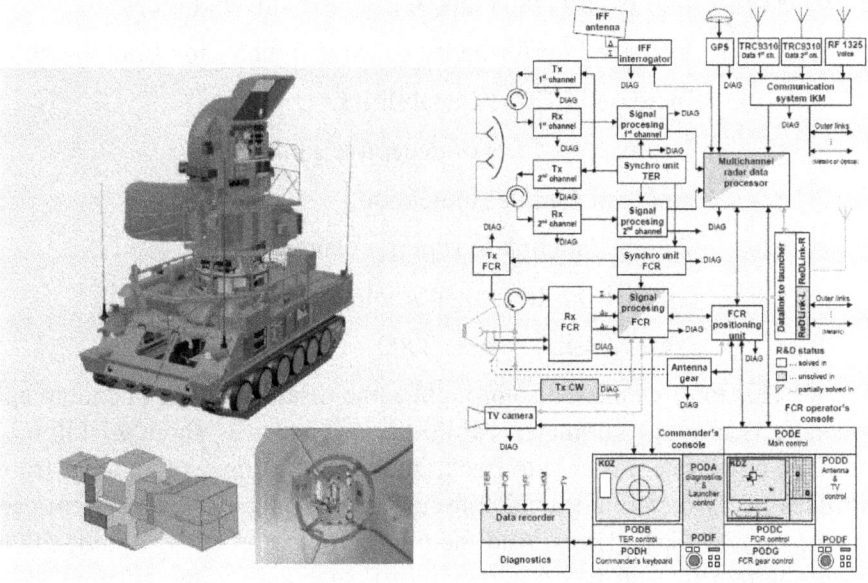

Figure 6-6: 1S91 SURN demonstrator (Source: Retia)

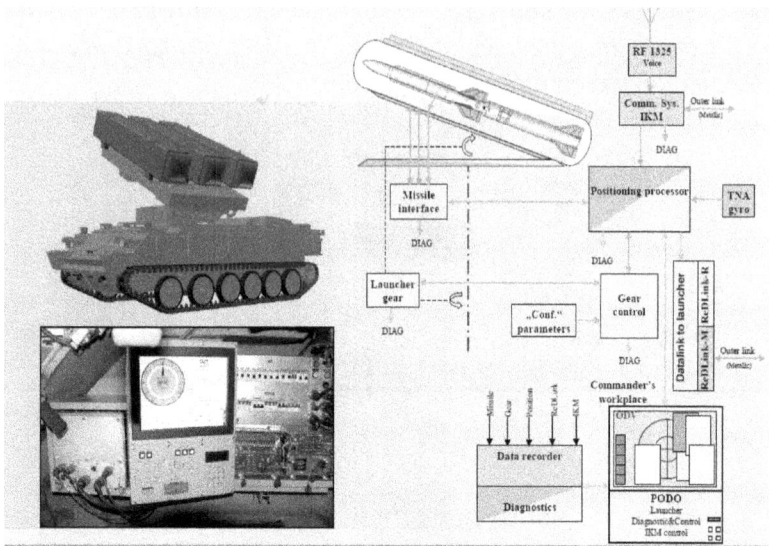

Figure 6-7: 2P25 launcher demonstrator (Source: Retia)

Main Upgrade Benefits Includes:

- Easier Operation, reduced crew load.
- Improved Parameters of Signal and Data Processing.
- Improved Performance of Day/Night Vision Equipment.
- Increased ECCM Capabilities.
- Decreased effects of deceptive Jammers.
- Angle of Jammer Indication.
- Digital data link to superior center.
- Mk XII IFF Interrogator integration.
- New Missile: Aspide 2000.

This improvement also brought some disadvantages. The intercept coverage is only 23 kilometers while the original was about 27 kilometers. The new system is able to track, intercept and engage the target from altitudes of 25 meters up to 12 kilometers while the original system can engage up to 14 kilometers. And the main problem with the Aspide 2000 missile is that the top speed is only at 1.8 Mach while the original 3M9 missile top speed is 2.8 Mach. In a key engagement ability, this version is still inferior in missile speed, range and maximum altitude comparing to the original Soviet-made system.

Polish and Hungarian modernization[61]

The modernization of Hungarian Air Force capabilities started in the middle 1990s. After the collapse of the Warsaw Pact, East European countries tried to solve their military defense problems. Earlier - during the Warsaw Pact era - all countries had their independent and Warsaw Pact integrated air defense systems. As the Cold War situation melted, Hungarian politicians and military experts decided to reduce the Hungarian air defense capabilities. First, they reduced the army organic air defense artillery, secondly, the home air defense missile capabilities were eliminated step–by–step, and later the army organic air defense missile units were integrated into one. So nowadays, only HUAF missile AD regiment "Arrabona" exists in Győr (Fig. 6-8 and 6-9).

Figure 6-8: Hungarian and Polish modification - RStON Straight Flush radar upgraded with Polish built WZU–2 day/night optical tracker on the illuminator antenna. (Source: Miroslav Gyűrösi)

The Polish company "WZU" modernized the 1S91 the Straight Flush radar and the Hungarian company "ARZENÁL" modernized 2P25 launchers. The main effects of the modernization and overhaul of this

---

61   Bozsoki Attila, Developmental Trends in the SA–6 (2K12 KUB) Air Defence Missile Systems and the Finalized Developments in the Hungarian Air Force Surface–To–Air Missile System Hungarian Air Force.

weapon system are as follows:

- Increased resistance to passive and active interference.
- Increased detection of low radar cross–section targets.
- Passive day and night target acquisition with long-range thermal vision and television cameras.
- Application of IFF8 (target identification) system (Mark XII Mode 4) standard).
- Use of advanced spare parts allowing the supply of replacement spare parts necessary for normal operations.
- Introduction of advanced methods and algorithms for digital data processing,
- Enhanced radio-electronic camouflage ECCM9 by application of radar sector blinking system.
- Elimination of adjustments and tuning for upgraded systems.
- Growth capability to launch state–of–the–art (fire and forget) missiles.
- Integration of dehumidification system.
- Air-conditioned crew cabin.

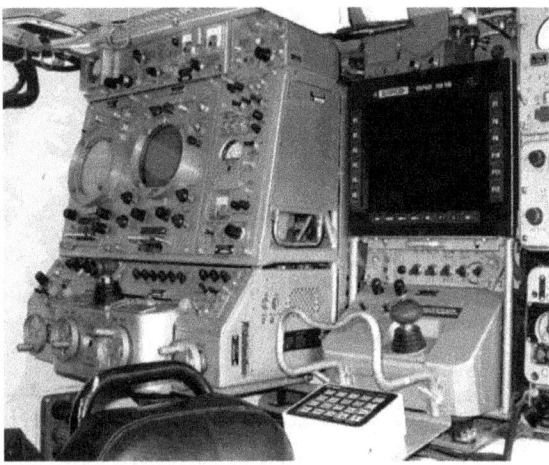

Figure 6-9: Modernized 1S91 operator stations - retrofitted digital flat panel displays provided by Hungarian Arzenal (Source: Miroslav Gyűrösi)

After the completion of the fire unit - level modernization, the Hungarian "Arzenal Company" commenced to modernize the former Soviet

K–1M SAM unit command post to a K–1P digitalized Wing (regiment)/ Group level Fire Distribution Centre. The K–1M was able to receive orders from the higher echelon and send them to subunits but it was not able to get RAP. It just used local radar signals as LAP. That is why combat operations were based on local sensors data.

As Hungary became a NATO member, this modernization had to be able to solve NATO requirements meaning that air defense missile unit employment had to be taken according to NATINADS rules and procedures. Thus the new K–1P was designed and built to meet these fire control requirements.

Serbian modernization

Serbian modernization was performed on the command vehicle and surveillance radar. 1S91M2 modernization included the installation of the new optical camera with thermal vision. Self-propelled surveillance radar 1RL128D, in Serbia, designated OARSt[62] is equipped with a new digital semiconductor moving targets selection system DBSO-128 (Digital constant reflector); the radar tract is replaced by a new one - digital semiconductor type. The radar transmission tract has been preserved. The new equipment also includes a new formation of digital data UFDM-128 (digital data creation device).

Digital extractors and trackers are also the new ones. All three original circular radar screens are replaced with new flat panel displays indicators based on a PK-51 panel computer. Modernized 1RL128D radar is equipped with the UM-RT-03 universal modem, which allows data transmission via radio station, radio relay connection, cable connection, or fiber optic cable connection.

The author of the UM-RT-03 universal modem is the Faculty of Technical Sciences FTN (Fakultet Tehničkih Nauka) from Novi Sad that carried out this work for the needs of Yugoimport SDPR. Part of the first stage of modernization work is also the adaptation of the radar altimeter PRV-16A to the possibility of remote surveillance radar control 1RL128D or from an automated UKUV command and control system. Visible change is the installation of the control panel UV-16 (Adjust the width for PRV-16), which is located in the lower parts of the radar operator console altim-

---

62 Osmatračko akvizicijska radarska stanica - Serbian acronym for Surveillance acquisition radar station.

eter PRV-16A (1RL132A).

Serbian modernization also includes installation of the IR guided missile (air-to-air missiles R-60 x 2 missiles at the side beams and R-73 x 1 missile in the center beam combined with TV and thermal vision system (Fig. 6-10 and 6-11).

Figure 6-10: Serbian modernized 2P25 launcher: central beam can fit triple launcher beams for R-60 and R-73 air-to air missiles. (Source: authors)

Figure 6-11: 2P25 IR control station screen. (Source: authors)

CHAPTER SEVEN

2K12 Kub/SA-6 Successor: 9K37 Buk (SA-11, SA-17)

Development of the 9K37 Buk / SA-11 Gadfly & SA-17 Grizzly battlefield self-propelled SAM system commenced in accordance with the Resolution of the Central Committee and USSR Council of Ministers dated 13 January 1972 and provided for cooperation between the main developers and manufacturers that had earlier developed the Kub system (Fig. 7-1).

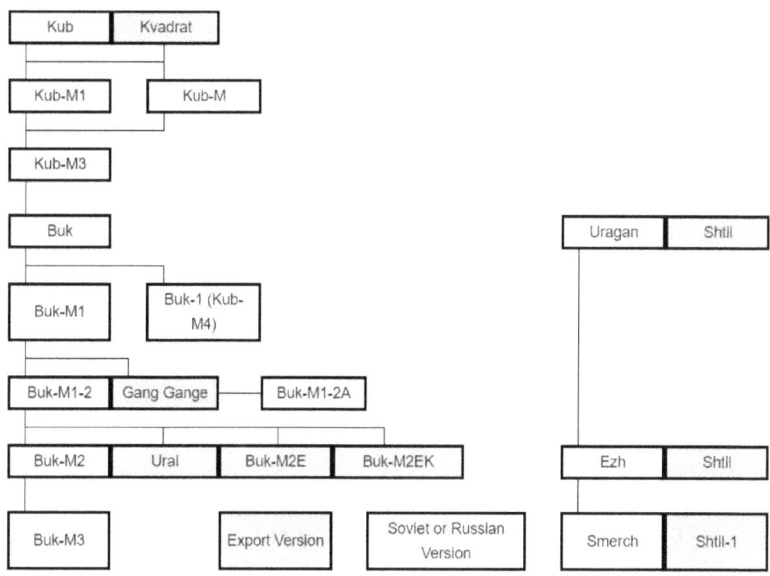

Figure 7-1: Kub and Buk system development. (Source: Wikipedia)

The Buk missile system was designed to surpass the 2K12 Kub in all parameters, and its designers, including its chief designer Ardalion Rastov, visited Egypt in 1971 to see Kub in operation. Both Kub and Buk used self-propelled launchers developed by Ardalion Rastov. As a result of this visit, the developers concluded that each Buk transporter erector launcher (TEL) should have its own fire control radar, rather than being reliant on one central radar for the whole system as in Kub. The result of this move from TEL to transporter erector launcher and radar (TELAR) was the development of a system able to shoot at multiple targets in multiple directions at the same time.

231

In 1974 the developers determined that although the Buk missile system is the successor to the Kub missile system, both systems could share some interoperability. The result of this decision was the 9K37-1 Buk-1 system. Interoperability between Buk TELAR and Kub TEL meant an increase in the number of fire control channels and available missiles for each system, as well as faster entry of Buk system components into service. The Buk-1 was adopted into service in 1978 following the completion of state trials, while the complete Buk missile system was accepted into service in 1980 after state trials took place between 1977 and 1979 (Fig. 7-2).

Figure 7-2: 9K37 Buk - M1/SA-11 TELAR (9A310) with 9M38M1 missiles is a further successful development of 2K12 system. (Source: authors)

Another modification to the Buk missile system was started in 1992 with work carried out between 1994 and 1997 to produce the 9K37M1-2 Buk-M1-2, which entered service in 1998. This modification introduced a new missile, the 9M317, which offered greater kinematic performance over the previous 9M38, which could still be used by the Buk-M1 (Fig. 7-2) and Buk-M1-2 (Fig. 7-3).

Such sharing of the missile type caused a transition to a different GRAU (Russian Main Missile and Artillery Directorate) designation 9K317, which has been used independently for all later systems. The previous 9K37 series name was also preserved for the complex, as was the Buk name. The new missile, as well as a variety of other modifications, allowed the system to shoot down ballistic missiles and surface targets, as well as enlarging the 'performance and engagement envelope' (zone of danger for potential attack) for more traditional targets like aircraft and helicopters. The 9K37M1-2 Buk-M1-2 received a new NATO reporting name distinguishing it from previous generations of the Buk system: SA-17 Grizzly. The export version of the 9K37M1-2 system is called 'Ural'; this name has also been applied to M2, at least to early, towed, export versions.

Figure 7-3: 9A310M1-2 Buk M1-2/SA-17. This TELAR can use 9M38, 9M38M1 and 9M317 missiles. (Source: Vitaly Kuzmin).

The further development includes Buk-M2 (9K317) which production started in 2008. The main visual difference between the M2 version and the previous one (comparing TELARs) is the flat radar dome that houses a phased array radar (Fig. 7-4)

Figure 7-4: 9A317 Buk M2/SA-17. The major visual difference from the version Buk M1 and M1-2 is that TELAR is equipped with phased array radar (Source: Almaz-Antey)

9K317M - BUK M3 VIKING

The latest modernization of the Buk family is 9K317M (Fig. 7-5), or the Buk-M3 also nicknamed 'Viking'. A medium-range surface-to-air missile system, it is a modernized version of the Buk-M2, features advanced electronic components and a deadly new missile and could be regarded as a completely new system. The system is designed, developed and manufactured by the Almaz-Antey. The Buk-M3 system boasts a new digital computer, high-speed data exchange system, and a tele-thermal imaging target designator instead of the tele-optical trackers used in previous models. A battery of Buk-M3 missiles can track and engage up to 36 targets simultaneously, while its advanced 9R31M missile is capable of knocking down all existing flying objects, including highly maneuverable ones, even during active electronic jamming. The Buk-M3 can launch vertically and can engage sea and land targets.

A Buk-M3 Viking missile battery consists of two TELAR 9A317M (Transporter Erector LAuncher and Radar) and one TEL 9A316M (Transporter Erector Launcher) vehicle. The TELAR is based on the GM-569 tracked armored chassis and carries six ready-to-fire missiles mounted on a turntable that can traverse a full 360°. The turret of the Buk-M3 TELAR includes fire control radar at the front and a launcher with six ready-to-fire missiles on top. In August 2018, at Army-2018 International Military Technical Forum in Moscow, the latest variant of the Buk-M3 was shown for the first time to the public with a new launcher turret equipped with two rows of three missile containers. The reloader vehicle of the Buk-M3 Viking is equipped with two blocks of six missiles using the same tracked chassis as the previous version of the Buk family.

The Buk-M3 Viking uses the new 9R31M missile radar-guided surface-to-air missile. The Buk-3M's target-destruction probability has been tested to 0.9999. It is able to destroy any type of air targets from a range of 2.5 to 70 km, with a speed of 3,000 m/s at altitudes of 15 meters up to 35 km. The Buk-M3 missile has been optimized for the interception of low-flying cruise missiles. The missile system includes a high-speed data exchange system and a thermal target imaging designator replacing optical trackers on previous Buk models. The 9M317M missile, stored in container, is fitted with a high-explosive fragmentation warhead (Fig. 7-5).

The most effective area defense is the Buk battalion (Fig. 7-6).

2K12 successor - Buk missile system

Figure 7-5: 9K317M Buk-M3 'Viking' with 9A317M TELAR and six 9R31M missiles stored in containers. (Source: Vitaly Kuzmin)

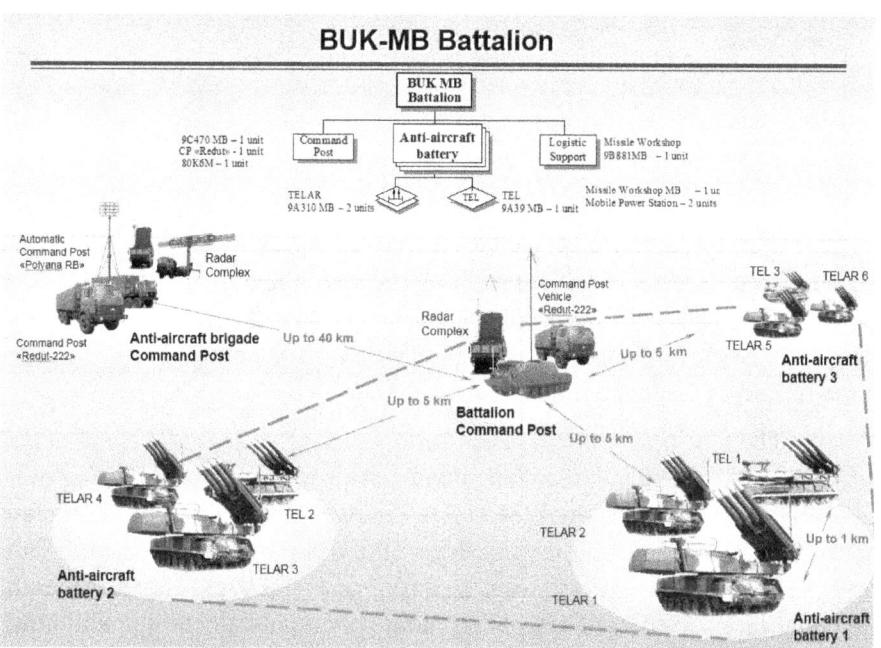

Figure 7-6: Typical composition of Buk MB battalion. (Source: authors)

The missile guidance system is very similar to the missile guidance system applied in the S-300V missile system, which led to a very inter-

235

esting modification with the integration of one launcher with 9A383 radar with four 9M83M missiles from the S-300V system (Fig. 7-7).

Figure 7-7: 9K17M Buk-M3 and S-300V integration.
(Source: authors)

In this configuration, the 9K17M Buk-M3 battalion can engage aerodynamic targets at distances up to 100 km, and ballistic targets at distances up to 40 km, with 9M83M missiles, so that the system can be also considered as an anti-ballistic system. These targets could be engaged with a maximum of 2 missiles at a time.

The working principle is as follows: target surveillance and acquisition are performed by the independent self-propelled target tracking radar 9S36M or by the individual 9A317M TELAR radar which scans the airspace and illuminates the targets. Upon the target is locked-on and when a 9M83M missile is launched by S-300V battery, a 9A317M radar on the launcher or a 9S36M self-propelled radar illuminates the target, and guide the S-300V launcher 9A383M radar antenna, and forms control commands that are sent to the missiles in a midway trajectory with the 9A383M radar.

In the final part of the missile guidance, 9A383M illumination radar on the S-300V system is activated, illuminating the target which enables the 9M83M missile final semi-active radar self-guidance to the target.

Guidance system: inertial & radio command & semi-active radar self-guidance. Guidance method: proportional navigation.

BUK Combat Service

Abkhaz authorities claimed that the Buk air defense system was used to shoot down four Georgian drones at the beginning of May 2008. Analysts concluded that Georgian Buk missile systems were responsible for downing four Russian aircraft – three Sukhoi Su-25 close air support aircraft and a Tupolev Tu-22M strategic bomber – in the 2008 South Ossetia war. US officials have said Georgia's SA-11 Buk-1M was certainly the cause of the Tu-22M's loss and contributed to the losses of the three Su-25s. According to some analysts, the loss of four aircraft is surprising and a heavy toll for Russia given the small size of Georgia's military. Some have also pointed out that Russian electronic countermeasures systems were apparently unable to jam and suppress enemy SAMs in the conflict and that Russia was unable to come up with effective countermeasures against missile systems that it had designed. Georgia bought these missile systems from Ukraine which had an inquiry to determine if the purchase was illegal.

The Buk-M1 system was used in the downing of Boeing 777 Malaysia Airlines Flight 17 (MH17) on 17 July 2014 in eastern Ukraine which resulted in 298 fatalities. Some of the evidence included pieces of warhead stuck in the wreckage, some with serial number remnants, and missile fragments recovered from the bodies of the flight crew (Fig. 7-8).

On 14 April 2018, American, British, and French forces launched a barrage of 105 air-to-surface and cruise missiles targeting eight sites in Syria. According to a Russian source, twenty-nine Buk-M2E missiles launched in response allegedly destroyed twenty-four incoming missiles. However, the American Department of Defense stated no Allied missiles were shot down ('déja vu' in previous conflicts).

In May 2018, during Operation House of Cards, the Israeli Air Force allegedly hit a Syrian Buk system. No independent source confirmed this. However, The Israeli military published a video of an attack on a Syrian/Iranian SA-22/Pantsir S1 vehicle which was not manned by the crew at that time.

Figure 7-8: Ukrainian Buk-M1 at the combat duty. One of these launchers is among the suspects involved in the downing of the Malaysian flight MH-17. (Source: authors)

According to the official Syrian media, during the recent conflict with Turkey, Syrian Buk-M2E systems shot down 20 Turkish UAVs (Fig. 7-9).

Figure 7-9: Syrian Buk-2ME TEL in action. (Source: https://en.topwar.ru/93760-buk-m2e-v-sirii.html)

APPENDICES

    Appendix A - Radar
    Appendix B - Anti radiation missiles
    Appendix C - Towed decoys
    Appendix D - Field orientation
    Appendix E - Lighting strike and protection
    Appendix F - NATO codification system

Appendix A

Radar Fundamentals

Radar is an acronym for radio detection and ranging, which tends to suggest that it is a piece of equipment that can be used to detect and locate a target. Modern radar does much more than just detection and ranging. It is used to determine the velocity of moving targets and also find out many more characteristics about the target such as its size, shape and other physical features including, for example, the type and number of engines used on an aircraft. Radar is extensively used in many civilian and military applications. Radar has been and will continue to be an essential capability for militaries worldwide. This Appendix chapter gives a very basic treatment to the radar fundamentals covering a wide cross-section of topics including basic radar functions, related performance parameters, radar range equation, radar waveforms, radar transmitters, receivers and displays, radar antennas and types of radar (Fig. A-1 and A-2).

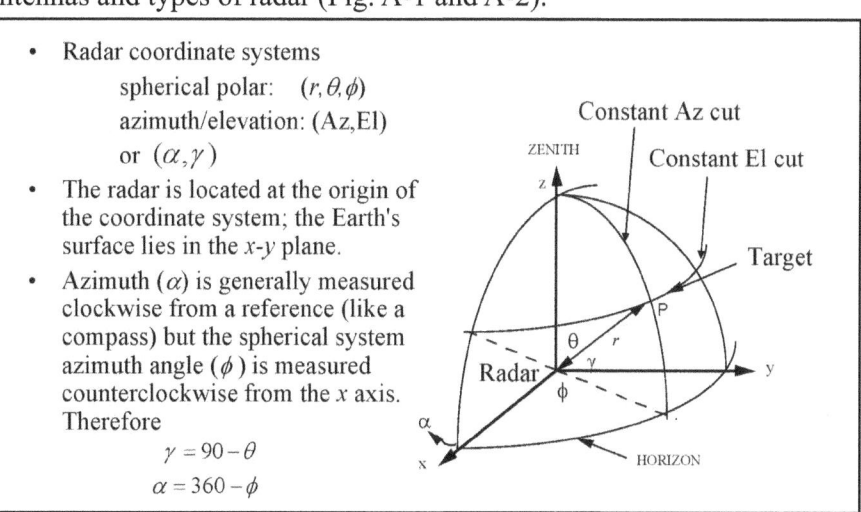

- Radar coordinate systems
    spherical polar: (r, θ, ϕ)
    azimuth/elevation: (Az,El)
    or (α, γ)
- The radar is located at the origin of the coordinate system; the Earth's surface lies in the x-y plane.
- Azimuth (α) is generally measured clockwise from a reference (like a compass) but the spherical system azimuth angle (ϕ) is measured counterclockwise from the x axis. Therefore
    $\gamma = 90 - \theta$
    $\alpha = 360 - \phi$

Figure A-1: Radar coordinate system. (Source: Naval Postgraduate School)

Radar System and Radar Range

Radar is a standalone active system with its own transmitter and receiver. It is primarily used for detecting the presence and finding the exact location of a far-off target. It does so by transmitting electromagnetic energy, in the form of short bursts in most of the cases, and then detecting the echo signal returned by the target.

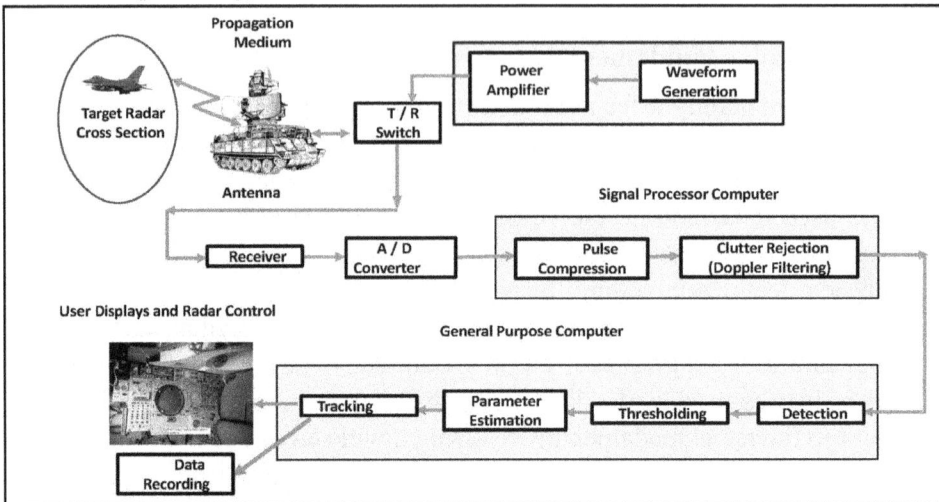

Figure A-2: Radar Cross Section processing. (Source: authors)

The radio waves used by radar are produced by a piece of equipment called a "magnetron". Radio waves are similar to light waves: they travel at the same speed, but their wavelengths are much longer and have much lower frequencies. Light waves have wavelengths of about 500 nanometers (500 billionths of a meter, which is about 100-200 times thinner than a human hair), whereas the radio waves used by radar typically range from about a few centimeters to a meter the length of a finger to the length of your arm or roughly a million times longer than light waves. Both light and radio waves are part of the electromagnetic spectrum, which means they are made up of fluctuating patterns of electrical and magnetic energy zapping through the air. The waves a magnetron produces are actually microwaves, similar to the ones generated by a microwave oven. The difference is that the magnetron in radar has to send the waves many miles, instead of just a few centimeters (inches), so it is much larger and more powerful.

The range of the intended target is computed from the time that elapses between the transmission of the energy and reception of the echo. The location of the target can be determined from the angle/direction of arrival of the echo signal by using a scanning antenna, preferably transmitting a very narrow width beam. As mentioned in the introductory paragraph, radar today does much more than just detecting a target and finding its location. Radar can be used to determine the velocity of a moving target, track a moving target and even determine some of the physical features of the target. Of course, no single radar type can be used to perform all the functions. There are different types that are best suited to different applications. In addition, radar is a principal source of navigational aid to aircraft and ships. It forms a vital part of overall weapon guidance or a fire-control system. Behind most of the radar functions lie its capability to detect a target and find its range and velocity.

The radar signal waveform as generated by the waveform generator modulates a high-frequency carrier and the modulated signal is raised to the desired power level in the transmitter portion. The transmitter could be a power amplifier employing any of the microwave tube amplifiers such as Klystron, Traveling Wave Tube (TWT), Crossed Field Amplifier (CFA) or even a solid state device. The radar waveform is generated at a low power level, which makes it far easier to generate different types of waveforms required for different radars. The average output power requirement of radar could be as small as a few tens of mill watts for very short-range radars to several megawatts for Over-The-Horizon-Radar (OTHR). The duplexer allows the same antenna to be used for both transmissions as well as the receptions.

It acts as a switch disconnecting the receiver from the antenna during the time the relatively much higher power transmitter is ON to protect the receiver from getting damaged. On reception, the weak received signal is routed to the receiver by the duplexer. The duplexer usually makes use of gas-filled transmit/receive tubes that are basically sections of transmission line filled with a low breakdown voltage gas. These tubes get fired due to the presence of high power to direct the transmitter output to the antenna. After the transmitter signal is radiated, these tubes de-ionize or recover quickly to direct any received signal to the receiver input. A circulator is sometimes used to provide further isolation between transmitter and receiver. A circulator as a component can also be used as a duplexer. The circulator duplexer contains a high-power RF circulator comprising of signal couplers and phase shifters such that a signal entering one port has a low attenuation path only to the next port in a particular direction. All other paths are high attenuation paths.

The antenna acts as an interface between the radar transmitter output and free space. Mechanically steered parabolic reflector antennas and electronically steered antenna arrays are commonly used. The echo signal received by the antenna is directed to the receiver input. The receiver is usually of the super heterodyne type. The receiver filters out-of-band interference. It also amplifies the desired signal to a level adequate for operating subsequent circuits.

Radar clutter is nothing but unwanted echoes. These undesired echoes could originate from a number of sources such as land or sea surfaces, insects, animals or birds, weather conditions like rain or atmospheric turbulences, objects deployed as countermeasures like chaff and decoys and so on. Clutter may be divided into three broad categories, including surface clutter originating from objects on land and sea surfaces; volume clutter produced by chaff and weather conditions such as rain and clutter originating from point targets such as birds, animals, vehicles and structures. The term "clutter" to an extent is application specific. Clutter in one application may be a genuine target in another. For example, for radar tracking a land target such as a tank to guide a missile to hit the target, scattering from vegetation on the land surface or from weather conditions such as rain would be a clutter. On the other hand, for airborne remote sensing radar, the reflection of radar energy from natural vegetation is the primary target. Also, backscattering from atmospheric particles and turbulences would be a genuine signal for weather radar.

Surface clutter includes both ground clutter and sea clutter. The magnitude of clutter, that is, the magnitude of undesired radar signal backscattered in the direction of the radar depends upon the nature of the material composition, surface roughness and the angle the radar beam makes with the surface in azimuth and elevation directions. The backscattered radar energy is also a function of radar signal wavelength and polarization. The reflected signal is the phasor sum of reflections from a large number of individual scatterers. These individual sources of scattering may be static such as in the case of buildings, tree trunks and so on, or moving like in the case of raindrops, leaves or ripples on the sea surface. Individual sources of clutter vary spatially and temporally.

It may be mentioned here that the reflection also occurs from ground and sea surfaces, atmospheric conditions like clouds, turbulence and so on. These reflections occurring in the direction of the radar constitute clutter. The backscattered energy travels back to the radar and a portion of it along with a portion of the clutter is intercepted by the radar's receiving antenna, which in the present case is the same as the transmitting antenna. The amount of the backscatter energy intercepted by the antenna depends upon the capture area of the antenna. The received signal is routed to the receiver by the duplexer. The signal that contains both the desired echo as well as the interfering signals and noise gets processed in the receiver.

The Antenna

The purpose of the radar antenna is to concentrate, or focus, the radiated power in a small angular sector of space. In this fashion, the radar antenna works much as the reflector in a flashlight. As with a flashlight, a radar antenna doesn't perfectly focus the beam. As the electromagnetic wave from the target passes the radar, the radar antenna captures part of it and sends it to the radar receiver.

The guided electromagnetic waves look more appropriate when the feeder connecting the output of the transmitter and the antenna or the input of the receiver and the antenna is a waveguide, which is generally true when we talk about microwave frequencies and microwave antennas. In the case of other antennas such as those at high frequency (HF) and very high frequency (VHF), the term guided electromagnetic waves mentioned previously would be interpreted as a guided electromagnetic signal in the form of current and voltage. Sometimes, an antenna is considered a system that comprises everything connected between the transmitter output or the receiver input and free space. This includes, in addition to the component that radiates other components such as the feeder line, balancing transformers and so on. An antenna is a reciprocal device, that is, its directional pattern as receiving antenna is identical to its directional pattern when the same is used as a transmitting antenna provided; of course, it does not employ unilateral and nonlinear devices such as some ferrites. Also, reciprocity applies, provided the transmission medium is isotropic and the antennas remain in place with only transmit and receive functions interchanged. Antenna reciprocity also does not imply that antenna current distribution is the same on transmission as it is on reception.

When a radio frequency (RF) signal is applied to the antenna input, there is current and voltage distribution on the antenna that leads to the existence of an electric and a magnetic field. The electric field reaches its maximum coincident with the peak value of the voltage waveform. If the frequency of the applied RF input is very high, the electric field does not collapse to zero as the voltage goes to zero. A large electric field is still present. During the next cycle, when the electric field builds up again, the previously sustained electric field gets repelled from the newly developed field. This phenomenon is repeated again and again and we get a series of detached electric fields moving outwards from the antenna. According to the laws of electromagnetic induction, a changing electric field produces a magnetic field and a changing magnetic field produces an electric field. It can be noticed that when the electric field is at its maximum, its rate of change is zero and when the electric field is zero, its rate of change is maximum. This implies that the magnetic field's maximum and zero points correspond to the electric field's zero and maximum points, respectively. That is, the electric and magnetic fields are at right angles to each other and so are the detached electric and magnetic fields. The two fields add vectorially to give one field that travels in a direction perpendicular to the plane carrying mutually perpendicular electric and magnetic signals back to the radar receiver. Interferences are signals from other electronic systems that when radiate will be received.

The common types of antenna radiation patterns include the (1) omnidirectional (azimuth plane) beam, (2) pencil beam, (3) fan beam and (4) shaped beam. The omnidirectional beam is commonly used in communication and broadcast applications for obvious reasons. The azimuth plane pattern is circular, and the elevation pattern has some directivity to increase the gain in horizontal directions. A pencil beam is a highly directive pattern whose main lobe is confined to within a cone of a small solid angle and it is circularly symmetric about the direction of maximum intensity. This is mainly used in the engagement, guiding and target tracking radars (fire control radars). A fan beam is narrow in one direction and wide in the other. A typical application of such a pattern would be in search or surveillance radars in which the wider dimension would be vertical and the beam is scanned in azimuth. The last application would be in height-finding radar where the wider dimension is in the horizontal plane and the beam is scanned in elevation. There are applications that impose beam-shaping requirements on the antenna. One such requirement, for instance, is to have a narrow beam in azimuth and a shaped beam in the elevation such as in the case of air search radar.

The typical antenna in the older surface to air missile systems is curved so it focuses the waves into a precise, narrow beam, but radar antennas also typically rotate so they can detect movements over a large

Appendices

area. The radio waves travel outward from the antenna at the speed of light 300,000 km (186,000 miles) per second and keep going until they hit something. Then some of them bounce back toward the antenna in a beam of reflected radio waves also traveling at the speed of light. The speed of the waves is crucially important. If a target is approaching at over 3,000 km/h (2,000 mph), the radar beam needs to travel much faster than this to reach the plane, return to the transmitter, and trigger the alarm in time. If for example, the target is 160 km (100 miles) away, a radar beam can travel that distance and back in less than a thousandth of a second.

As the antenna is the emitter of electromagnetic waves, it is a primary target for the anti-radiation missiles such as HARM which were guided to the electromagnetic sources.

Radar Displays

Some of the more commonly used radar displays in the military radars include the A-Scope or A-Scan, B-Scope, F-Scope and Plan Position Indicator (PPI) (Fig. A-3).

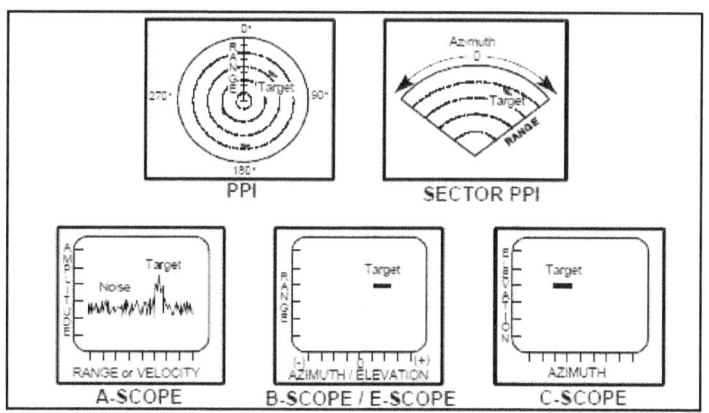

Figure A-3: Most common radar displays. (Source: Radar source)

A-Scope: target signal amplitude vs. range or velocity. Displays all targets along the pencil beam for selected range limits. Displays tracking gate. Some modern radars have raw video A-scopes as an adjunct to synthetic video displays.

B-scope: range vs. azimuth or elevation. Displays targets within selected limits.

247

C-Scope: azimuth vs. elevation. Displays targets within selected limits of azimuth and elevation.

E-Scope: elevation vs. range similar to a B-scope

Radar Classification

Radars can be classified on the basis of:
1. Operational frequency band,
2. Transmit wave shape and spectrum,
3. PRF (Pulse Repetition Frequency) class and
4. Intended mission and mode.

Operational Frequency Band

Radars typically operate in a frequency range of a few tens of MHz to few tens of GHz.

Radars operating up to about 30 MHz make use of ionospheric reflection as a means to detect targets lying beyond the radar horizon. Over-The-Horizon-Radar (OTHR) belongs in this category. Very long-range early warning radars are found in the VHF and UHF bands (30 MHz to 1 GHz).

- L band (D Band in the new designation) radars operating in the 1–2 GHz frequency band are usually long-range military radars and air traffic control radars.
- S band (E/F band in the new designation) radars operating in the 2–4 GHz band are usually the medium-range ground-based and shipboard search radars and air traffic control radars.
- C band (G Band in the new designation) radars operating in the 4–8 GHz frequency band are usually search and fire-control radars of moderate range, weather detection radars and metric instrumentation radars.
- X band (I/J band in the new designation) radars operating in the 8–12.5 GHz frequency band are mostly airborne multimode radars.
- Ku, K and Ka bands (J, K and L bands in the new designation)

operating in the 12.5–18 GHz frequency band (Ku), 18–26.5 GHz frequency band (K) and 26.5–40 GHz frequency band (Ka) are used for short-range applications due to severe atmospheric attenuation in these bands. These include short-range terrain avoidance and terrain following radars and space based radars.

- Radars operating in the infrared and visible bands (Laser radars) are mainly used as range finders and designators.

Basic Radar Functions

The basic functions that radar can perform include target detection, identifying target location in range and angular position and determining target velocity. The radar performs these tasks provided that the target echo signals after signal processing are sufficiently stronger than the interfering signals like noise generated in the receiver; clutter that is unwanted signal echo due to reflections from land, sea, clouds and so on; a jamming signal, which is an intentional interference; electromagnetic interference (EMI), which is an accidental interference from friendly sources such as communication systems, other radars and spillover, which is due to leakage from the transmitter into receiver occurring mainly in CW radars. It may also be mentioned that not all radars are capable of measuring all these listed parameters.

Target Location

The target location is expressed in terms of its range, azimuth angle and elevation angle. The range is the shortest distance of the target from the radar regardless of direction. The azimuth angle is the angle between the antenna beam's projection on the local horizontal and some reference. The azimuth reference in the case of land-based radars is usually the true north. Ship-borne radars usually reference the ship's head, which is a line parallel to the ship's roll axis. Airborne radars reference the roll axis on the local horizontal plane. The elevation angle is the angle between the radar antenna's beam axis and the local horizontal. Local horizontal in the case of land-based radars is the plane passing through the antenna's center of radiation and perpendicular to Earth's radius passing through the same point.

249

Military Applications of Radar Systems

Though radar systems are extensively used in a wide range of civilian applications in the areas of science, meteorology and air traffic control, the use of radars by law enforcement agencies and military applications outnumber all other radar applications. Major radar systems in use by the armed forces and law enforcement agencies include the police radar used for detecting traffic rule violations, surveillance-based radar systems including battlefield surveillance radar, ground penetration radar, air surveillance radar and tracking based applications such as air defense radar, weapon locating radar and ballistic missile defense radar. Military radars are also used for navigation, weather forecasting and Identification Friend or Foe (IFF). This appendix will discuss only the application of the radars in air defense.

Surveillance-Based Applications

Surveillance radar sensors are used to monitor activity surrounding critical and/or strategic assets such as military installations, border crossings, airports, ports and harbors, nuclear research and nuclear power generation facilities, missile and satellite launch stations, oil refineries, ammunition storage depots and so on. Surveillance functions may include intended targets underneath ground level, on ground level or in the air space surrounding the critical asset. There are primary radars and secondary surveillance radars. While primary radar systems measure only the range and bearing of intended targets by detecting the transmitted radio frequency signal reflected off the target, secondary surveillance radar (SSR) relies on targets equipped with a radar transponder that replies to each interrogation signal by transmitting a response containing encoded data. Air traffic control (ATC) radar is an example of a secondary surveillance radar system. ATC radar not only measures the range and bearing of the aircraft, but it also requests additional information from the aircraft itself such as its identity and altitude. The IFF system is another example of an SSR system. Common surveillance-based military radar systems include ground (or area) surveillance radar, air surveillance radar, and ground penetration radar (GPR).

State-of-the-art ground (or area) surveillance radar scans track movements of targets such as an individual walking or crawling towards a facility with precision, speed, and reliability. Such radars typically have ranges of several hundred meters to over 10 km. Battlefield surveillance radar is the most commonly used application of ground surveillance. These radars are generally suitcase sized tripod-mounted portable systems. Those with longer ranges are mounted on a vehicular platform. There are hundreds of other ground surveillance radars with similar or enhanced features available from major international manufacturers of defense and security equipment.

Military application of air surveillance radar primarily involves monitoring the airspace to detect hostile aircraft and directing defensive measures against them. Conventional air surveillance radar called two-dimensional (2D) radar measures the location of a target in two dimensions including range and azimuth. Air surveillance radar capable of determining the elevation angle in addition to the target range and the azimuth angle is known as three-dimensional (3D) radar. The elevation angle allows the computation of target height. The 3D air surveillance radar measures range in a conventional manner but has an antenna that is mechanically or electronically rotated about a vertical axis to obtain a target's azimuth angle and has either fixed multiple beams in elevation or a scanned pencil beam to measure its elevation angle. There are other types of radar such as electronically scanned phased arrays and tracking radars that measure the target location in three dimensions. It is essential for air surveillance radar to be able to look "around the corners" to provide better coverage and capability to detect ground-hugging airborne targets. Over-the-horizon-radar (OTHR) exploits certain features of Earth's atmosphere enabling it to detect low-flying aircraft over ranges of thousands of kilometers. Air surveillance radars are generally located on elevated platforms to maximize coverage area. Coverage area and capability to detect ground-hugging aircraft can be further enhanced by mounting radar on an airborne platform. The Airborne Warning and Control System (AWACS) is one such example. State-of-the-art air surveillance radars are designed to detect, locate, track and classify a wide range of targets including traditional fixed and rotary-wing aircraft, non-traditional targets like ultra-lights, "Para Gliders" and "Unmanned Aerial Vehicles" (UAVs) also referred to as drones), ballistic missiles and even birds, thereby providing early warning, situational awareness, and tactical ballistic missile surveillance and defense. Radars used by air traffic controllers for both approach phase surveillance and on-route surveillance are also examples of air surveillance radars.

Tracking Radar-Based Applications

Tracking radar detects and follows the intended targets so as to determine their trajectory, a function that is put to use in a wide range of civilian and

military applications. One such widely used application of tracking radar is for air traffic control. Air traffic controllers rely on systems installed both at airports as well as at strategic spots on the ground beneath air traffic lanes for effective air traffic control extending to hundreds of kilometers. Tracking radars installed at airports are generally short-range radars that are intended to track airplanes, vehicles and even individuals on the surface in and around the airport. There is a large number of military applications that rely on their functioning on tracking radars. Armed forces use tracking radars to keep track of friendly and enemy platforms, which include land-based vehicles such as tanks, airborne targets such as aircraft, unmanned aerial vehicles, missiles, rockets, and ships. Radar is used to monitor enemy targets to determine if they represent an immediate threat. In case of an imminent threat, radar may track the target and then use the track information to employ suitable defensive or offensive countermeasures such as using guided missiles or aircraft to intercept the enemy targets. Another important application of tracking radars is in the removal of space debris. Space debris comprises used rocket stages and leftovers from completed missions, fragmented and inactive satellites and asteroids. Tracking radar may be used to track the space debris to determine if it poses any threat to major space assets such as space stations. The spacecraft may be maneuvered to get out of the way in the case of any possibility of collision. Common military radars employing tracking radar concept or a combination of tracking and surveillance concepts include fire-control radar, weapon locating radar also called counter-battery radar or shell tracking radar.

Engagement and fire-control radar is a "tracking radar" specifically designed for integration with air-defense weapon systems. The radar component of the platform measures the coordinates of the intended target or targets in terms of their azimuth, elevation, height, range, and velocity, which may be used to determine the target trajectory and to predict its future position. These radars provide continuous position data on single or multiple targets enabling the associated guns or guided weapons to be directed and locked onto targets.

Radar Cross Section (RCS)

RCS of a target, denoted by "σ" (sigma), is measured as a ratio of the transmitted radar signal power backscattered from the target per unit solid angle in the direction of radar to the radar signal power intercepted by the target. Conceptually, RCS is measured by comparing the strength of a reflected signal from the target to the reflected signal from a perfectly smooth conducting metal sphere with a frontal or projected area of 1 m². RCS is measured in m² and is, therefore, the projected area of an isotropically radiating perfectly conducting sphere that would reflect the same power in the direction of radar as the one that is actually reflected by the target for a given incident power. RCS is also measured in dBsm (or dBm²), which is decibels relative to 1 m². RCS in dBsm or dBm² is expressed as 10 log σ where σ is RCS in m² (Fig. A-2 and A-4).

A sphere is used for comparison while computing RCS as a sphere projects the same area irrespective of its orientation. Also, RCS of a sphere is independent of frequency provided that the operating wavelength is much smaller than both the range as well as the radius of the sphere. Most structures including a sphere exhibit different RCS dependence on the operating frequency.

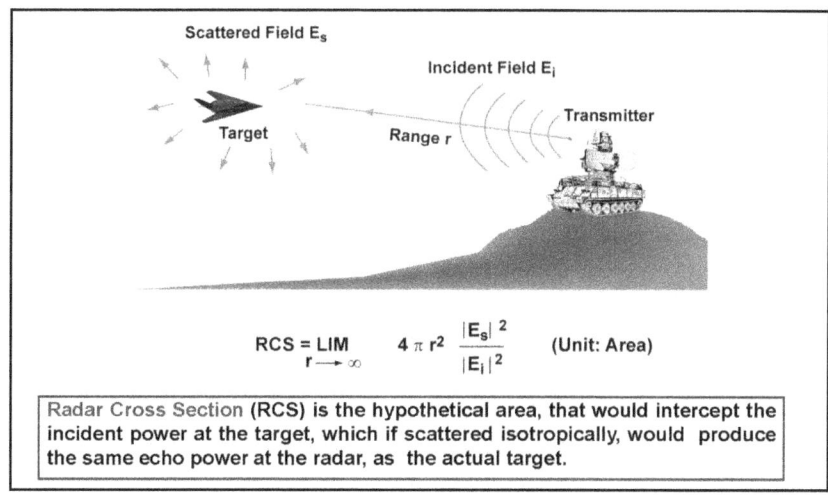

Figure A-4: Radar Cross Section processing. (Source: authors)

Target Size and Shape

RCS is directly proportional to the target size. Larger the target, greater is its RCS value. In addition to the absolute size of the target, its shape also influences the RCS. Different shapes present different incident angles to the radar signal. Radar waves that make large angles of incidence are reflected away from the direction of the radar and therefore contribute to reducing the RCS. Very large incidence angles produce equally large angles of reflection leading to forward scattering. This makes the target stealthier. In comparison with the fighter aircraft, passenger jetliner has far larger RCS simply because the size and no effort are ever made to hide any potential sources of radio wave reflections.

Target Material

The materials used in the construction of the target and also the materials used to coat the surfaces play a significant role in determining the RCS. There are materials such as metals that are strong reflectors of radar waves. Even a thin layer of metal coating makes the object a strong reflector of radar energy. Chaff that is often made of metalized plastic or glass is a good example. There are materials such as wood, plastic, and fiberglass that are less reflective. The use of radar-absorbent materials significantly reduces the RCS. Radar-absorbent materials minimize the reflection of radar waves thereby reducing the RCS. There are two broad categories of radar absorbing materials; namely impedance matching absorbers and resonant absorbers. There are other absorbing material configurations that have features of both classifications.

Operating Wavelength

RCS is a strong function of operating frequency or wavelength. There are three frequency regimes, namely the low frequency or Rayleigh regime, mid-frequency or "Mie" regime and high-frequency or optical regime. RCS is a function of the relative size of the target with respect to operating wavelength and is approximately equal to the real area of the target when the target size is much smaller than the operating wavelength. For a target size roughly equal to the operating wavelength, the RCS may be greater or smaller than the real area depending upon operating wavelength before it approaches the real value in the optical region.

Target Orientation

Target orientation with respect to radar line-of-sight strongly influences the RCS. For example, a fighter aircraft presents a much larger area when viewed from the side than when it is viewed from the front. The fact that military targets such as fighter aircraft have many reflecting elements and shapes and also that targets move relative to radar line-of-sight, relative orientations of various reflecting elements and shapes on the target structure make RCS dependence on target orientation a very complex phenomenon.

Appendices

Appendix B

Anti – Radiation Missile (ARM) Against the Radar

Since the middle of the twentieth century radars have been destroyed by specialized weapons designated as anti-radiation missiles (ARM) homing in on the electromagnetic radiation of the radars. Over the decades the radars have been modified and modernized. New ones have been constructed and different exploitation techniques have been developed. The technical progress of these devices is a never-ending competition.

The anti-radiation missiles destroy radars which are elements of the opponent's air defense system. This allows for the free operation of friendly aircraft in the enemy's airspace. Aircraft carrying these missiles attempt to fulfill the task without entering the striking distance of the ground elements of the enemy's air defense system (rockets and barrel artillery). Such operations demand proper evaluation of the space striking abilities of the system and to ensure the system is equipped with weapons of the proper strike range needed for destroying the defense system elements. Air defense system elements are attacked while crossing the border of their strike range. Also, the weapons systems protecting important objects within the opponent's territory are eliminated (Fig. B-1).

While estimating the influence of the anti-radiation missiles' strike range one cannot neglect the inseparable parameter of the missile flight speed. These two parameters determine the time in which the missile reaches the target after being launched from the plane. Anti-radiation missiles can be divided roughly according to their range into short-range (maximum 100 km), mid-range (maximum 200 km) and long-range (over 200 km).

Another important parameter of anti-radiation missiles is the efficiency of target damage done by the warhead exploding; this is significant for the radar's survival on the battlefield. In the 1950s the low accuracy of anti-radiation missiles was compensated by using warheads of high explosive power, large enough for strategic aircraft to carry them. During the 1960s three new weight categories of warheads appeared (approximately 150 kg, 86-90 kg and 66 kg); these are mostly still in use. Accuracy was improved and the distance (altitude) of the fuse from the target was optimized.

255

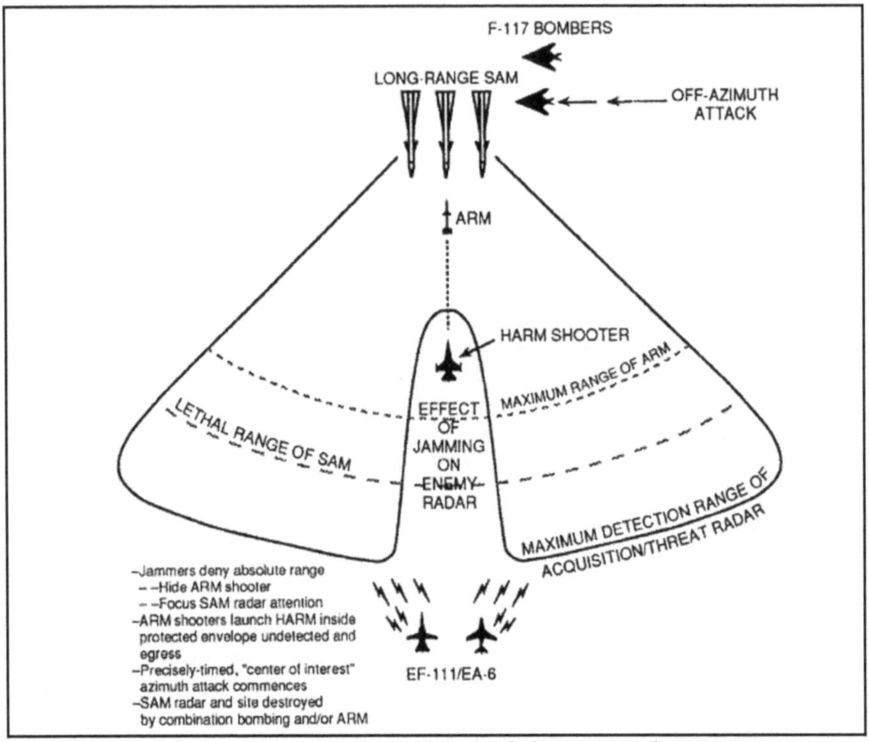

Figure B-1: Attacking the air defense missile site.
(Source: Setting the Contest: SEAD and Joint War Fighting)

At the beginning of the 1990s, the British ALARM missile appeared, which could attack a radar with one meter of accuracy (without GPS). The AGM-45 Shrike missile (with a 66 kg warhead) was striking radars with 15 meters of accuracy. Its 'A' version was equipped with high explosives containing 20,000 cubic piercing fragments. The Ch-58UszE missile (with a 150 kg warhead) could hit radars within twenty meters. The target accuracy of the Ch-15P and Ch-58UszE missiles is 5 to 8 meters, of the Ch-31P missile up to 7 meters, and of the AGM-88 A/B HARM missile target accuracy is estimated between 7.3 and 9 meters. For the Ch-58UszE the target hitting probability within 20 meters is 0.8. The AGM-88C HARM warhead is equipped with 12,845 tungsten cubes of 5 mm able to perforate a ½ inch soft metal sheet or a ¼ inch armored plate from a distance of 6 meters. The German ARMIGER missile has quite a small warhead, only 20 kg, but its target accuracy is less than 1 meter. Probably the accuracy of the American AGM-88E AARGM missile is on a similar level to that of the ARMIGER since both are based on the same construction (AGM-88D

HARM) and both represent the same technological advancement level.

To deploy the missile within efficient strike range it must be equipped with a proper guidance system. Missiles produced in the 1950s and 1960s were homed to the electromagnetic radiation of the radars with the support of the inertial guidance system only. The whole process was controlled by a technologically simple autopilot. In the 1970s the dynamic development of miniature transistor-circuit systems began, and they were employed by the constructors of the anti-radiation missiles homing systems. The following two decades were characterized by the improvement of the existing electronics of the missiles, the aim being the possibility of constructing devices equipped with programmable databases. They allowed for the comparison of the parameters of detected radars and thus the ability to choose those most dangerous or those predefined to a specific combat task.

A conventional anti-radiation missile is homed primarily to the radar's main lobe emission, but also to the emission of its horizontal sidelobes and backlobes emission – depending on the distance between the radar and the missile. However, in the case of the older radars, the primary target is their high horizontal sidelobe and backlobe emissions, which radiate continually. This allows the missile to have uninterrupted tracking of the radar and the passive anti-radiation homing receiver does not become saturated. Modern radars with very low horizontal sidelobe and backlobe emissions are a 'blinking' target for a missile, the 'blinking' being the result of the intervals in receiving the radar main lobe emission during the turn of its antenna. In such a situation, the onboard systems of missiles without GPS are forced to estimate the radar's position on the basis of an intermittently received emission. When the turn speed of the antenna is low (long intervals in receiving the emission), the guidance system of the missile is supported by its inertial system, especially during the final phase of flight, which often results in a bigger margin of error (a few meters) in detecting the position of the radar than was assumed beforehand. The error is usually increased to such an extent that at the moment hitting the target the warhead is not set off by a contact fuse but by a proximity fuse. To maintain the attack efficiency, the warhead must be equipped with a much stronger explosive.

In 1973, during the Yom Kippur War, conventional anti-radiation missiles of the 1950s' generation were used. At that time, Egyptian Tu-16 bombers fired thirteen KSR-2 and twelve KSR-11 (KSR-2P) missiles from above the Mediterranean towards the targets located on the coast and inside Israeli territory. Most of the missiles (about twenty) were intercepted and destroyed by either the air force or HAWK surface-to-air missiles. Five of them penetrated the Israeli air defense system and reached their targets. Three radars and one logistic point on the Sinai Peninsula were eliminated.

Missiles of the 1970s' generation were used during the Iran-Iraq war (1980-88) by Iraqi aircraft targeting Ch-28 missiles towards the radars of the Iranian HAWK systems. The effects of these attacks have not been revealed, unlike the results of the Ch-22MP BURJA missiles which were launched from the Iraqi Tu-22K bombers. Despite numerous launchings towards the HAWK radars, only one missile hit its target. The reason was the poor training of the Iraqi bomber crews, the low efficiency of the guiding system (on the missiles and the deck systems of the bombers), as well as difficulties in efficiently detecting the radars' position from a long distance. Therefore, later the launchings took place at a distance of 60 km or less and the missiles were carried by the Tu-16 bombers. The targets attacked were near Teheran oil refineries and some other places protected by anti-aircraft systems.

Missiles of the 1980s' generation were used for the first time on 15 April 1986 during the US bombing of Libya (Tripoli and Benghazi), Operation El Dorado Canyon. AGM-88A Harm anti-radiation missiles were homed, very efficiently eliminating the radars of Libyan air defense system missile launchers SA-2 Guideline (S-75), SA-3 Goa (S-125 Pechora) and SA-5 Gammon (S-200 Angara) around the Gulf of Sidra.

In the 1990s the British ALARM missile introduced some changes in the context of fighting radars. ALARM can be used in the same way as conventional missiles, but in addition, it is able to detect and destroy radars independently. It climbs to an altitude of 12,000-21,000 meters within the task zone. There its motor is turned off, the parachute opens, and the missile starts diving slowly while its passive anti-radiation homing receiver searches for the target radar. When detected, the parachute detaches itself and the missile, directed by the guidance system, falls towards the radar. The ALARM missile was created before GPS started to be used in such constructions and its operating method has its reasons. The so-called vertical attack of this missile is the result of an assumption made before the ALARM project appeared. Its passive anti-radiation homing receiver independently homes itself towards the radar emission radiating vertically up, i.e. towards the vertical sidelobes. Since most radars had become able to locate the air objects with high accuracy, the emission level of the horizontal sidelobes and backlobes had lowered in comparison to the high emission level of the vertical sidelobes. Regardless of the direction of the mainlobe emission of the radar, the ALARM passive anti-radiation homing receiver is able to continuously track the fluctuating microwave emission leaking upwards from the radar's antenna.

Guiding to the vertical sidelobes (vertical attack at an angle of 90 degrees) has an additional aspect, namely reducing the influence of emission coming from radiation reflected by ground objects, which in case of attack at an angle of 20-40 degrees normally widens the margin of error. Taking advantage of it, the ALARM missile is able to attack the target with high accuracy. The accuracy is 1 meter, so the explosion should be initiated 1 meter from the radar antenna for maximum explosive power. The programmable warhead of this missile can have a database containing information on the general construction of every type of radar, which shows, among other details, where the antenna is located. This enables the missile to initiate a precise explosion destroying the antenna system or the main electronic systems located in the main blocks of the radar's board (depending on what task has been programmed before). It is of special importance when eliminating radars whose antennas are raised high, for detecting air objects flying at low altitudes. The warhead of an anti-radiation missile equipped with a smaller explosive exploding close to the antenna will result in the same destructive level as a warhead with a bigger explosive exploding at a greater distance.

ALARM missiles were used for the first time during the First Gulf War (1990–91). British Tornado aircraft launched 121 missiles in 24 missions aimed only at destroying the Iraqi air defense system and 52 SEAD missions (Suppression of Enemy Air Defenses) operating in enemy airspace. In a few cases, the launching of the ALARMs of the first experimental series was unsuccessful. To eliminate the Iraqi air defense system, coalition forces used also HARM anti-radiation missiles. During Operation Desert Storm about 2,000 were launched at Iraqi radars. A question might be asked as to whether Iraq really had so many air defense radars. One can conclude that these missiles were often used only as a precaution. Some sources prove that the initiators of such launchings were mainly the pilots of the US Navy (F/A-18 planes), who were using an imprecise warning system – the first version of ALR-67 RWR – while the crews of aircraft designed especially for the SEAD missions carried out well-planned target selection, had more time for destroying their targets (it was their main task); and they were better trained and equipped, with much better electronics.

During the First Gulf War ALARM missiles, climbing vertically, were a novelty for many allied pilots. Quite often the missiles speeding upwards (aiming at reaching maximum speed and starting the parachute dive) were mistaken for Iraqi air defense system rockets, which would alarm the battle group unnecessarily, with accounts of such events becoming transformed into various anecdotes.

The analysis of the conflict of the 1990s and experiences resulting from it led to the upgrading of some of the missiles by equipping their guidance systems with additional elements.

AGM-88 HARM

Figure B-2: US Navy F/A-18 Hornet armed with HARM during the first Gulf War. (Source: US DoD)

One of the most important experiences came from the period of NATO operating over the Balkan Peninsula. During NATO Operation Deliberate Force of 1995, American first-version AGM-88 HARM missiles were used. The American F-16 aircraft were equipped with the Harm Targeting System (HTS), which was used then for the first time in combat. During 1999, ALARM, AGM-88B HARM and AGM-88C HARM missiles were launched all over Serbia, but they were not able to do serious damage to the extremely mobile Yugoslavian air defense forces. The damage was symbolic and resulted from the too low accuracy of the inertial guidance systems homing the missiles. This provided a strong impulse for the use of GPS in the guidance systems.

NATO planes launched 743 HARM missiles, six ALARMs and eight ARMATs at the radars of the Yugoslavian air defense forces. About 115-130 ground targets emitting electromagnetic radiation were attacked. Yugoslav air defense limited the time of radar radiation emission to ten seconds, constantly changed the position of anti-aircraft weapons, and used many different methods of field camouflage. The NATO official reports state that the efficiency of the HARM missiles was 3 to 6.6%, depending on the operation's phase. The high efficiency of the Yugoslavian forces was proved by the fact that during the operations the Americans decided to deploy to Italy their experimental Tiger Team from China Lake Weapons Division (USA), an institution testing new weapons. For thirty-six days its pilots tested 400 HARM missiles and worked on developing new tactics. According to the US Navy more targets were then destroyed, however, this is not confirmed (Fig. B-2 and B-3).

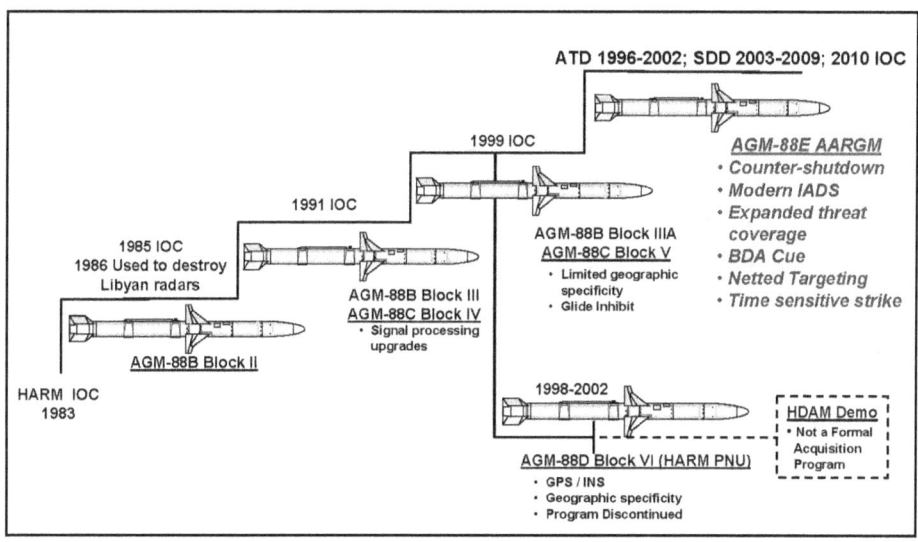

Figure B-3: Evolution of AGM-88 HARM. (Source: ATK)

This confirms that NATO used this campaign to test and develop new systems. Yugoslavia was the laboratory for testing and developing new systems. After the war when one of the authors moved to North America he had a chance to speak with people from different branches and development centers in the USA and several confirmed that during the bombing they were stationed in Italy and performed on-site evaluation and testing of their equipment.

HARM can be launch from F/A-18, F-16, Tornado, EA-6B. Attacking aircraft used them on daily basis. The missile has a range of 150 km but is usually launched much closer to the target. It can fly at over 2,200 km/h, so the crew at the fire control station doesn't have much time to react before they are hit. From 30 km, just outside SAM effective engagement zone, the crew in the fire control station has about 49 seconds to impact. If the airplane is flying at supersonic speed towards the target and within the range of the missile, then the crew will have a maximum of 25 seconds to turn on the target guidance radar, acquire the target, lock on, and launch. Those few seconds were just enough time to turn off the radar before HARM hit it.

The blast-fragmentation type warhead in HARM is designed to destroy enemy radars and vehicles such as command modules. When the missile carrying the warhead reaches a position close to an enemy missile control radar or other targets, a pre-scored or pre-made band of metal on the warhead is detonated and pieces of metal are accelerated with high velocity and strike the target. Approximately 30% of the energy released by the explosive detonation is used to fragment the case and impart kinetic energy to the fragments. The balance of available energy creates a shock front and blast effects. The fragments overtake and pass through the shock wave after a short distance. The rate at which the velocity of the shock front decreases is generally much greater than the decrease in the velocity of the fragments. The radius of effective fragment damage, although target dependent, thus considerably exceeds the radius of effective blast damage in an air burst. The radar, the guidance station and everything on the way are showered with fragments.

The missile consists of four sections: guidance, warhead, control and rocket motor. The AGM-88A missile is powered by a Thikol SR113-TC-1 dual-thrust (boost/sustain) low-smoke solid-fuel rocket motor and has a 66 kg (146 lb) WDU-21/B blast-fragmentation warhead (25,000 steel fragments) in a WAU-7/B warhead section. The warhead is triggered by an FMU-111/B laser proximity fuse. The seeker of the WGU-2/B guidance section has to be pre-tuned to likely threats at depot-level maintenance, so every base or ship has to store a selection of differently tuned HARM seeker heads. In flight, the AGM-88 is controlled by the WCU-2/B control section using four movable BSU-59/B mid-body fins and stabilized by fixed BSU-60/B tailfins (Fig. B-4).

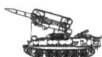

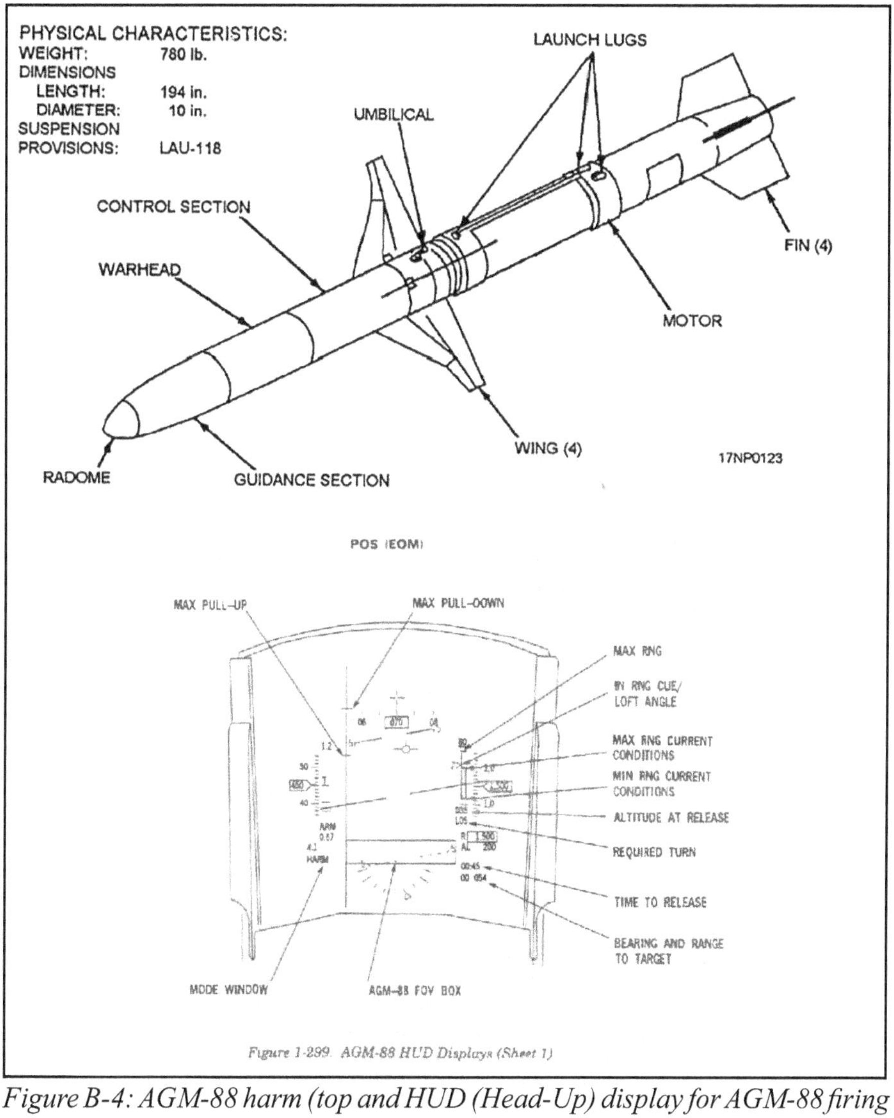

Figure 1-299. AGM-88 HUD Displays (Sheet 1)

Figure B-4: AGM-88 harm (top and HUD (Head-Up) display for AGM-88 firing mode on F-16CJ HARM shooter (bottom). (Source: T.O.GR1F-16CJ-34-1-1)

The HARM can be used in three different operational modes, known as Pre-Briefed (PB), Target-of-Opportunity (TOO), and Self-Protect (SP). In PB mode, the long-range (up to 150 km) of the AGM-88 is used to launch the missile on a lofted trajectory towards a known threat. When the HARM reaches lock-on range and detects the radar emission, it can home in on the target. If the target radar is switched off before a lock can be acquired, the missile destroys itself to avoid possible friendly casualties by the now unguided missile. In SP mode, the aircraft's radar warning receiver is used to detect enemy emissions. The CP-1001B/AWG HARM Command Launch Computer (CLC) then decides which target to attack, transmits the data to the missile, and launches the AGM-88. TOO mode means that the seeker of the AGM-88 itself has detected a target, and the missile can be fired manually if the radar emission is identified as a threat. In SP and TOO modes, the AGM-88 can even be fired at targets behind the launching aircraft, although this of course significantly reduces the missile's range. The AGM-88 missile has an inbuilt inertial system so that whenever it has acquired a lock once, it will continue towards the target even if the emitter is shut down (although the CEP is larger in this case) (Fig. B-5).

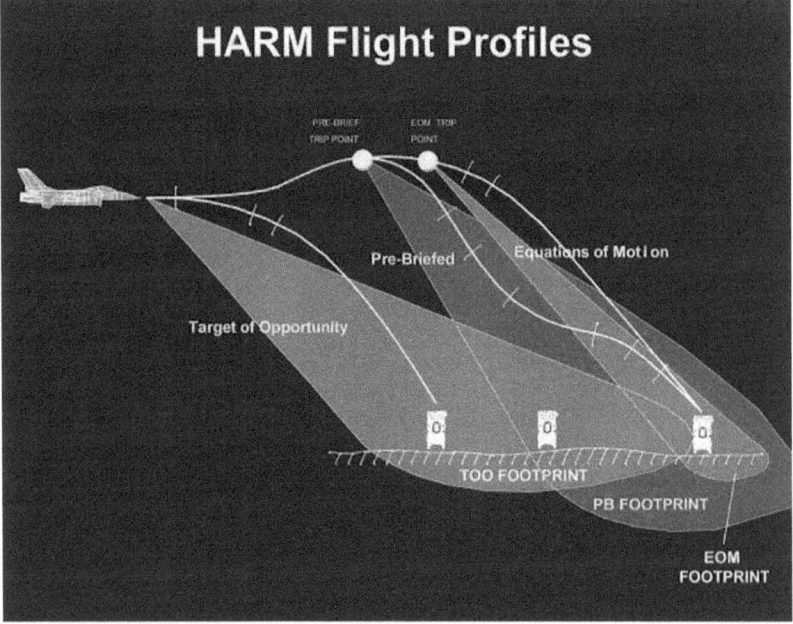

Figure B-5: AGM-88 HARM flight profiles. (Source: ausairpower.net)

The basic protection from HARM attacks is relatively simple. Most missile units applied tactics of short radar emissions which worked very well.

HARM has a proportional guidance system that homes in on enemy radar emissions through a fixed antenna and seeker head in the missile nose. To confuse HARM's guidance system, reflectors were raised 5-6 m above the ground (as high as possible) to try to activate the proximity fuses in the warhead before impact. Reflectors placed around the firing position can reflect the signals and create a saturated picture which may initiate the explosion. There were some articles in the press and on the internet mentioning the use of ordinary kitchen microwaves to confuse HARM's sensors and that Yugoslav's used them extensively. That was never applied in practice. Theoretically, it is possible, but microwaves need a power supply. Hundreds of meters of power cables would have been needed. Air defense units struggled to find enough cables to power the equipment they had.

Large numbers of radar reflectors, log protection and camouflage and false firing control radar emitters were the optimal solution against HARM. And of course, short cycle radar emissions. Another solution is decoys. The aim of using decoys is to lure a HARM to detonate where it does not cause harm to the radar, and, if possible, to the decoys either. The decoy itself is a transmitter that repeats the same wave-form as the protected radar. The passive seeker of the HARM cannot distinguish between the transmissions of the decoys and those of the radar based on modulation, pulse width, carrier frequency etc. A desirable feature of the decoys is that the radar can continue transmitting in order to provide surveillance information. Another feature is that in the case of successful deceiving, the same decoys can be reused against a new HARM.

The effectiveness of decoys depends on their transmission power and location. If the transmission power is set too low compared to the side lobe level of the antenna of the radar, the decoys fail to lure the HARM. Setting the power too high makes the decoys vulnerable to the HARM. Similarly, regarding the locations, decoys that are too far from the flight path of the HARM may not lure it, whereas being too close makes the decoys vulnerable. Although it is better to sacrifice a single decoy instead of the radar, the best outcome is that both survive. In studies, the locations of the decoys are usually assumed to be known or there are few possible locations, but the decoys are not assigned to the locations optimally. As the locations may considerably affect the outcome of survival, there is a need for an approach for determining the best possible locations. In reality, such planning is also affected by the geographical area which limits where the decoys can be placed (Fig. B-6).

What was more dangerous than HARM missiles were NATO laser-guided bombs or even ordinary gravity bombs.

How this works: a laser is kept pointed at the target and the laser

Figure B-6: Fire control radar imitator - anti-radiation missile decoy system - very effective way to "confuse" the anti-radiation missile guidance system. (Source: authors)

radiation bounces off it and is scattered in all directions. The missile, bomb, etc., is launched or dropped somewhere near the target. When it is close enough for some of the reflected laser energy from the target to reach it, a laser seeker detects which direction this energy is coming from and adjusts the projectile trajectory towards the source. While the projectile is in the general area and the laser is kept aimed at the target, the projectile should be guided accurately to the target. However, this does not work against targets that do not reflect much laser energy, including those coated in a special paint which absorbs laser energy. Countermeasures to laser guidance are laser detection systems, smokescreen and anti-laser active protection systems. Some of the missile battalions were hit in this way and the equipment obliterated, and in some cases, the people got killed. The attack could be avoided if the laser locked the weapon onto the decoy. That is where camouflage plays a crucial role.

 *Appendices*

Appendix C

Towed Decoys

Towed decoys can be used to thwart a missile attack during the last phase of guidance. These decoys are towed by a fighter or bomber airplane on a cable which length can vary (Fig. C-1). When stowed, the decoy is located in a special compartment. A towed decoy is equipped with amplifying repeaters and passive reflectors that increase the value of its radar cross section (RCS) to that of the carrier airplane. Their effectiveness is high if, at the initial moment of missile (or fighter) guidance, the protected airplane and the decoy are represented as a single target (i.e., they are not resolved into angles, ranges and Doppler frequencies). The use of towed decoys has a number of specifics. The distance of the towed decoy from the airplane basically is determined by the angle and velocity resolution of the system being jammed[62].

Figure C-1: AN/ALE-50 AAED Advanced Airborne Expendable Decoy towed by B-1B (an artistic impression).

The advantage of the airborne towed decoy is that its jamming sig-

---

[62] S. Vakin, L. Shustoc, R. Dunwell: Fundamentals of Electronic Warfare. Artech House, 2001

nal is inherently provided with the same Doppler content of the aircraft target, and thus is sufficient for its transmitted energy to exceed the target return in order to lure the CW (continuous wave) semiactive missiles' tracking gates. Airborne TDs can be either of the repeater type or RF fed at low power via a fiber-optic cable.

The AN/ALE-50 towed decoy system was developed by Raytheon to protect multiple US military aircraft from radar-guided missiles. The ALE-50 consists of a launch controller, launcher and towed decoy. It can be used on a variety of platforms without modification. When deployed, the ALE-50's expendable aerial decoy is towed behind the aircraft. The decoy protects the host aircraft providing a more attractive target and steering the radar-guided missile away from the aircraft and right to the decoy (Fig. C-2).

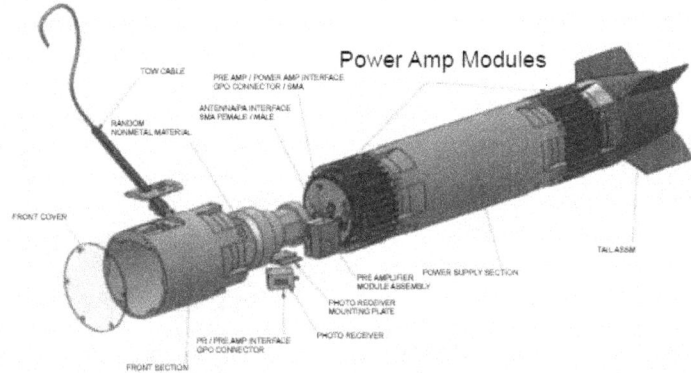

Figure C-2: The core of towed decoys is a transmitter that amplified and retransmit all signal it received thus it appear like an attractive target with high RCS on adversary radar. In layman term, towed decoys are small transmitters being drag behind aircrafts. A solid state decoy with a pair of solid state GaN amplifier.

Fiber-optic towed decoys have a remote transmitter (usually a mini-TWT power amplifier) to which both RF modulating signals (via fiber-optic cables) and high-voltage power supply (HVPS) via an inner core of the cable that is generated internally to the towing aircraft) are provided via the same towing cable. As such, they are able to exploit a large variety of jamming programs available from the onboard RECM technique generator (and are able to counter more advanced threats than just those from CW semiactive missiles[63].

The towed decoy technique presents two conical regions within which an approaching missile will fuse on and destroy the aircraft. They result from the fact that the missile, while tracking the decoy signal, passes close enough to the aircraft to fuse on and destroy it either before or after passing the decoy. The cone aperture is usually small in relation to the large towing cable length. Indeed if the aircraft and the towed decoy are aligned with respect to the direction of arrival of the missile in the forward sector of the aircraft, the missile will prevalently home on the aircraft and its Doppler-based fuse system will explode in proximity of it. In the aircraft rear sector, if the missile is homing onto the towed decoy but for any reason is not exploding in its proximity, it may continue its course and explode in the proximity of the aircraft (Fig. C-3 and C-4).

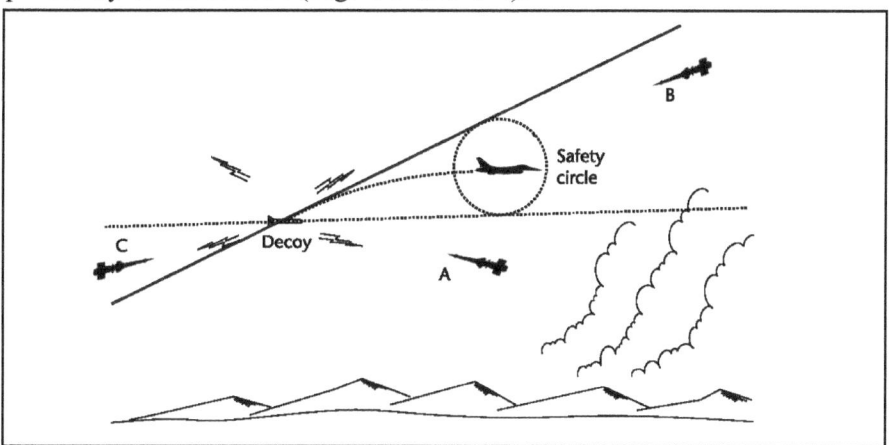

Figure C-3: Towed decoy is effective but with the certain limitations. In the front and rear sectors (missiles B and C) it is not capable of assuring a valid defense.

To avoid such inconvenience, as soon as a missile lock-on is detected the pilot performs a gentle weave maneuver (such as to not dramatically

---

[63] Andrea De Martino: Introduction to Modern EW Systems, Second Edition, Artech House, 2018.

increase the aircraft RCS as viewed by the missile) to prevent the aircraft and the towed decoy from being aligned with the direction of arrival of the missile.

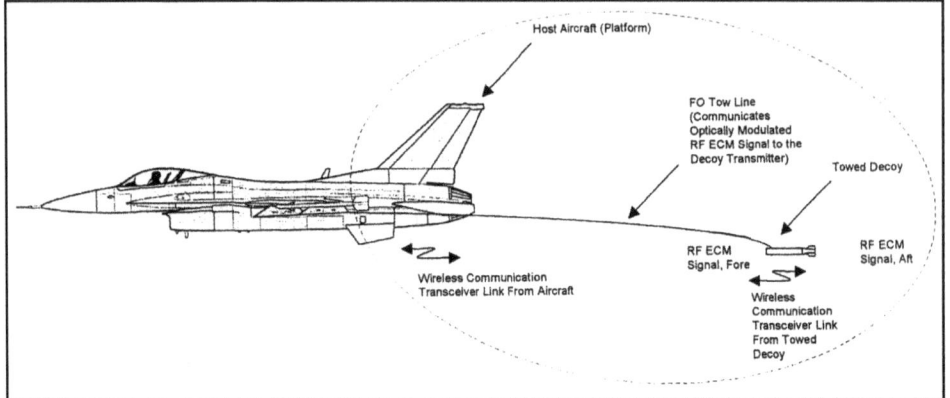

Figure C-4: F-16 towed decoy. (Source: ausairpower.net)

Because the towed decoy body activates the missile's fuse, it is possible that the missile explosion will damage or destroy the towed decoy. In that case, the aircraft is usually provided with at least a further decoy, which is immediately deployed to protect the aircraft against a second attack.

As discussed above, the airborne towed decoy is very effective against the CW semiactive missiles but is less effective (unless provided with a much larger effective radiated power - ERP) against AAA tracking radars, which can exploit frequency agility and LE range gate tracking.

Towed decoys are likely to be less effective against command-guided missiles, whose operator can easily discriminate between the aircraft and the decoy and, in general, against radars exploiting frequency agility. This is proven in practice when manual tracking operators on S-125M Neva/SA-3 were able to discriminate the decoy from F-16CG which resulted in the successful hit and downing of the fighter bomber. [64]

During the war in Kosovo, towed decoys were used with success in many missions. It has been reported that during the war period several thousand decoy ammunitions had been used. This generated criticism over the operational life cost of the towed decoy ECM technique.[65]

---

64   Mike Mihajlović, Djordje Anicić: Shooting Down the Stealth Fighter: Eyewitness Accounts of From Those Who Were There, Pen and Sword Books, 2021
65   Filipo Neri: Introduction to Electronic Defense Systems, Artech House, 2018

Appendix D

Field orientation

To understand what the orientation means in the military applications and which unit of measurement is used, the very same unit need to be explained.

Military use radian and milliradian units.

Radian describes the plane angle subtended by a circular arc as the length of the arc divided by the radius of the arc. One radian is the angle subtended at the center of a circle by an arc that is equal in length to the radius of the circle. More generally, the magnitude in radians of such a subtended angle is equal to the ratio of the arc length to the radius of the circle; that is, $\theta = s/r$, where θ is the subtended angle in radians, s is arc length, and r is the radius. Conversely, the length of the enclosed arc is equal to the radius multiplied by the magnitude of the angle in radians; that is, $s = r\theta$.

One radian is equal to $180/\pi$ degrees. Thus, to convert from radians to degrees, multiply by $180/\pi$.

A milliradian (mrad, also abbreviated as mil) is a measuring unit for angular measurement which is defined as a thousandth of a radian (0.001 radian). Milliradians are generally used for very small angles, which allows for precise mathematical simplifications to more easily calculate back and forth between the angular separation observed in an optic, linear subtension on target, and range. In such applications, it is useful to use a unit for target size that is a thousandth of the unit for range, for instance by using the metric units millimeters for target size and meters for range. This coincides with the definition of the milliradian where the arc length is defined as 1/1000 of the radius.

For maps and artillery, three rounded definitions are used which are close to the real definition, but more easily can be divided into parts. The different map and artillery definitions are sometimes referred to as "angular mils", and is 1/6000 for Soviet/Russian systems. NATO systems use 1/6400. Old Swedish is 1/6300, but Soviet/Russia and western/NATO are much more in use today.[66]

---

66 https://en.wikipedia.org/wiki/Milliradian.
In military use, this is written as 60-00, 64-00 or 63-00. In Russian measuring system, for example a full circle of 360 degrees have 60-00.

Terrain topographical preparation

The missile battery, preparation includes:

- Battery command post coordinates determination;
- Battery command post navigation equipment preparation for the combat engagement;
- Individual combat vehicle orientation.

Battery long-range surveillance radar orientation

Determining the angle of the compass

The compass sighting device is preliminarily combined with the initial stroke of the limb, and then it is sighted in the direction of the left side of the measured angle and, without changing the position of the compass, a count is taken against the direction of the right side of the angle. This will be the value of the measured angle or its complement up to 360° (60-00), if the signatures on the dial go counterclockwise.

The angle of the compass can be determined more accurately by measuring the azimuths of the directions of the sides of the angle. The difference in azimuths of the right and left sides of the angle will correspond to the value of the angle. If the difference turns out to be negative, then it is necessary to add 360° (60-00). The average error in determining the angle in this way is 3-4°.

Determination of the angle of artillery compass PAB-2

To measure the horizontal angle, the compass is installed above the terrain point, the level bubble is drawn to the middle and the pipe is sequentially pointed first to the right, then to the left object, precisely combining the vertical thread of the cross-hair of the grid with the point of the observed object (Fig. D-1 and D-2).

With each hover, a countdown is taken along the compass ring and the drum. Then perform the second method of measurement, for which the compass is rotated at an arbitrary angle and the actions are repeated. In both methods, the angle is obtained as the difference between the samples: the count on the right object minus the count on the left object. For the final result take the average value.

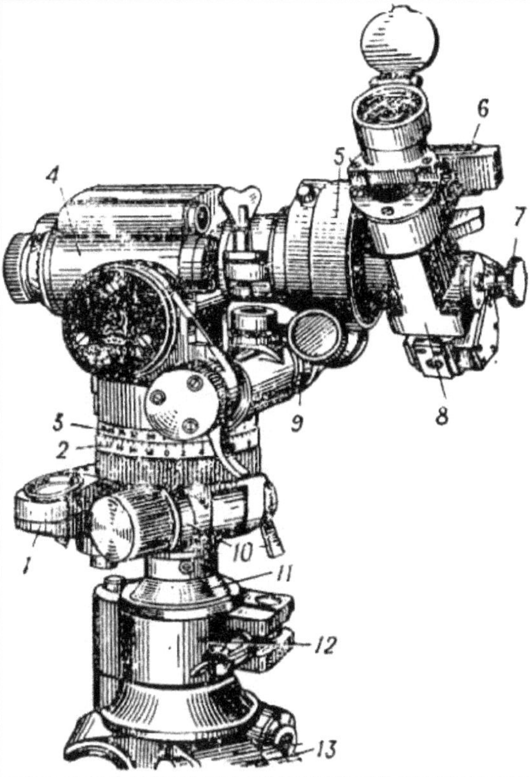

Appendices

1. orientation compass
2. goniometer ring
3. compass ring
4. monocular
5. azimuth attachment
6. level
7. hand-wheel for turning the reticle head (sight)
8. sight
9. body of the counting worm mechanism
10. body of the installation worm mechanism
11. vertical gear axis
12. clamp
13. tripod head

Figure D-1: Periscope Artillery Compass (перископическая артиллерийская буссоль) PAB-2 used in artillery and air defense units for orientation. (Source: Spravochnik Oficera Artilerii)

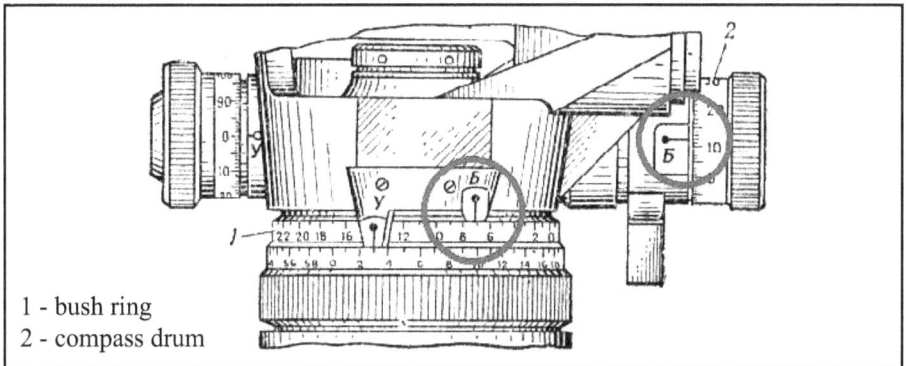

1 - bush ring
2 - compass drum

Figure D-2: Bussole reading device used to measure horizontal angles. (Source: PAB-2 manual)

When measuring angles with a compass, each count is made up of a count of large divisions of the compass ring according to the pointer marked with the letter "Б" and small divisions of the compass drum indicated by the same letter. An example of counts in Fig. D-2 for the compass ring - 7-00, for the compass drum - 0-12; full countdown - 7-12.

By the rule, battery long-range surveillance radar is always oriented taking in the consideration the true north (geographical) azimuth and the direction of the target is determined in correlation with the true azimuth.

To provide the proper airspace surveillance, the position and orientation of the long-range surveillance radar shall be precisely determined (Fig. D-2). This includes:

- Radar coordinates (x and y) and altitudes – geographic north direction, and directional azimuths from the starting points of the battery command post, surveillance radar and each launcher as well as available geographical orientation objects such as the predetermined geolocation objects or individual objects such as trees, religious objects, industry stacks or anything that can be used for this purpose.

- Angles and distances for the determination of the radar base definition for each of the individual launchers in relation to the command post and surveillance radar.

- Determination of the elements for the integration into the battery automation control system for the positioning and repositioning- taking over the position and relocation to the next one.

- The data necessary for the combining of the missile unit position elements are the coordinates of the source (reference) point. Each reference point (one or two) are chosen on that way so that from the chosen position the antenna of the surveillance radar is visible. Coordinates of the base point are usually predetermined exact coordinates of one of the prepared geolocations which are stored in the database or catalogues. What kind of orientation angles will be used, depends on what angle system will be used which is in direct relation with the structural features and type of the missile system.

Appendices

Battery command post orientation

Battery command post coordinates are determined based on the military-grade topographical maps (usually 1:50000 or 1:25000 scale) and/or GPS equipment. Older systems do not have GPS equipment and it still taking maps and compass for orientation while hand-held GPS may be used as a secondary option. More advanced digitalized versions have fully integrated GPS navigation equipment. Direction angles (azimuths) are determined based on the known orientation objects or based on the maps and compass taking into consideration magnetic azimuths (Fig. D-3, D-4

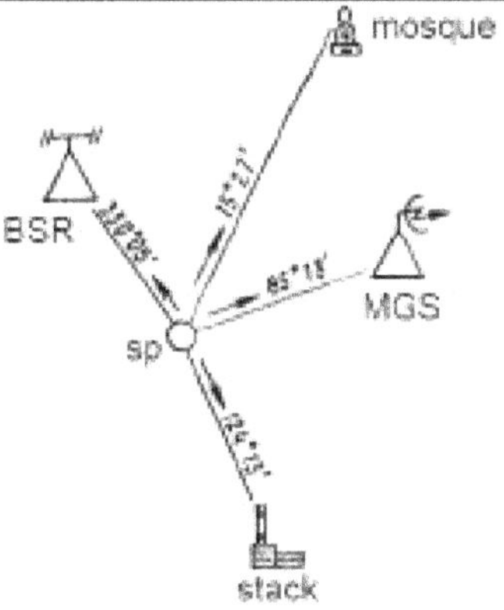

Standing point	Orientation object	True azimuth	x	y
sp	mosque	$12°27'$		
	stack	$126°13'$		
	MGS	$85°13'$		
	BSR	$330°05'$		

MGS - missile guidance station
BSR - battery surveillance radar

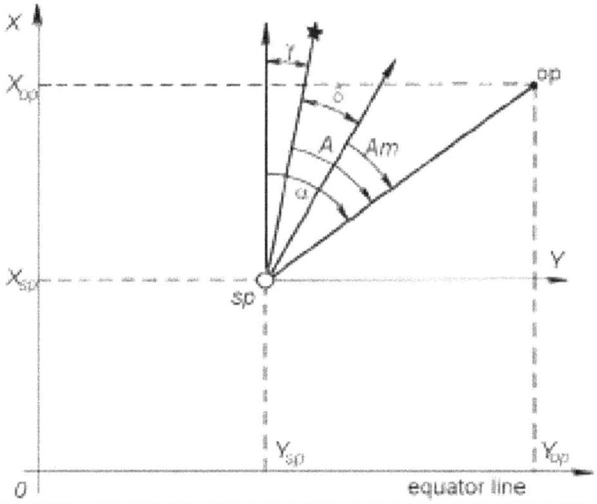

Figure D-3: Battery radar orientation based on the topographical location, characteristics landmarks and measurements.
(Source: Spravochnik Oficera PVO)

and D-5).

Directional angles (azimuths) are determined with the use of optical instruments (compass, collimator, aiming circle for example) or by taking measurements for the topographical maps. The first step in any missile battery orientation is to determine the true north – geographical north direction.

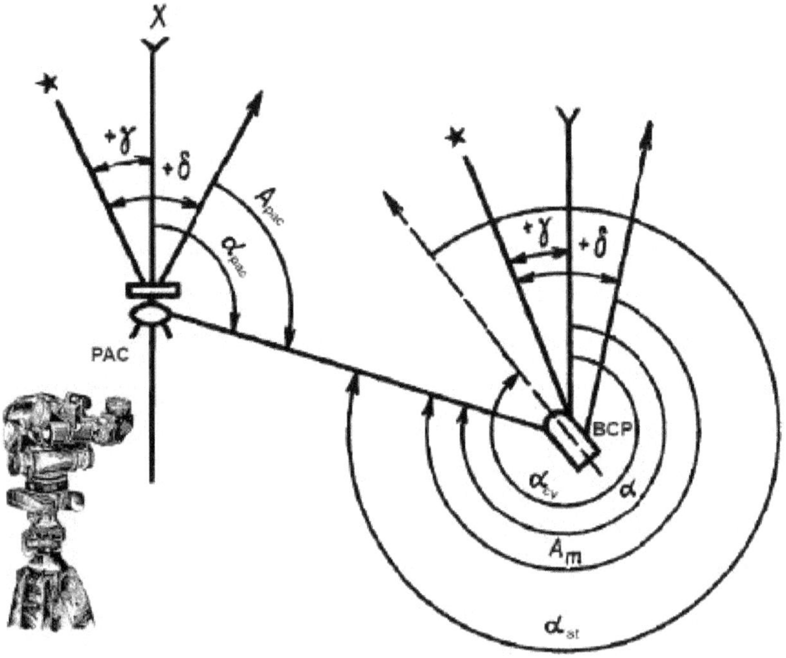

α_{pac} - directional angle of the PAC (periscopic artillery compass)
α_{cv} - directional angle of the combat vehicle – launcher
α_{st} - directional angle of the vehicle sight
PAC – Parametric Artillery Compass or orientation circle
BCP - Battery command post

Figure D-4: Battery combat post orientation based on the measures. PAB is used to precisely determine the angles of orientation.
(Source: Spravochnik Oficera Artilerii)

To get the azimuth, the optical device shall be positioned at the standing point and stabilized. Tripod provide the best stabilization device. Compass sight shall be pointed toward the orientation object. This object can be anything that is distinguished on the horizon. Important thing is that the compass shall be moved far from any magnetic source such as metal surfaces – free from magnetic attractions. When the orientation object is in the sight, from the compass scale azimuth can be read. The difference between the true north (magnetic azimuth) and the directional azimuth can be calculated by simple formulas or with the use of graphic schematics.

The procedure for the battery command post is as follow:

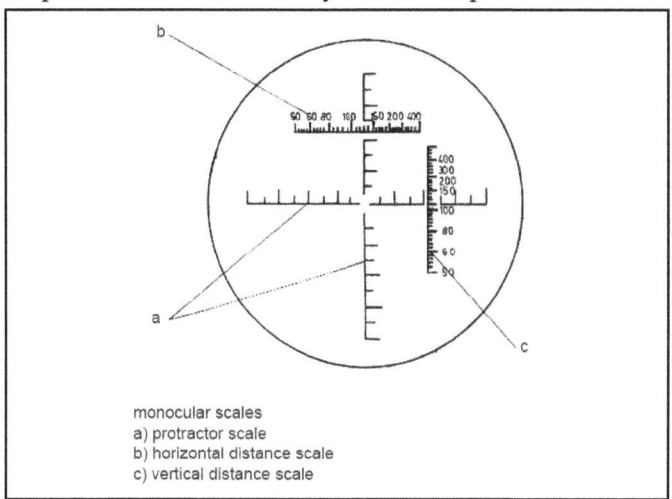

Figure D-5: Monocular scale showing protractor, horizontal and vertical scales. (Source: PAB-2 manual)

The compass shall be positioned away from any magnetic source – 30-40 m (minimum) from the battery command post vehicle. The monocular of the compass is aimed at the vehicle and the azimuth measure is taken from the circle on the device drum (Fig. D-4 and D-5). Measured azimuth shall be changed to 30-00 (based on the previously described description of the angular mills). Directional angle a with the correction DA can be calculated with the formulas:

$\alpha = Am + \Delta Am$

$\Delta Am = \delta - \gamma + \Pi$

Where:

γ - rapprochement of meridians, determined by the topographic location

δ - magnetic deviation of the compass pointer, determined by the topographic location

α - directional angles (α_{pac}, α_{cv}, α_{st})

A - azimuth

Am - magnetic azimuth, determined by compass

ΔAm - current change in compass correction

П – correction for the embedded compass error (determined through the factory check)

To determine the BCP (directional angle battery command post) the next step is to align the sight on the battery command vehicle and align it with the PAC and take the measurements for the directional angle of the vehicle sight (α_{st}), taking in the consideration the clockwise direction.

The next step is to calculate the directional angle of the battery command post vehicle longitudinal axis with the use of the formula:

$$\alpha_{cv} = \alpha \pm \alpha_{st}$$

Combat vehicle – launcher orientation

Even the orientation is very similar for the different launchers, there are small differences between systems in calculations.

The orientation of the combat vehicle is similar to the BCP orientation and is finished with determining the initial angle Qc and installing it on the vehicle directional setter (vehicle computer). The system will be oriented through the selsyn[67].

The initial angle (own bearing) is measured in the horizontal plane from the main direction clockwise to the longitudinal axis of the combat vehicle. For the main direction, the north direction of the abscissa axis (x axis) is applied.

To determine the Qc angle, it is necessary to:

- set the optical device at 20-50 m in front of the launcher,
- position the vehicle with the optical sight or by the sight on the compass,
- read the angle qn from the block scale,
- point the monocular of the compass into the vehicle optical sight or the compass sight and read the combat vehicle azimuth

---

[67] Selsyn or synchro is an electro-mechanical device used for the easy and precise transmission of angular data between two or more remote points.

Acv on the compass black ring and drum,

- based on the readings, change the launcher azimuth Acv 30-00 (if Acv is more than 30-00, to Am = Acv − 30-00). Or if Acv is less than 30-00 to Am=Acv + 30-00

- compute the direction angle a and put the correction of the azimuth values compass:

    $\alpha = \Delta Am + Am$

- calculate the value of the initial angle Qc by the formula:

    $Qc = \alpha - qn$ if a is more than qn or

    $Qc = (60\text{-}00 + \alpha) - qn$ if α is less than qn

How this really looks in practice: assume we have a reading of 14-45. To convert this reading into degrees, the first 15 need to be multiplied by 6. The result is 90 degrees. The next step is to multiple 45 with 3 which is equal to 135. The next step is to convert that number to minutes: 135 shall be divided with 60 (number of minutes in one degree) which give us 2 degrees and the remaining 15 minutes. These 2 degrees we shall add to the 90 degrees previously calculated which now give us 92 degrees. The next step is to multiply 45 with 36 which is 1620. Dividing this number with 60 will give us 27 minutes. These 27 minutes shall be added to the previously obtained 15 minutes, which is 42. This conversion 15-45 will give us 92 degrees and 27 minutes (920 47"). This value shall be set into the acquisition radar which shall be without the power. Once when the power is turned on, selsyn will take that position and the radar is oriented.

Appendix E

Lighting strike and protection[68]

The highest probability for lightning attachment to an airplane is the outer extremities, such as the wing tip, nose, or rudder. Lightning strikes occur most often during the climb and descent phases of flight at an altitude of 5,000 to 15,000 feet (1,524 to 4,572 meters). The probability of a lightning strike decreases significantly above 20,000 feet (6,096 meters).

Seventy percent of all lightning strikes occur during the presence of rain. There is a strong relationship between temperatures around 32 degrees F (0 degrees C) and lightning strikes to airplanes. Most lightning strikes to airplanes occur at near freezing temperatures.

Conditions that cause precipitation may also cause electrical storage of energy in clouds. This availability of electrical energy is associated with precipitation and cloud creation. Most lightning strikes affecting airplanes occur during spring and summer.

Although 70 percent of lightning-strike events occur during precipitation, lightning can affect airplanes up to five miles away from the electrical center of the cloud. Approximately 42 percent of the lightning strikes reported by airline pilots were experienced with no thunderstorms reported in the immediate area by the pilots.

During the initial stages of a lightning strike on an airplane, a glow may be seen on the nose or wing tips caused by ionization of the air surrounding the leading edges or sharp points on the airplane's structure. This ionization is caused by an increase in the electromagnetic field density at those locations (Fig. E-1).

In the next stage of the strike, a stepped leader may extend off the airplane from an ionized area seeking the large amount of lightning energy in a nearby cloud. Stepped leaders (also referred to as "leaders") refer to the path of ionized air containing a charge emanating from a charged airplane or cloud. With the airplane flying through the charged atmosphere, leaders propagate from the airplane extremities where ionized areas have formed.

---

68 Source: https://www.boeing.com/commercial/aeromagazine/articles/2012_q4/4/#:~:text=Lightning%20protection%20on%20airplanes%20may,fabric%2C%20and%20bonded%20aluminum%20foil.

Appendices

Once the leader from the airplane meets a leader from the cloud, a strike to the ground can continue and the airplane becomes part of the event. At this point, passengers and crew may see a flash and hear a loud noise when lightning strikes the airplane. Significant events are rare because of the lightning protection engineered into the airplane and its sensitive electronic components.

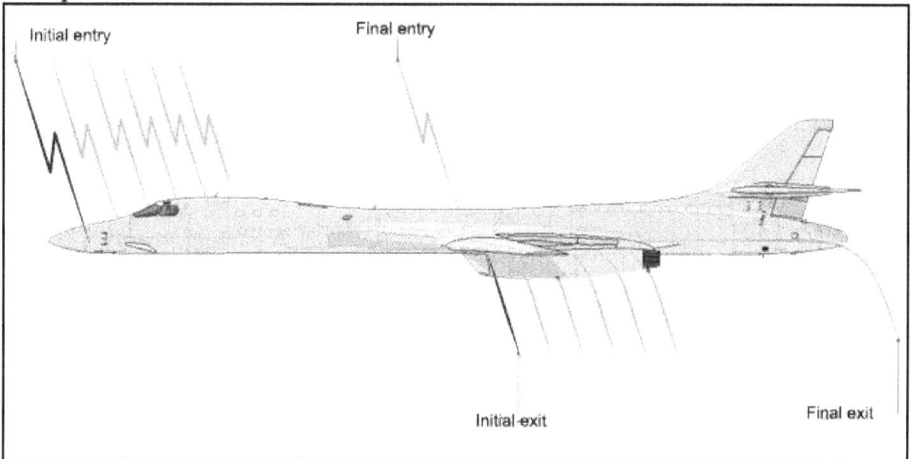

Figure E-1: Aircraft lighting strike. (Source: Authors)

After attachment, the airplane flies through the lightning event. As the strike pulses, the leader reattaches itself to the fuselage or other structure at other locations while the airplane is in the electric circuit between the cloud regions of opposite polarity. Current travels through the airplane's conductive exterior skin and structure and exits out another extremity, such as the tail, seeking the opposite polarity or ground. Pilots may occasionally report temporary flickering of lights or short-lived interference with instruments.

Airplane components made of ferromagnetic material may become strongly magnetized when subjected to lightning currents. Large current flowing from the lightning strike in the airplane structure can cause this magnetization.

While the electrical system in an airplane is designed to be resistant to lightning strikes, a strike of unusually high intensity can damage components such as electrically controlled fuel valves, generators, power feeders, and electrical distribution systems.

Most of the external parts of legacy airplanes are metal structure with sufficient thickness to be resistant to a lightning strike. This metal assembly is their basic protection. The thickness of the metal surface is sufficient to protect the airplane's internal spaces from a lightning strike. The metal skin also protects against the entrance of electromagnetic energy into the electrical wires of the airplane. While the metal skin does not prevent all electromagnetic energy from entering the electrical wiring, it can keep the energy to a satisfactory level.

By understanding nature and the effects of lightning strikes, Boeing works to design and test its commercial airplanes for lightning-strike protection to ensure protection is provided throughout their service lives. Material selection, finish selection, installation, and application of protective features are important methods of lightning-strike damage reduction.

Areas that have the greatest likelihood of a direct lightning attachment incorporate some type of lightning protection. Boeing performs testing that ensures the adequacy of lightning protection. Composite parts that are in lightning-strike prone areas must have appropriate lightning protection.

The large amount of data gathered from airplanes in service constitutes an important source of lightning-strike protection information that Boeing uses to make improvements in lightning-strike damage control that will reduce significant lightning-strike damage if proper maintenance is performed.

Lightning protection on airplanes may include:

Wire bundle shields; ground straps and composite structure expanded foils, wire mesh, aluminum flame spray coating, embedded metallic wire, metallic picture frames, diverter strips, metallic foil liners, coated glass fabric, and bonded aluminum foil.

Abbreviations

Appendix F

NATO Codification System

- SA-1 'Guild' (S-25 Berkut)
- SA-2 'Guideline' (S-75 Dvina/Volkhov/Desna)
- SA-3 'Goa' (S-125 Neva)
- SA-4 'Ganef' (9M8 Krug)
- SA-5 'Gammon' (S-200 Volga)
- SA-6 'Gainful' (3M9 Kub/Kvadrat)
- SA-7 'Galosh' and 'Grail' (9K32 Strela-2)
- SA-8 'Gecko' (9K33 Osa)
- SA-9 'Gaskin' (9K31 Strela-1)
- SA-10 'Grumble' (S-300P/PS/PT)
- SA-11 'Gadfly' (9K37 Buk)
- SA-12 'Gladiator' and 'Giant' (S-300V)
- SA-13 'Gopher' (9K35 Strela-10)
- SA-14 'Gremlin' (9K36 Strela-3)
- SA-15 'Gauntlet' (9K330/9K331/9K332 Tor)
- SA-16 'Gimlet' (9K310 Igla-1)
- SA-17 'Grizzly' (9K37 Buk-M1-2)
- SA-18 'Grouse' (9K38 Igla)
- SA-19 'Grison' (2K22 Tunguska)
- SA-20 'Gargoyle' (S-300PM/PMU Favorit)
- SA-21 'Growler' (S-400 Triumf)
- SA-22 'Greyhound' (Pantsir-S1)
- SA-23 'Gladiator/Giant' (S-300VM 'Antey-2500')
- SA-24 'Grinch' (9K338 Igla-S)
- SA-25 (9K333 Verba)

- Viking (9K317 BUK M3)
- S-500 Prometheus

The US DoD has different designations for naval surface-to-air missiles (SAN series) with Soviet designations. However, these are not standard NATO names. NATO uses the regular SA series for naval SAM. The US DoD refers to them by these names:

- SA-N-1 Goa (4K90 Volna) [SA-3]
- SA-N-2 Guideline (M-2 Volkhov-M) [SA-2]
- SA-N-3 Goblet (4K60/4K65 Shtorm)
- SA-N-4 Gecko (9M33 Osa-M) [SA-8]
- SA-N-5 Grail (9K32 Strela-2) [SA-7]
- SA-N-6 Grumble (S-300F Fort) [SA-10]
- SA-N-7 Gadfly (9M38/9M38M Uragan)[[SA-11]
- SA-N-8 Gremlin' (9K34 Strela-3) [SA-14]
- SA-N-9 Gauntlet (3K95 Kinzhal) [SA-15]
- SA-N-10 Grouse (3M38 Igla) [SA-18]
- SA-N-11 Grison (3M87 Kashtan) [SA-19]
- SA-N-12 Grizzly (3K37 Smerch/Shtil) [SA-17]
- SA-N-14 Grouse (9K38 Igla) [SA-18]
- SA-N-20 Gargoyle (S-300FM) [SA-20]

Soviet/Russian radar code names (used in this book)

- Flat Face (P-15 Tropa)
- Spoon Rest (P-18 Terek)
- Long Track (P-40)
- Thin Skin (PRV-16)
- Low Blow (SNR-125)

Glossary and Abbreviations

The following are typical terms used in radar, electronic warfare, and air defense. Often, abbreviations are used immediately after the full meaning.

Not all the terms in this list are used in this book, but it is worth having them all in one place as it may help the reader to understand the meaning of abbreviations and terminology often used in these fields.

1S91 - self-propelled fire control and engagement unit, same as RStON and 'Straight Flush'.

2P25 - self propelled missile launcher.

Active homing guidance - A system of homing guidance in which both the source for illuminating the target, and the receiver for detecting the energy reflected from the target as the result of illumination, are carried within the missile.

Airborne Warning and Control System (AWACS) - An aircraft suitably equipped to provide control, surveillance, and communications capability for strategic defense and/or tactical air operations.

Air defense - All defensive measures designed to destroy attacking enemy aircraft or missiles in the earth's envelope of atmosphere, or to nullify or reduce the effectiveness of such attack.

Air Surveillance Radar (ASR) - A radar displaying range and azimuth that is normally employed in a terminal area as an aid to approach and departure control.

Air-to-air missile (AAM) - A missile launched from an airborne carrier at a target above the surface.

Air-to-surface missile (ASM) - A missile launched from an airborne carrier to impact on a surface target.

Amplifier - An electronic circuit usually used to obtain amplification of voltage, current, or power.

Antenna - A device used for transmitting or receiving RF energy. The function of the antenna during transmission is to concentrate the radar energy from the transmitter into a shaped beam that points in the desired direction. During reception, or listening time, the function of the antenna is to collect the returning radar energy, contained in the echo signals, and deliver these signals to the receiver. Radar antennas are characterized by directive beams that are usually scanned in a recognizable pattern. The primary radar antenna types in use today fall into three categories: parabolic, Cassegrain, and phased array antennas.

Anti-aircraft artillery (AAA) - Guns used to shoot unguided projectiles at airborne aircraft. Usually used in the air defense system.

Anti-radiation missile (ARM) - A missile that homes passively on a radiation source.

Area defense - The concept of locating defense units to intercept enemy attacks, remote from, and without reference to, individual vital installations, industrial complexes, or population centers.

Azimuth -
1. the direction of a celestial object from the observer, expressed as the angular distance from the north or south point of the horizon to the point at which a vertical circle passing through the object intersects the horizon.
2. the horizontal angle or direction of a compass bearing.

Azimuth – Search – Command to start searching with the tracking and/or fire control radar in a designated direction.

Azimuth resolution - The ability of a radar to distinguish two targets in close azimuth proximity and distance.

Backlobe - The portion of the radiation pattern of an antenna that is oriented 180° in relation to the main beam. The antenna backlobe is a result of diffraction effects of the reflector and direct leakage through the reflector surface.

Bandwidth - The range of frequencies within which performance, with respect to some characteristics, falls, with specific limits (i.e., the width of frequency of a barrage noise package).

Beam rider - A missile guided by an electronic beam.

Beamwidth - The width of a radar beam measured between lines of half-power points on the polar pattern of the antenna. This width is measured at the 3 dB points.

Clutter - Unwanted signals, echoes, or images on the face of a scope that interfere with the observation of desired signals. Also called noise. This tends to mask the true target from detection or cause a tracking radar to break lock.

Clutter elimination - The clutter eliminator circuit discriminates against any target echo that exceeds three times the transmitted pulse width, and will not display it on the indicator. It is normally employed on the lower beams of a high frequency radar. This will allow targets above a preset signal strength to be presented, while the clutter (land) will be eliminated.

Command and control warfare (C2W) - The integrated use of operations security (OPSEC), military deception, psychological operations (PSYOP), electronic warfare (EW), and physical destruction, mutually supported by intelligence to deny information, influence, degrade, or destroy adversary C2 capabilities while protecting friendly C2 capabilities.

Command, control, communications, and computer systems (C4) - The process of, and means for, the exercise of authority and direction by a properly designated commander over assigned forces in the accomplishment of the commander's mission.

Command guidance - A guidance system in which intelligence transmitted to the missile from an off-board source causes the missile to traverse a directed flight path.

Communications intelligence (COMINT) - Intelligence derived from the interception of enemy communications signals.

Conical scan (CONSCAN) - A type of scanning in which the axis of the RF beam is tilted away from the axis of the reflector and rotated about it, thus generating a cone.

CW - Continuous Wave - is an electromagnetic wave of constant amplitude and frequency.

CW jamming - The transmission of constant-amplitude, constant-frequency, unmodulated jamming signals to change the signal-to-noise ratio of a radar receiver.

Data-link - A communications link which permits automatic transmission of information in digital form.

Deception - Those measures designed to mislead the enemy by manipulation, distortion, or falsification of evidence to induce him to react in a manner prejudicial to his interests. (See Electronic Deception, or Manipulative Deception.)

Defense suppression - A term applied to weapons systems that are intended to eliminate or degrade enemy detection, acquisition, or tracking equipment.

DoD - Department of Defense also means Ministry of Defense.

Doppler (effect) - Continuous wave (CW) Doppler radar modules are sensors that measure the shift in frequency created when an object moves. A transmitter emits energy at a specific frequency which, when reflected, can indicate both speed and direction of the target. When objects move closer to the Doppler source, they increase in shift (positive value), and when they move further away, they decrease in shift (negative value).

Doppler radar - A radar system that measures the velocity of a moving object by the apparent shift in carrier frequency of the returned signal as it approaches or recedes.

Downlink - The signal from a transponder beacon located on a surface-to-air missile (SAM) used to provide a traceable radar return for missile guidance.

Downlink jamming (DLJ) - Some command guidance missiles carry a beacon (downlink) which is used by the parent radar to track the missile. If this beacon reply can be hidden from the parent tracking radar, the missile guidance solution can be defeated. Hence, downlink (beacon) jamming is intended to screen the missile beacon signal from the parent radar's view.

Dummy antenna - A device that has the necessary impedance characteristics of an antenna and the necessary power-handling capabilities, but does not radiate or receive radio waves. Note: In receiver practice, that portion of the impedance not included in the signal generator is often called a dummy antenna.

Early warning radar - A radar set or system used near the periphery of a defended area to provide early notification of hostile aircraft approaching the area.

EA pod - A jamming system that is designed to be carried externally on an aircraft. Effective radiated power (ERP) - Input power to antenna time

multiplied by the gain of the antenna, expressed in watts.

Electromagnetic deception - The deliberate radiation, reradiation, alteration, absorption, or reflection of electromagnetic radiations in a manner intended to mislead an enemy in the interpretation of, or use of, information received by his electronic systems. There are two categories of electronic deception:

1. Manipulative deception - The alteration or simulation of friendly electromagnetic radiation to accomplish deception.

2. Imitative deception - The introduction of radiations into enemy channels that imitate his own emissions.

Electromagnetic interference (EMI) - Any electromagnetic disturbance that interrupts, obstructs, or otherwise degrades or limits the effective performance of electronic systems. EMI can be induced intentionally, by way of jamming, or unintentionally because of spurious emissions and modulations.

Electromagnetic pulse (EMP) - The generation and radiation in a transmission medium of a very narrow and very high-amplitude pulse of electromagnetic noise. The term is associated with the high-level pulse because of a nuclear detonation and with an intentionally generated narrow, high-amplitude pulse for EA applications. In nuclear detonations, the EMP signal consists of a continuous spectrum with most of its energy distributed throughout the low frequency band of 3 to 30 kHz.

Electromagnetic radiation - Radiation made up of oscillating electric and magnetic fields and propagated with the speed of light. Includes gamma radiation, x-rays, ultraviolet, visible and infrared radiation, plus radar and radio waves.

Electromagnetic spectrum - The total range of frequencies (or wavelengths) over which any form of electromagnetic radiation occurs.

Electronic attack (EA) - The use of electromagnetic energy, directed energy, or antiradiation weapons to attack personnel, facilities, or equipment with the intent of degrading, neutralizing, or destroying enemy combat capability. Action taken to reduce the enemy's effective use of the electromagnetic spectrum. EA is a division of electronic warfare (EW).

Electronic combat (EC) - Action taken in support of military operations against the enemy's electromagnetic capabilities. EC is task-oriented and includes electronic warfare (EW), command and control warfare (C2W), and suppression of enemy air defenses (SEAD).

ECM - Electronic countermeasure.

Electronic protection (EP) - Active and passive means taken to protect personnel, facilities, and equipment from any effects of friendly or enemy employment of electronic warfare that degrade, neutralize or destroy friendly combat capability. EP is a division of electronic warfare (EW).

Electromagnetic deception - The deliberate radiation, reradiation, alteration, absorption, or reflection of electromagnetic radiations in a manner intended to mislead an enemy in the interpretation of, or use of, information received by his electronic systems. There are two categories of electronic deception:

1. Manipulative deception - The alteration or simulation of friendly electromagnetic radiation to accomplish deception.
2. Imitative deception - The introduction of radiations into enemy channels that imitate his own emissions.

Electronic intelligence (ELINT) - The intelligence information product of activities engaged in the collection and processing for subsequent intelligence purposes of foreign, noncommunications, electromagnetic radiations emanating from other than nuclear detonations or radioactive sources.

Electronic jammers –

1. Expendable - A transmitter designed for special use such as being dropped behind enemy lines.
2. Repeater - A receiver-transmitter device that, when triggered by enemy radar impulses, returns synchronized false signals to the enemy equipment. The returned impulses are spaced and timed to produce false echoes or bearing errors in the enemy equipment.

Electronic jamming - The deliberate radiation, reradiation, or reflection of electromagnetic energy with the object of impairing the use of electronic devices, equipment, or systems.

Electronic order of battle - A listing of all the electronic radiating equipment of a military force giving location, type function, and other pertinent data.

Electronic reconnaissance - Specific reconnaissance directed towards the

Glossary

collection of electromagnetic radiations. Examples:

    COMINT Communications Intelligence

    ELINT Electronic Intelligence

    OPINT Optical Intelligence

    RINT Radiated Intelligence

    SIGINT Signal Intelligence

Electronic warfare (EW) - Military action involving the use of electromagnetic energy and directed energy to control the electromagnetic spectrum. EW has three divisions: electronic attack (EA), electronic protection (EP), and electronic warfare support (ES).

Electro-optics (EO) - The interaction between optics and electronics leading to the transformation of electrical energy into light, or vice versa, with the use of an optical device.

Electro-optic counter-countermeasures (EOCCM) - Actions taken to ensure the effective friendly use of the electro-optic spectrum despite the enemy's use of countermeasures in that spectrum.

Endgame - The period of military engagement 3-5 seconds before missile impact.

Equivalent - The command 'Equivalent' is to 'turn off' the high frequency energy emission into the space, but not turn off the radar.

EW - Electronic warfare

Expendable jammer - A nonrecoverable jammer. Early expendables were limited to chaff and flare deployments; however, various radiating jamming systems exist that use noise or repeater techniques. These are dispensed by aircraft or other delivery systems and are designed to disrupt or deceive a victim radar for a short period of time.

Extremely high frequency (EHF) - Frequencies in the range of 30 to 300 GHz.

False target – A radiated bundle of electromagnetic energy that is displaced in time from the echo that creates a response in the receiver where no reflecting surface exists.

False target generator - Device for generating electromagnetic energy of the correct frequency of the receiver that is displaced in time from the reflected energy of the target.

Fire control radar - Specialized radar systems used to locate and track airborne and surface targets, compute an optimum weapons firing point, and control the firing and sometimes guidance of its weapons.

FM jamming – A technique consisting of a constant amplitude RF signal that is varied in frequency around a center frequency to produce a signal over a band of frequencies.

Frequency spectrum - The entire range of frequencies of electromagnetic radiation.

G, g - Acceleration due to gravity (32.2 ft/sec^2).

Gain (manual) - The receiver gain control allows the operator to vary the receiver sensitivity. It is not designed as an AJ feature; however, when properly employed it may greatly reduce the effects of jamming. The radar detection capability is also reduced by an equal amount.

Gain (transmission gain) - The increase in signal power in transmission from one point to another under static conditions. Note: Power gain is usually expressed in decibels.

Get the High Down – This command means that the high voltage is turned off but the emitter is still working in normal mode but there is no high energy emission into space.

GRAU - Main Missile and Artillery Directorate of the Ministry of Defense of the Russian Federation.

Ground controlled intercept (GCI) - Vectoring an interceptor aircraft to an airborne target by means of information relayed from a ground-based radar site that observes both the interceptor and target.

Guidance system (missile) - A system that evaluates flight information, correlates it with target data, determines the desired flight path of the missile, and communicates the necessary commands to the missile flight control system.

Guided missile - An unmanned vehicle moving above the surface of the earth whose trajectory of flight path is capable of being altered by an external or internal mechanism.

Height finder - A radar used to detect the angular elevation, slant range and height of objects in the vertical sight plane. An air defense ground radar used specifically to accurately determine aircraft altitude for tracking and ground controlled intercepts.

Hertz (Hz) - The unit of frequency, equal to one cycle of variation per second. It supersedes the unit cycle per second (cps).

High frequency (HF) - Frequencies from 3,000 to 30,000 kHz.

Homing guidance - A system by which a missile steers itself towards a target by means of a self-contained mechanism which is activated by some distinguishing characteristics of the target.

Identification, friend or foe (IFF) - A system using radar transmission to which equipment carried by friendly forces automatically responds, for example, by emitting pulses, thereby distinguishing themselves from enemy forces. It is the primary method of determining the friendly or unfriendly character of aircraft and ships by other aircraft and ships, and by ground forces employing radar detection equipment and associated identification, friend or foe units.

IGR - Illumination and Guidance Radar.

Image frequency - An undesired input frequency capable of producing the selected frequency by the same process. NOTE: An image frequency is a frequency which differs from, but has a certain symmetrical relationship to, that which a superheterodyne receiver is tuned. Consequently, the image frequency can be mistakenly accepted and processed as a true frequency by the receiver.

Infrared (IR) - That portion of the frequency spectrum lying between the upper end of the millimeter wave region and the lower (red) end of the visible spectrum. In wavelength, the IR lies between 0.78 and 300 microns; in frequency, it lies between one and 400 terahertz (THz).

Infrared counter-countermeasures (IRCCM) - Actions taken to effectively employ our own infrared radiation equipment and systems in spite of the enemy's actions o counter their use.

Infrared countermeasures (IRCM) –

1. Countermeasures used specifically against enemy threats operating in the infrared spectrum.
2. Actions taken to prevent or reduce the effectiveness of enemy equipment and tactics employing infrared radiation.

Intercept point - A computed point in space towards which an interceptor is vectored to complete an interception.

Interference (electronic) - An electrical or electromagnetic disturbance that causes undesirable responses on electronic equipment. Electrical interference refers specifically to interference caused by the operation of electrical apparatus that is not designed to radiate electromagnetic energy.

Intermediate frequency (IF) –
1. A fixed frequency to which all carrier waves are converted in a super-heterodyne receiver.
2. A frequency to which a signaling wave is shifted locally as an intermediate step during transmission or reception.
3. A frequency resulting from the combination of the received signal and that of the local oscillator in a superheterodyne receiver.

Klystron - A very stable microwave amplifier that provides high gain at good efficiency. This is accomplished by velocity modulating (accelerating a beam of electronics flowing from its cathode to its anode.

LAP - Local Air Picture

Laser target designation - The use of a laser to direct a light beam onto the target so that appropriate sensors can track or home on the reflected energy.

Light amplification by stimulated emission of radiation (LASER) - A process of generating coherent light. The process uses a natural molecular (and atomic) phenomenon whereby molecules absorb incident electromagnetic energy at specific frequencies. It then stores this energy for short but usable periods, then releases the stored energy as light at particular frequencies, and in an extremely narrow frequency band.

Lobe - One of the three-dimensional sections of the radiation pattern of a directional antenna bounded by 1-2 cones of nulls.

Low frequency (LF) - Frequencies from 30 - 300 kHz.

Magnetron - A radar microwave device whose operation is based on the motion of electrons (AC) under the influence of combined electric and magnetic fields.

Mainlobe - The lobe of a transmitting or receiving antenna centered on the directivity axis of the antenna.

Medium frequency (MF) - Frequencies from 300 to 3,000 kHz.

Micron - A unit of length equal to a micrometer (10^{-6} meters).

Millimeter waves - Frequencies (30 GHz to 300 GHz) in the millimeter portion of the electromagnetic spectrum.

Miss distance - The distance measured between the closest paths of a target and interceptor (i.e., aircraft and missile). One objective of self-protection jamming systems is to increase the miss distance to avoid destruction if missile launch cannot be prevented.

Modulator - A device (such as an electron tube) for modulating a carrier wave or signal for the transmission of intelligence of some sort.

Monopulse - A method of pulse generation that allows the simultaneous determining of azimuth, elevation and range, and/or speed from a single pulse.

Monopulse radar - A radar using a receiving antenna system having two or more partially overlapping lobes in the radiation patterns. Sum and difference channels in the receiver compare the amplitudes or the phases of the antenna outputs to determine the angle of arrival of the received signal relative to the antenna boresight. A well-designed monopulse tracking system will achieve a more accurate track under conventional jamming techniques than on the skin return. Certain monopulse trackers are susceptible to angular jamming techniques such as skirt and image jamming. Techniques such as 'CROSS EYE' are designed to attack all monopulse tracking systems. Monopulse deception is a major area of advanced R&D with no clear 'best technique' yet in sight.

Moving Target Indicator (MIT) - A radar presentation that shows only target s that are in motion. Signals from stationary targets are subtracted out of the return signal by the output of a suitable memory circuit.

Multiband radar - Radar that simultaneously operates on more than one frequency band through a common antenna. This technique allows for many sophisticated forms of video processing and requires that a jammer must jam all channels simultaneously.

Noise –

1. Any unwanted disturbance within a dynamic electrical or mechanical system, such as undesired electromagnetic radiation, and any transmission channel or device.

2. Uncontrolled random disturbances that arise in a guided missile system because of various physical phenomena.

Noise jamming - Direct (straight) AM or FM noise on a carrier frequency

that has a highly variable bandwidth for the purpose of increasing (saturating) the radar receiver's noise level.

OARSt - Osmatračko akvizicijska radarska stanica - Serbian acronym for Surveillance acquisition radar station.

Oscillator - Electronic circuit or device capable of converting direct current (DC) into alternating current (AC) at a frequency determined by the inductive and the capacitive constants of the oscillator.

Passive detection and tracking - By combining azimuth data on jamming strobes from several stations, intersections are obtained which indicate the position of the jammers. The number of ghosts can be reduced by increasing the number of friendly stations and obtaining elevation angles of strobes when available.

Passive electronic countermeasures - Electronic countermeasures based on the reflection, absorption or modification of the enemy's electromagnetic energy. This distinction between active and passive countermeasures is not currently used, but is based on the presence or absence of an electronic transmitter.

Point defense - The defense of specified geographical areas, cities, and vital installations. One distinguishing feature of point defense missiles is that their guidance information is received from radars located near the launching sites. Polarization - The direction of an electrical field is considered the direction of polarization. When a half-wave dipole antenna is horizontally oriented, the emitted wave is horizontally polarized. A vertical polarized wave is emitted when the antenna is erected vertically.

Pulse Doppler radar - A highly complex radar system that employs a very high pulse repetition frequency (usually 10,000 PPS or higher) to reduce 'blind speeds' and measure the Doppler frequency shift to resolve target velocity. Pulse Doppler is applied principally to radar systems requiring the detection of moving targets in a ground clutter environment. It uses pulse modulation to achieve higher peak power, greater range, less susceptibility to unfriendly detection, and enhanced range resolution.

Pulse Repetition Frequency (PRF) - the number of pulses of a repeating signal in a specific time unit, normally measured in pulses per second.

PVO - Yugoslav/Serbian abbreviation for Air Defense (Protiv Vazdušna Odbrana)

Radar beacon - A receiver-transmitter combination that sends out a coded signal when triggered by the proper type of pulse enabling determination of range and bearing information by the interrogating station or aircraft.

Radar cross section - The equivalent area intercepted by a radiated signal and, if scattered uniformly in all directions, produces an echo at the radar receiver equal to that of the target. Typical radar cross sections of aircraft vary from one to over 1,000 square meters. The RCS of ships may exceed 10,000 square meters.

Radar definition - The accuracy with which a radar obtains target information such as range, azimuth, or elevation.

RF - Radio Frequency.

Radar homing - Homing on the source of a radar beam.

Radar homing and warning (RHAW) - Typically consists of an airborne, wideband video receiver designed to intercept, identify, and display the direction to pulsetype emitters.

Radar resolution - A measure of a radar's ability to separate targets that are close together in some aspect of range, azimuth, or elevation into individual returns.

Radar warning receiver (RWR) - A receiver onboard an aircraft that analyzes the hostile radar environment and determines radar threat by type, frequency, relative bearing, and relative distance. The threat is displayed to the aircrew by means of display lights, video symbols, and aural tones.

Radio frequency (RF) - Electromagnetic energy radiated at some frequency. Radio frequency interference - An unintentional interfering signal capable of being propagated into electronic equipment, usually derived from sources outside the system.

Range - The distance from one object to another.

RECM technique - Radar Electronic Countermeasure technique. RECM systems can work in different ways, for example creating electronically false targets, or blinding the platform to be protected from the view of enemy radars.

RStON - Radarska Stanica Osmatranja i Navodjenja' which is an abbreviation for the translated meaning of 'Radar Station for Surveillance and Guidance'.

SAM - Surface-to-air missile.

Scan - The process of directing a beam of RF energy successively over a given region, or the corresponding process in reception.

Scan interval - The time interval from the peak of one mainlobe in a scan pattern to the peak of the next mainlobe.

Scan period - The time period of basic scan types (except conical and lobe switching) or the period of the lowest repetitive cycle of complex scan combinations. The basic unit of measurement is degrees/mils per second or seconds per cycle.

Scan type - The path made in space by a point on the radar beam, for example, circular, helical, conical, spiral, or sector.

Search –
1. A term applied to that phase of radar operation when the lobe, or beam of radiated energy, is directed in such a way to search for targets in the area.
2. A systematic examination of space to locate and identify targets of interest.

Sector scan - A scan in which the antenna sweeps back and forth through a selected angle.

Semiactive radar homing - Semiactive homing guidance combines principles from both the beam rider and the active radar homing missile. Track on the target is established by the AI's radar; the missile is launched when the target comes within its effective range. During missile flight, the AI maintains track on the target. Radar returns from the target are received by the missile. Guidance commands are generated within the missile from the radar returns.

Sidelobe - Part of the beam from an antenna, other than the mainlobe. Sidelobe gain is usually less than mainlobe gain. Given that the mainlobe radiates most of the power at zero degrees azimuth, sidelobes inherently radiate significant power in the direction of +20°, 90°, and 150° relative to the mainlobe.

Sidelobe jamming - Jamming through a sidelobe of the receiving antenna in an attempt to obliterate the desired signal received through the mainlobe of the receiving antenna at fixed points.

Sidelobe suppression - The suppression of that portion of the beam from a radar antenna other than the mainlobe.

Signal intelligence (SIGINT) - Intelligence derived from the interception of enemy communications and noncommunication signals. A generic term that includes both COMINT and ELINT.

Signal-to-jamming ratio (S/J) - The ratio of the signal power to the jamming power or intentional interference at some point in the system. This ratio is often expressed in decibels.

Signal-to-noise ratio (S/N) - Ratio of the power of the signal to the power of the noise. Signature - The set of parameters that describes the characteristics of a radar target or an RF emitter and distinguishes one emitter from another. Signature parameters include the RF of the carrier, the modulation characteristics (typically the pulse modulation code), and the scan pattern.

SPAAG - Self propelled anti aircraft gun

Straight Flush - self-propelled fire control and engagement radar unit, same meaning as RStON and 1S91.

Super high frequency (SHF) - Frequencies from 3 to 30 GHz.

Suppression of enemy air defenses (SEAD) - That activity which neutralizes, destroys, or temporarily degrades enemy air defense systems in a specific area by using physical attack, deception, and/or electronic warfare.

Surface-to-air missile (SAM) - A missile launched from a surface launcher at a target above the surface.

TELAR - Transporter, Erector LAuncheR - acronym for the mobile launchers. It also includes radar component.

Terminal guidance –

1. The guidance applied to a guided missile between mid-course and arrival in the vicinity of the target.
2. Electronic, mechanical, visual, or other assistance given to aircraft pilots to facilitate arrival at, operation within or over, landing upon or departure from an air landing or air drop facility.

Tracking - The continuous monitoring of range, velocity, or position of a target in space from a reference position. This is accomplished via radar and/or optical means.

Tracking radar - A radar that measures the range, azimuth, elevation, and/

or velocity of the target and provides data that may be used by the fire control computer to determine the target path and predict its future position.

TOV - Television Optical Sight (In local terminology called 'visor;.

UAV - Unmanned Aerial Vehicle, drone

Ultra high frequency (UHF) - Frequencies from 300 to 3,000 MHz.

Very high frequency (VHF) - Frequencies from 30 to 300 MHz.

Very low frequency (VLF) - Frequencies from 3 to 30 kHz.

Video frequency –

1. A band of frequencies extending from approximately 100 Hz to several MHz.

2. The frequency of the voltage resulting from television scanning. Range from zero to 4 MHz or more.

VIKO - name for the detached radar screen located in the UNK cabin of SA-3/S-125 system.

Warning receiver - A receiver with the primary function of warning the user that his unit is being illuminated by an electromagnetic signal of interest.

WO - Warrant officer

References and Bibliography

Books:

1. Aleksandar Razinger, Elektronsko izviđanje i maskiranje, drugo dopunjeno izdanje, VINC, Beograd, 1989.
2. Benjamin Lambetha, NATO`s Air War for Kosovo, A Strategic and Operational Assessment, RAND Corporation, 2001.
3. Bojan B. Dimitrijević, Jovica Draganić, Vazdušni rat nad Srbijom 1999. godine, drugo izmenjeno i dopunjeno izdanje, MC Odbrana, Beograd, 2013.
4. Bojan B. Dimitrijević, Jugoslovensko Ratno vazduhoplovstvo i Protivvazdušna odbrana, ISI, Beograd 2017.
5. Bojan B. Dimitrijević, Vazdušni rat nad Republikom Srpskom i Republikom Srpskom Krajinom, Društvo istoričara Srbije, Beograd, 2017.
6. Col. Christopher E. Haave, USAF, Lt. Col. Phil M. Haun, USAF, A-10s over Kosovo, Maxvell Air Force Base, Alabama, December 2003.
7. Danko Borojević, Paklena krila, mlazni lovački avioni u ratu 1943-2004, SGC, Beograd, 2009.
8. Danko Borojević, Dragi Ivić, Orlovi sa Vrbasa – istorija vojnog vazduhoplovstva na teritoriji Republike Srpske, D.O.O. „Štampa", Ruma, 2014.
9. Danko Borojević, Dragi Ivić, Vojska Republike Srpske, 12. maj 1992-31. decembar 2005., SRVČ, Beograd, 2014.
10. Danko Borojević, Dragi Ivić, Željko Ubović, Vazduhoplovne snage bivših republika SFRJ 1992-2015, D.O.O. „Štampa", Ruma, 2016.
11. Generalštab Jugoslovenske narodne armije, I uprava, Četvrti Izraelsko-arapski rat oktobra 1973, interno, Vojna štamparija, Beograd, 1974.

12. General Spasoje Smiljanić, Ratno vazduhoplovstvo i protivvazdušna odbrana u odbrani otadžbine, treće izdanje, Vesti d.o.o, Beograd, 2012.
13. Joseph S. Doyle, squadron leader, Royal Air Force, The Yom Kippur war and the Shaping of the United States Air Force, Air University Press Curtis E. LeMay Center for Doctrine Development and Education Maxwell Air Force Base, Alabama, Presented to the faculty of SAASS in June 2016, Published by Air University Press in February 2019.
14. Kenneth P. Werrell, Archie to SAM A Short Operational History of Ground-Based Air Defense, Second Edition, Air University Press Maxwell Air Force Base, Alabama, August 2005.
15. Komanda RV i PVO, Avioni, helikopteri, bespilotne letelice i projektili u naoružanju zemalja NATO i Švedske, Zemun, decembar 1965. godine.
16. Novica Simić, Operacija Koridor 92, BORS, Banja Luka, 2011.
17. Thomas Withington, B-1B Lancer Units in Combat, Osprey Combat Airfcraft, Botley-Oxford, 2006.
18. Mike (Mihajlo) Mihajlović, Djordje Aničić: Missileers Against the Stealth: The First Downing of the Stealth Fighter in History., MSM publishing, Toronto, 2019.
19. Skolnik, M.I. (2002), Introduction to Radar Systems, McGraw-Hill Education.
20. Richards, M.A., Scheer, J.A. and Holm, W.A. (2010), Principles of Modern Radar-Basic Principles, SciTech Publishing.
21. Georg M. Siouris, (2004), Missile Guidance and Controls Systems, Springer.
22. Arhangelski I. I., (2001) Proektirovanie Zenitnih Upravlyaemih Raket, Moskovskii Aviacioni Institut (MAI)
23. Yanushevsky, Rafael, (2011) Guidance of Unmanned Aerial Vehicles, CRC Press
24. Nerri, Filippo (208), Introduction to Electronic Defense Systems, Artech House.
25. Adamy, David L. (2011), Electronic Warfare Pocket Guide,

Scitech Publishing.

26. Pokorni, Slavko (2001), Tendencije Razvoja Pasivnih Mamaca, Vojno Tehnicki Glasnik, Serbia.

27. Mihajlović, Mihajlo, (1994) Proporcionalno vodjenje - Proportional Guidance), Faculty of Technical Sciences (Fakultet Tehničkih Nauka) Novi Sad, Serbia 1993.

28. Mike (Mihajlo) Mihajlović, Djordje Aničić: Shooting Down the Stealth Fighter: Eyewitness Accounts From Those Who Were There, Pen and Sword Books, 2021.

29. Mike (Mihajlo) Mihajlović, Jetliner Down: Tor-M1 Missile System Which Downed Ukrainian Flight PS752, MSM publishing, Toronto, 2020.

30. Vakin, Sergei A., Shustov, Lev N., Dunwell, Robert H. (2001), Fundamentals of Electronic Warfare, Artech House.

31. T.O.GR1F-16CJ-34-1-1 Avionics and Nonnuclear Weapons Delivery Flight Manual, F-16C/D (1997).

32. T.O.GR1F-16CJ-1-1 Flight Manual F-16C/D (2003).

33. Pervov, Mikhail (2012) Raskazi o Ruskih Raketah, Stolichnaya Enciklopedia, Moskva.

34. Leonov, A.P. and others (2015) Voiskovaya Protivvozdushanay Oborona 1915-2015, Zbornik.

35. ZRK Kub, Ruskie Tanki, (2013) Eaglemoss Collection.

36. Voruzhenie PVO I RES Rossii (Air Defense Weapons and Electronic Systems of Russia) (2011) Rosoboronexport, Moskva.

37. Andersen. Yu. A., Drozhkin A. I., Lozik P.M. (1979) Protivvozdushnaya Oborona Suhoputnih Voisk, Voeno Izdatestvo Ministerstvo Oboroni SSSR, Moskva.

38. Zenitni Raketni Kompleksi PVO Suhoputniy Voisk, (1997), Tehnika i Voruzhenie.

39. Balkani 1991-2000, Voina v Vazduhe 10.

40. Mihajlović Mihajlo, Arsić Stanislav (2003) Specijalne Snage Sveta (World Special Forces) Novinsko Izdavački Centar Vojska, Beograd.

41. Teperin L.L.,Vozhdaev V. V. (2018) Kharakteristiki Radiolokatsionnoy Zametnosti Letatelnih Aparatov, FizMatLit, Moskva.

42. Banjac Dušan (1986): Elektronska Borba u Protivvazdusnoj Odbrani, Vojno Tehnicki Izdavački Centar, Beograd.

43. Andrea De Martino (2018), Introduction to Modern EW Systems, Second Edition, Artech House.

Magazines and videos:

1. Aeromagazin br. 93, oktobar 2013, Danko Borojević, Nebeski štit sa zemlje, samohodni raketni sistem zemlja-vazduh 2K12 Kub.

2. Danko Borojević, Dragi Ivić, Raj i pakao obećane zemlje, obećana zemlja kao večito žarište, ili: rajski vrt kao predvorje pakla, 28 jun 2010.

3. Danko Borojević, Ratna krila Mojsijevih sinova, 18. jun 2010.

4. Grigoriy Yashkin, 'Beneath the Hot Sun of Syria', Journal of Military History/ Voenno-istoricheskii zhurnal, No. 4, 1998.

5. Henry A. Kissinger, The White House, Memorandum Of Conversation, Monday, October 22, 1973.

6. Ivan Brigović, Odlazak Jugoslavenske narodne armije s područja Zadra, Šibenika i Splita krajem 1991. i početkom 1992. godine, Hrvatski memorijalno-dokumentacijski centar Domovinskog rata, Zagreb, 2011.

7. Jerusalem Post, Israel News, Uri Milstein, Operation Mole Cricket 19: 34 years later, the IAF's most decisive victory remains the standard, 18 Jul 2016.

8. Vladimir Voronov, The Sirian Nemesis, Russia studias centre, January 2017, Translated by Arch Tait.

9. Bozsoki Attila, Developmental Trends in the SA–6 (2K12 KUB) Air Defence Missile Systems and the Finalized Developments in the Hungarian Air Force Surface–To–Air Missile System Hungarian Air Force, AARMS Vol. 13, No. 2 (2014) 283–293.

References and bibliography

10. Tehnika i Voruzhenie (1999-2018).
11. Vojnotehnički glasnik, Vol. 52, No. 2, mart-april 2004, str. 171-181, dr. Čedomir Gacović, pukovnik, dipl. inž., Vojna akademija Beograd, Ispitivanje uticaja oblaka smetnji na monoimpulsni nišanski radar i protivradarske rakete.
12. Вестник ПВО, авторскй проект Саида Аминова, 22.05.2009.
13. Николай Юрьев „Будни полигона", Техника и вооружение №3, 2004.
14. Eric Schmidt, 'The World; Bombs Are Smart, People Are Smarter', New York Times, 4 July 1999.
15. Video material: 'Sdelano v SSSR'.
16. Video material: 'Zastava Film'.
17. Video Material: 'Dozvolite'.
18. Video Material: 'RTS'.

Index

230th regiment 59, 135, 146, 155, 167, 214

240th regiment 59, 109, 136, 146, 155, 167, 168, 187, 192-194, 214

250th Missile Brigade 145, 146, 156, 218

310th regiment 59, 108, 136, 146, 155, 167, 170, 192, 193, 198, 214

311th regiment 59, 69, 71, 141, 146, 155, 167, 168, 170, 184, 214, 215

60th regiment 59, 107, 135, 136, 141, 146, 155, 158, 166, 170, 185, 201, 214, 215, 217

1RL-128D-1 60

1S11 12, 13, 15, 42, 45, 160, 162, 224

1S31 12-15, 46, 160, 162, 224

1S91 12, 15, 16, 27, 31, 34, 36, 42, 44, 47, 49, 60, 60, 62, 89, 111, 113, 147, 160, 200, 207, 212

1S91, modernization 213, 218, 219, 222, 224, 227

2K11 Krug (SA-4 Ganef) 1, 4, 7, 18,

2K12 1, 3-8, 11, 18, 21, 31, 33, 34, 42, 53, 58, 70, 71, 73, 104, 107, 108, 110, 111, 135, 146, 156, 161, 173, 180, 187

2K12 modernization 219-223, 231,

2P25 6, 11, 15, 16, 31, 34, 36, 37, 49, 60, 62, 131, 219, 222, 223, 227

2T7, transloader 6, 31, 37, 51, 52, 131, 222

3rd battalion (Neva) 169, 210

3M9 6, 11, 15, 18-21, 23, 30, 31, 33, 34, 35, 42, 60, 62, 86, 89, 104, 115, 142, 175, 188, 222, 224

9K37 34, 231-233

9K317 232, 234

9S417 35, 39, 42

A

A-4 Skyhawk 77, 83, 97

A-10 180-186

Allied Force, operation, 145, 177, 178, 203-206

An-2 108

An-26 128, 129

AN/ALE-50 175, 176, 192, 268

Angolan border war 99,

antenna 12-15, 20, 23, 40-42, 46, 48, 65, 67, 97, 102, 115, 126, 162, 200, 202, 227, 236, 241-247, 249, 251, 257, 259, 265, 274, 286

Armenia, war 104, 15

Artsakh (Nagorho Karabakh) 104

Aviano, air-base 115, 119, 121, 153, 191

AWACS 98, 251

Azerbaijan, war 104

azimuth 14, 15, 39, 41, 42, 45, 46, 48, 49, 170, 202, 244, 246-249, 251, 252, 272, 274-279,

B

B-1B 173, 174, 176-180, 267

B-52 103, 152

Batajnica, air base 145,

beam rider 29,

Bekaa Valley 89, 90, 92, 94, 97

Belgrade 55, 110, 138, 166, 167, 173,

198, 200
Bear (the radar) 36, 40, 60, 61, 63-67, 69, 70, 108, 160, 166, 201, 215
Buk/SA-11 33, 34, 71, 231-233, 237, 238
Buk M3 Viking 234-236

C
C-130 112
camouflage, field 125, 142, 166, 170, 171, 186, 197, 205, 206, 208, 228, 261, 265, 266
Chad, war 100-103,
chaffs 86, 97, 118, 123, 173, 179, 180-182, 244, 254
Clark, Wesley 206, 207

D
deception 95, 150, 203, 205, 206, 208
decoy 25, 33, 86, 95, 104, 166, 170, 174, 175, 179, 190, 192, 205-209, 244, 265, 266
decoy-towed 267-270
Desert Storm 126, 149, 150, 156, 181, 204, 259

E
E-2C 95, 97, 99
EC-130 125
E-3 Sentry 152
EA-6B 153, 191, 210, 262
Egypt (wars with Israel) 32, 73-86, 89, 231, 267
electronic warfare 83, 126, 153, 168, 170, 267
ELINT 201

F
F-4 15, 75-77, 96, 97, 103
F-14 103

F-15 98, 104, 126, 153, 199
F-16 115, 116, 118-123, 151, 163, 169, 185, 191, 198, 210, 211, 260, 262, 263, 270
flares 29, 86, 118, 123, 149, 179, 222
frequency 13-15, 21, 30, 40, 42, 67, 115, 117, 121, 180, 243, 245, 248-250, 253, 254, 265, 270

G
guidance, CLOS 29
guidance, command 28-30
guidance, missile 24, 25, 27-30, 31, 32, 46, 49, 62, 96, 130, 131, 146, 147, 150, 160, 162-166, 175, 186, 187, 189, 190, 222, 236, 237, 243, 257, 258, 260-262, 264, 266, 267

H
HARM 129, 159, 162, 182, 190, 197, 198, 200, 210-212, 221, 247, 256, 258-264

I
IAF (Israeli Air Forces) 73, 86, 88, 89, 98, 99
IKO, circular indicator 46
institute 20 2
integrated air defense 126, 227
Iran 68, 103, 258
Iraq 68, 103, 258

J
Jaguar 100, 101, 103
jamming 25, 30, 39-42, 56, 62, 72, 77, 90, 95, 97-99, 115, 131, 160, 168, 170, 201, 221, 223, 234, 249, 267, 269

K
Karabakh 104

Index

Kosmos, repair center 68, 69, 108, 110, 111, 125, 129-131
Kosovo 109, 137-141, 144, 146, 161, 164, 166, 167, 173, 174, 177, 184, 188, 190, 201, 203-206, 212-215, 270
KUB/SA-6 1, 3-8, 18, 34, 42, 71

L
Libya, war in Chad 100-103

M
Mirage F1 101, 103
magnetron 66, 242
MiG-21 98, 128, 206
MiG-29 153, 207
MQ-9 104

N
NATO 11, 12, 36, 40, 42, 55, 112-114, 119, 121, 125, 126, 129, 131, 132, 135, 136, 138-145, 149-154, 158-161, 170, 187, 188, 190, 192, 193, 197, 198, 203-215, 219, 229, 260, 261, 265, 271
Neva, system 4, 145, 146, 156, 160, 167-170, 210, 270

O
Operation Dugman (IAF) 83
Operation Model (IAF) 88
Operation Mole Cricket (IAF) 19 89
Operation Tagar (IAF) 81

P
P-15 (Flat Face) 36, 38, 41, 42, 160, 166, 168, 169, 188, 199, 201, 202, 213, 215
P-18 (Spoon Rest) 37, 222
P-40 (Long Track) 36, 38, 40, 60, 61, 110

Pechora 258
Praga, M53/59 61, 148, 159, 184, 205
PRF 13, 248
proportional guidance 237, 264
PRV-16 (Thin Skin) 36, 38, 40, 41, 60 , 62, 157, 160, 166, 170, 201, 213, 215, 222, 229, 230

R
R-27 104
R-60 147, 222
radar (general) 2-4, 6, 7, 12, 13, 15, 16, 24, 25, 27, 29, 32-37, 39-42, 45, 46, 49, 59, 62-73, 77, 83, 89, 90, 95-99, 102, 103, 108, 110, 111, 115, 121, 122, 125, 126, 128-131, 142, 143, 146, 147, 149, 150, 153, 156, 160, 162-172, 174, 185, 186-190, 193-195, 201, 202, 210-215, 222, 229
radar absorbing materials 254
radar cross section 150, 228, 242, 252, 253267, 296
radar display 247
radar fundamentals 241
radar imitator 131, 170-172, 210, 266
radar range 66, 88, 99, 241
radar range equation 241
radar warning receiver 222, 264
radar, applications 250
readiness 44, 49, 70, 72, 129, 141, 145, 162, 185, 192, 201, 205
Republika Srpska 68, 110-114, 125-127, 130-133

S
S-125 4, 56, 74, 76, 77, 86, 145, 146, 156, 160, 167, 210, 258, 270
S-300V 236, 237
S-75 (S-75) 56, 111, 145
SA-3 GOA 4, 56, 73, 74, 76, 77, 80,

309

86, 99, 100, 145, 146, 150, 168, 210-212, 258, 270
SA-7/Strela 2 77, 86, 99, 100, 148, 149
SAAF 100
SEAD 95, 117, 149, 169, 186, 191, 256, 259, 260
Serbia, Serbian 35, 40, 107-110, 112-115, 125-128, 131, 135, 137-141, 144-149, 173-174, 177, 182, 203-205, 207, 210, 212, 215-218, 229, 230, 260
Syria (Yom Kippur war) 73, 80, 83-85, 87-89
Syria (Bekaa valley) 89-91, 95-99
Syria (Buk use) 237, 238

T
three point, guidance 29
Tikhomirov, Vikor Vasilyevich 3, 4
Toropov, Ivan Ivanovich 3, 4, 10,
Tornado 104, 210, 259, 262
TOV 15, 47, 161-166, 182, 183, 185, 186, 213,

U
U-2 55, 121

Y
Yemen, war 104
Yom Kippur 58, 73, 77, 89, 257
Yugoslavia 32, 40, 41, 56, 59, 68, 70, 72, 110, 112, 127, 132, 135, 136, 139, 141, 144, 147, 148, 152, 154, 156, 176, 177, 188, 206, 207, 214, 216, 217, 260, 261

Z
ZSU 23/4 85, 86, 103

www.ingramcontent.com/pod-product-compliance
Lightning Source LLC
Chambersburg PA
CBHW071301110426
42743CB00042B/1129